The Souls of Jewish Folk

The Souls of Jewish Folk

W. E. B. Du Bois, Anti-Semitism,
and the Color Line

James M. Thomas

The University of Georgia Press
ATHENS

Designed by Kaelin Chappell Broaddus
Set in 10.5/13.5 Garamond Premier Pro Regular
by Kaelin Chappell Broaddus

Most University of Georgia Press titles are
available from popular e-book vendors.

Printed digitally

Library of Congress Cataloging-in-Publication Data

Names: Thomas, James M., 1982– author.
Title: The souls of Jewish folk : W. E. B. Du Bois, anti-
    Semitism, and the color line / James M. Thomas.
Description: Athens : The University of Georgia Press,
    [2023] | Series: Sociology of race and ethnicity |
    Includes bibliographical references and index.
Identifiers: LCCN 2023010439 | ISBN 9780820365060
    (hardback) | ISBN 9780820365077 (paperback) | ISBN
    9780820365084 (epub) | ISBN 9780820365091 (pdf)
Subjects: LCSH: Du Bois, W. E. B. (William Edward Burghardt),
    1868–1963—Sources. | Du Bois, W. E. B. (William Edward
    Burghardt), 1868–1963—Knowledge—Antisemitism. |
    Antisemitism—Germany. | African Americans--Relations
    with Jews. | Jews—Germany—History—1800–1933. |
    African Americans—Social conditions—To 1964. | Racism
    in the social sciences. | Germany—Intellectual life—19th
    century. | United States—Intellectual life—1865–1918.
Classification: LCC E185.97.D73 T46 2023 |
    DDC 323.092—dc23/eng/20230411
LC record available at https://lccn.loc.gov/2023010439

This book is dedicated to the memory of my mother, Marcia Markowitz Thomas (December 2, 1944–April 4, 2021). Mom, I never ever had to guess how proud you were of me or whether you loved me because you never failed to let me know. May your memory forever be a blessing.

CONTENTS

ACKNOWLEDGMENTS

I have a lot for which to be thankful. Rather than simply list the names of folks to whom I owe a debt of gratitude, I'd rather say a bit about why I'm so thankful. But before I give thanks, allow me to give my confession.

I began writing this book in 2017 while on a summer residential fellowship at the University of Massachusetts's W. E. B. Du Bois Center. My aim was to complete a full draft by the end of my sabbatical, which was in the spring of 2020. The world had other plans.

In the fall of 2018, I became the target of a right-wing troll campaign. My mistake? Suggesting, with clear humor, that senators who detain migrant children in cages and give safe harbor to sexual predators through appointment to the Supreme Court ought to be confronted by their electorate. Salads the world over wilted in fear (you had to be there). In hindsight, I should have been far more forceful in condemning these senators' actions.

My remarks, made via Twitter, were amplified by the then chancellor of the University of Mississippi, who used his own social media platform to condemn my comments and put distance between me and the institution. To the mob, the former chancellor gave carte blanche.

For weeks I received hundreds of email messages and voicemails to my office phone spewing hatred. Several of those messages contained clear threats to me and my loved ones. Someone posted my home address to Twitter and encouraged their followers to pay me a visit while my family was home. My department placed a security detail on the floor of the academic building in which the department is housed, in no small part because my colleagues feared for their own safety.

This all unfolded the year I was up for tenure and promotion. My dossier was complete, and my recommenders' letters were secured. My department was just about to take its vote, after which my candidacy would make its way through the usual institutional channels. I was encouraged by well-intentioned (though misguided) folks to lay off social media. The implication was clear, even if unspoken.

By the end of the fall semester, and in spite of the Far Right's efforts, I had cleared every institutional hurdle with flying colors. My department's vote on my tenure and promotion was unanimous. The college and provost's office likewise approved without reservations. The previous chancellor had resigned that November, and the interim chancellor signed off on my advancement without hesitation. But I live and work in Mississippi. And in Mississippi, things often have a way of going south.

Mississippi's colleges and universities are governed by the Institutions of Higher Learning Board of Trustees, or just the IHL. In May 2019, and in an unprecedented move, the IHL's board of directors voted to remove my name from the consent agenda, which included the names of seventy-six other academics up for tenure and promotion across its eight public colleges and universities, and consider my case separately in a closed executive session. After several hours of private deliberation out of public view, I was granted tenure and promotion on a 7–5 split vote, with the IHL commissioner noting in a public statement that some members "dissented." Tenured, with dissent.

Or tenured, nonetheless. With this all now seemingly behind me, I recalibrated and recommitted to writing this book. I wrote feverishly that summer, in part because it allowed me to feel that I was putting distance between myself and what had happened to me. Forging ahead, Mississippi be damned. I taught that fall, looking forward to the spring semester, when I would be on sabbatical and have all the time in the world to write, to think, to take long walks, and to dream. And I did all of those things . . . for about six weeks.

Then, in March 2020, the world shut down. My children—then ages seven and four—were "transitioned to virtual learning." That's how it was explained to us, at least. I am reminded of the late comedian George Carlin's bit on euphemisms and "soft language" from his 1990 stand-up special, *Parental Advisory*. Americans, according to Carlin, struggle with the truth. "So," he professes, "they invent a kind of soft language to protect themselves from it." Soft language "takes the life out of life": the CIA neutralizes or depopulates an area instead of murdering dissenters; the government engages in misinformation rather than lying; and children "transition to virtual learning." What this meant was that both of my children needed to be in front of a working computer for several hours each weekday, trying as hard as they could to focus on the little boxes on the screen that contained their friends and teacher. Something like a dystopian *Hollywood Squares* for school-age children. Whatever plans I had for this book were now on hold indefinitely.

By the fall of 2020, things had begun to open back up, albeit prematurely. My children returned to school. I returned to teaching, though now remotely. Still, I had a plan for writing this book and was confident it would unfold without a hiccup.

But did I mention that I live and work in Mississippi? And that in Mississippi, things have a way of going south?

That fall, and in response to a summer defined by even more police violence toward Black and Brown communities, including the murder of George Floyd by the Minneapolis police, I joined hundreds of other academics across North America in what was known as #ScholarStrike. I informed my students that we would not meet for one day in class and instead provided them with resources on structural racism, police violence, and abolitionism.

Word of my participation made its way to a right-wing think tank and from there to the Mississippi Office of the State Auditor. The auditor issued a letter to my university declaring that by participating in #ScholarStrike I had violated state law (reader: I had not). Moreover, the letter demanded that the university withhold my pay for the two days of my participation and terminate my employment. As of the writing of this sentence, I remain employed, and my money remains in my pocket where it belongs.

The culmination of this and other efforts to get me fired from my academic post has led to my being named among the ten "most America-hating professors" by a David Horowitz–backed organization. I'm ranked ninth, right behind Cornel West. Not too shabby for a kid from Kansas City with a state school education.

So here we are today. We're still not quite on the other side of the pandemic. Yet I have my health, my family, and now this book, of which I am tremendously proud. I wish I could take full credit for it, but I cannot. Like all things, *The Souls of Jewish Folk* has been a collective effort. Remaining faults notwithstanding, this book would not be half of whatever it is and might later become without the support of so many other individuals.

That's my confession. Now for my thanks.

The ideas for this book were first seeded while I was writing about and thinking through the histories of German Jews and Black Americans with the esteemed historian Sander L. Gilman. Sander is among the most brilliant and generous people with whom I have ever had the pleasure of knowing and writing. His early encouragement of this project meant the world to me. Thank you, Sander.

A 2017 summer residential fellowship at the University of Massachusetts at Amherst and its W. E. B. Du Bois Center provided me the necessary time and access to primary sources to begin to understand what kind of book I wanted to write and how I might go about doing it. I remain forever grateful to Dr. Whitney Battle-Baptiste for her support of me as a scholar, for her efforts to create a true cohort of Du Boisian scholars built upon mutual respect and generosity, and for just being a fearless force of nature within academia. Among those with whom I had the pleasure of sharing the Du Bois archives, I want to especially thank Michael Saman, Charisse Burden-Stelly, and Gaidi Faraj for their intellectual and political camaraderie during our summer residency.

Over the past several years I have had opportunities to workshop many of the ideas in this book with academic audiences around the country. The 12th Social Theory Forum, held in 2017 at the University of Massachusetts in Boston, was especially formative for my thinking. Many thanks to José Itzigsohn in particular for his kindness and generosity toward my ideas when they were still nascent.

Likewise, I want to thank the faculty and students affiliated with Dartmouth University's Jewish Studies Program, in particular Susanah Heschel, for their thoughtful and insightful comments. Likewise, I'm thankful for the support of the Tufts University Center for Humanities and its director, Kamran Rastegar. Kamran invited me to speak to the center's wonderful faculty affiliates as I began to craft some of the substantive chapters of this manuscript. That invitation likely would not have been possible without my friend and colleague Freeden Ouer Blume. Freeden is a fellow Du Boisian scholar, far more talented than I am, and among the kindest souls in all of academia. Every time we speak, I walk away feeling wiser and better. Thank you, Freeden.

During this time in which I was honing my analysis, I also benefited tremendously from sharing my ideas and writings with friends like Melissa Weiner. Melissa's encouragement and excitement for my project sustained me throughout the writing of this book.

I'm especially thankful for the skillful editing provided to me by Kate Lechler. When I had looked for too long with tired eyes at these chapters, Kate was able to lend a fresh perspective and suggest important changes. Kate's kind and careful attention to detail has made this book far more readable than I could have ever done on my own. Later, Mary M. Hill helped further sharpen my sentences and clarify my sourcing. Any remaining deficiencies are mine alone.

I especially need to give thanks to my friends and mentors, David L. Brunsma and David G. Embrick. Their support for this project, their encouragement of me at every turn, and their steadfast belief in me as a scholar and human being are simply life-sustaining. I am, because they are.

I am also quite thankful for Mick Gusinde-Duffy and the University of Georgia Press. Mick, you have been so incredibly patient with me, especially when my progress stalled. Thank you for continuing to believe in me and this project.

To my dear scholar-friends in Oxford—Marcos, Conor, Jesse, Darren, Catarina, Derrick—thank you for the conversations about Du Bois and for always being willing to lend your eyes and insights to my ideas, no matter how half-baked they may be. Likewise, these friends and their families—Alice, Carey, Laura, Will, and April—have given me and my own family tremendous strength and support over these past several years as my trials and tribulations were under way. For similar reasons, I give thanks to my dear friend no longer in Oxford, Brian Foster. The University of Virginia is better for having you.

I want to give a special thanks to attorney Rob McDuff and the Mississippi Center for Justice, who have in response to the efforts of the Mississippi state auditor provided me with legal support pro bono. Without that support, I would not have completed this book. Thank you, Rob, sincerely.

To Olive and Noah, my heart and soul, my sun and moon. There is a lot of joy in writing a book. There's also a lot of grief, frustration, and worry. As much as I hope to impart the joyous parts to you both, I know I cannot keep you from the less exciting parts of the journey. Just know that on those more frustrating, grief-filled days, your smiles and laughter lifted me and sustained me. You both make my whole wide world go round.

Finally, Afton. You get my most special thanks and my enduring love. You have been with me on every step of this journey and many others. Thank you for being my ride-or-die, always. You know, and have, my whole heart. Oscar Mayer, always (I love you).

The Souls of Jewish Folk

On Roots and Routes

Herein lie buried many things which if read with patience
may show the strange meaning of being black here at the
dawning of the Twentieth Century. This meaning is not
without interest to you, Gentle Reader; for the problem of
the Twentieth Century is the problem of the color line.

—W. E. B. Du Bois, "The Forethought," in
The Souls of Black Folk (1903)

W. E. B. Du Bois was just thirty-five years old when
he was approached by the publisher A. C. McClurg and Company to compile a
set of his previously published writings into a volume titled *The Souls of Black Folk*.
Du Bois did not have high expectations for the volume. For one thing, these writings were, by his own description, "fugitive essays"—works with no apparent relationship to any larger volume or project. More generally, Du Bois was skeptical because he felt that "books of essays almost always fall flat."[1]

Yet by 1903 Du Bois was a known American intellectual. He had earned his
doctorate from Harvard University in 1895, becoming the first Black American
to do so. Just a few short years later, Du Bois published a comprehensive social-
scientific study of Black American life in the United States under the title *The
Philadelphia Negro*. This work earned high praise in academic circles and served
in part as the catalyst for his move to Atlanta University. Moreover, Du Bois was
quickly becoming known—and praised—on an international scale. He had already amassed a number of bylines in some of the most widely read print magazines of his time, such as the *Atlantic Monthly*, *The Independent*, *The Nation*, and

Harper's Weekly. He was invited to serve as chairman of the committee on the address for the First Pan-African Conference, held in London's Westminster Town Hall in 1900. In this role Du Bois helped draft a letter from the conference leadership to European nations that boldly announced: "The problem of the twentieth century is the problem of the colour line, the question as to how far differences of race, which show themselves chiefly in the colour of the skin and the texture of the hair, are going to be made, hereafter, the basis of denying to over half the world the right of sharing to their utmost ability the opportunities and privileges of modern civilisation."[2]

Given his stature, it doesn't surprise contemporary readers—nor should it have surprised Du Bois—that the praise bestowed upon *Souls* following its publication was anything but flat. Indeed, Du Bois's collection of essays left an indelible impression on scholars and laypersons alike. William James, the American psychologist, philosopher, and Du Bois's mentor and professor at Harvard, wrote, "The whole makes a tremendously strong impression, both for matter and manner. Few men can combine statistics with personal and emotional suggestion as you do, and I think you can count on this book having a recognized place in literature hereafter."[3] After receiving the page proofs, Du Bois's editor, Francis G. Browne, informed Du Bois, "My faith in the book increases with every page of proof that I read. That it will make an impression on the country I am certain, and that before very long it will be selling largely I am also equally sure."[4]

The first edition was released in April, and the publisher issued a second edition just one month later. Major American newspapers, including the *Chicago Herald*, the *San Francisco Post*, and the *Chicago Tribune*, would heap praise (with some criticism) upon *Souls* over the next several months. On June 10, 1903, Browne informed Du Bois that his press "had never published a volume which has had more serious attention or greater praise, and we are very proud to have our imprint on it." The press had ordered paper for a third print edition. By May 1904 the book was on its fourth edition; by April 1905 the press was arranging for both French and German editions.[5]

The positive reception to *Souls* went well beyond its book sales. Black newspapers across the country—from the *Ohio Enterprise* to William Monroe Trotter's *Boston Guardian*—celebrated the text. Black luminaries, including James Weldon Johnson and Langston Hughes, lauded Du Bois for his elegant prose and sharp commentary on the matter and weight of the color line. Ida B. Wells wrote to Du Bois from her Anti-Lynching League office to invite him to attend a discussion of his book in Chicago "with a few friends." Camillus Phillips, associate editor of *The Independent*, wrote to Du Bois that *Souls* "has recently made some distinct impression upon the reading public" and compared Du Bois to the likes of Rudyard Kipling, Andrew Lang, Booth Tarkington, John Fox Jr., and Humphrey Ward, among others.[6]

Du Bois and his newly published book were not without their detractors, of course. Among those who were particularly harsh were the *New York Times*, the *Chicago Tribune*, and the *New York World*. Yet *The Nation* praised Du Bois for "the emotion and the passion throbbing here in every chapter, almost every page." The *Los Angeles Times* declared that *Souls* was "the cry of a race struggling against fearful odds" and among the best books of the year.[7] Its detractors were in the clear minority, and praise for *Souls* only grew in the years following its 1903 publication.

At the University of Massachusetts at Amherst's library, where the W. E. B. Du Bois Papers are housed, personal letters to Du Bois praising his work abound. In February 1907 Hallie E. Queen, an African American and one of only two women of color students at Cornell University, wrote to inform Du Bois that a movement had been started at Cornell to make a study of Du Bois's works. The idea began not with her but "in the mind of a Philadelphia white girl who had heard you speak before the Ethical Culture Society." Queen noted that the Co-Operative Society (the students' store) had ordered many copies of *Souls*, with which the group began its work. A copy of the book was also sent to the wife of Ambassador Andrew White, who lived on the campus, and other copies were sent to a variety of groups with whom Queen and her comrades were hoping to build solidarity.[8]

At the time of Queen's letter, the group had read three essays from *Souls*: "The Passing of the First Born," "The Coming of John," and "Of Our Spiritual Strivings." Queen noted that, among other comments, one girl stated that "Of Our Spiritual Strivings" reminded her of the 137th Psalm. Queen also reported that because of her familiarity with the literary department of Cornell, she was asked to serve as the critic of the club. Queen told Du Bois that his book was now in Cornell's library and was constantly referred to by Dean Walter Willcox of the College of Arts and Sciences. Queen said that when they discussed "The Coming of John," "I believe that the discussing of that one essay has done much toward broadening the racial spirit of Cornell—that is, the best kind of racial spirit." She described how membership was growing and how the club hoped to become incorporated: "Surely the 'Veil' is lifting, surely the day is not so far off. The horizon is broadening here, somewhere the sun is already high."[9]

In a different letter dated March 1909, a Miss Winifred Myser of Savannah, Georgia, expressed her desire to give copies of *Souls* to her White friends in the North: "If more white people would read it they might see what a cruelly unnecessary thing the Veil is. . . . [Whites] too must feel the effects of its shadows."[10]

The praise and regard for *Souls* only grew. In fact, from its publication to the present, *Souls* has been the subject of so much scholarly attention that it would be unfair to continue a summary in this space. My own interests, in any event, are not in the place of *Souls* within W. E. B. Du Bois's canon. Instead, my aim in this book is to examine what the cultural theorist Paul Gilroy would describe as the "roots" and "routes" of *Souls*, including those that demonstrate its continued significance for revealing the contours of the color line today.[11]

In particular, my interests are in those roots that extend back toward Du Bois's time spent in Germany, from 1892 to 1894, and then the routes in which traces of this German experience are found thereafter. In this way, *The Souls of Jewish Folk* complements recent considerations of Du Bois's intellectual legacy.

In *Lines of Descent: W. E. B. Du Bois and the Emergence of Identity*, Kwame Anthony Appiah demonstrates how Du Bois's German education shaped some of the key ideas found within *Souls*. Elsewhere, in *Dark Voices: W. E. B. Du Bois and American Thought, 1888–1903*, Shamoon Zamir examines the roots of *Souls* by way of Du Bois's undergraduate training at Fisk University through his years in Germany. In both texts, Germany is a lynchpin of sorts in Du Bois's ongoing understanding of the race concept and the plight of Black Americans.

Du Bois studied in Germany at Friedrich-Wilhelms-Universität, then known as the University of Berlin (and, after World War II, renamed Humboldt University). He was mentored and taught by some of the greatest German scholars and public intellectuals of the late nineteenth century. Gustav von Schmoller and Adolph Wagner cotaught a seminar on political economy. Du Bois sat in on the lectures given by the German firebrand historian and Reichstag member Heinrich von Treitschke. In this environment and situated within the larger German scene at the time—politically, culturally, and socially—Du Bois could not help but give new consideration to the set of questions that preceded his German adventure and shaped his trajectory thereafter. The problem of the color line, the dichotomy between race and nation, spurred his questioning cry, "When these loyalties diverge, where shall my soul find refuge?"[12]

While serving as theoretical inspiration, Du Bois's German university training also provided him with an empiricist's tool kit that would guide his approach to the social sciences and shape the tradition of American sociology. Du Bois received training from Schmoller in the careful and inductive method for social-scientific analysis that, to this day, marks his 1899 *Philadelphia Negro* as a pioneering treatment of Black social life. That same training is also evident in the volumes of social-scientific research Du Bois and his students produced in the Atlanta Sociological Laboratory at Atlanta University in the first decades of the twentieth century. To be clear, Du Bois's German training did not replace or diminish his lyrical voice;

instead, it complemented it. Zamir reveals Du Bois's contrasting and, at times, conflicting roles: those of philosopher, social scientist, and lyricist whose body of work refuses and refutes sweeping generalization. Even in just the short period following Du Bois's return to the United States from Germany and the publication of *Souls*, his refusal of scholarly compartmentalization is evident. *The Philadelphia Negro*, "The Conservation of the Races," and "The Strivings of the Negro People," the latter of which would later become the well-known chapter "Of Our Spiritual Strivings" in *Souls*, are as stylistically different as one can imagine. All were all published within one year of each other.[13]

The early twentieth-century German social theorist Karl Mannheim, in his treatise on the sociology of knowledge, rejected conceptualizing individuals as distinct and separate from the times in which they live. According to Mannheim, every society, every epoch has a particular *Zeitgeist*, an ideology that guides and shapes the actors within it. Mannheim's contribution was the acknowledgment that our ideas and beliefs are structured by the contexts and social positions we inhabit. The major social, political, and economic events through which we live form the ground that then seeds and gives force to the ideas of our time.[14]

The University of Berlin and its service to the "roots" of Du Bois's intellectual legacy have been subject to several treatments. Yet the majority of these works focus on Du Bois's training within the classroom, his tutelage within the German historical-empiricist tradition lauded by Schmoller, and the influence of German philosophy and literature. Few, if any, scholarly works examine the larger sociopolitical contexts of late nineteenth-century Germany—the soil in which Du Bois's roots were nurtured. An important exception is Kenneth Barkin's analysis of German imperialism and Du Bois's fascination with some of Germany's imperialist symbolism. This, however, is just the tip of a rather large iceberg.[15]

A large body of scholarship makes clear that the late nineteenth-century German scene was rampant with anti-Semitism. By the time Du Bois arrived in 1892, a populist brand of German nationalism had tethered its calls for national unity to a resounding rejection of the Jew within the German body politic. The rejection of all things Jewish in the name of German purity would remain unrivaled in German history until the rise of the Third Reich. Meanwhile, German academia, including the University of Berlin, where Du Bois studied, served as a kind of ground zero for entrenched medical and social-scientific discourse on Jewish pathology and inferiority, both fueling and fueled by the political anti-Semitism of that era. Many of the leading racialist minds of western Europe were trained or taught at German institutions of higher education. While racialists' views of how best to resolve the "Jewish question" differed widely, there was general consensus for a scientific rationale on German Jewry's inability to properly assimilate into the German nation-state. To date, these wider sociopolitical contexts have largely gone underexamined and undertheorized for how they affected Du Bois's own thinking and writing.

There has been a resurgence of interest in the life and works of W. E. B. Du Bois since 2000. Across the humanities and the social sciences, scholars have been re-examining his large body of work. These scholars hope to reassert Du Bois's rightful place among the great intellectual figures of the twentieth century and to determine what those works might tell us about our present condition, including the persistence of the color line in the twenty-first century. This reexamination is long overdue, of course. Du Bois was among the most prolific intellectuals of his era. Yet while his work was widely read by his contemporaries, it was rarely cited. We know, for example, that in 1905 German political economist and sociologist Max Weber wrote to Du Bois with high praise for *Souls* and expressed a hope that the text would soon be translated for a German audience. And we know that by the time the jubilee edition of *Souls* was published, it had gone through twenty-four editions in the United States alone, along with several concurrent printings abroad.[16]

Souls, of course, is far from the only work for which Du Bois was renowned, especially in the early twentieth century. Du Bois's Atlanta studies were lauded nationally and internationally and by both academics and laypersons, including the United States Department of Labor and reviewers at the *Boston Herald*, *The Guardian*, and the *London Spectator*, to name but a few. Social scientists from the top colleges and universities wrote to Du Bois to praise his scholarship and request copies of his works for their own departments. Charles Ellwood, University of Missouri sociologist and later president of the American Sociological Association, asked Du Bois for copies of his Atlanta studies to be placed in the University of Missouri Department of Sociology's own collections. Mary Roberts Smith, the first full-time American professor of sociology, requested that Du Bois send her the "bulletins published by the Atlanta University" on Black America for her course Race Problems, to be taught to sophomores at Stanford University. Smith further noted, "I have found your book on the Philadelphia Negro invaluable for the use of students, since it serves to correct many misstatements and extreme views found in other authors."[17]

The highly regarded economist Frank William Taussig of Harvard University wrote to Du Bois to inform him that, in Taussig's estimation, "no better work is being done in the country" than that taking place in the Atlanta Sociological Laboratory. Furthermore, "no better opportunity is afforded for financial support on the part of those who wish to further the understanding of the negro problem." Taussig had taught Du Bois at Harvard, and two years prior, as president of the American Economic Association, he had extended an invitation to Du Bois to speak at the association's annual meeting on the "negro problem." Taussig's praise for Du Bois's scholarship is even more extraordinary, considering Taussig was known not only for his advancements in economic theory but also for his advocacy of the forced sterilization of Black and poor people, whom Taussig considered parasites of "poor physical and mental endowment."[18]

Broadly, I believe the revival of contemporary interest in Du Bois's life and works has been driven by two desires: first, to assert Du Bois's rightful place as a founder of the American sociological tradition, and second, to better situate Du Bois's intellectual contributions within the contemporary study of race and racism. We find these motivations within the recent works of Aldon Morris, Earl Wright II, and Kwame Anthony Appiah, for example. In Appiah's work, we even see consideration given to Du Bois's experiences in Germany as shaping his intellectual thought in the United States and later his global framework for studying the color line.[19]

The Souls of Jewish Folk is motivated by similar desires, but with some important differences. Like other books, this book seeks to provide a proper intellectual history of Du Boisian scholarship. Where this book is different, however, is in its focus on the sociopolitical climate of Germany and western Europe, in particular, the anti-Semitism that defined the political and academic scene in which Du Bois lived and studied. The primary thesis of *The Souls of Jewish Folk* is that Germany's ongoing struggle with what it considered its Jewish question—what to do with Germany's Jews—served as an important and to-date undertheorized influence on Du Bois's subsequent considerations of Black people's social position within the American racial landscape at the turn of the twentieth century. The roots and routes of Du Bois's considerations of the color line are haunted by the specter of the Jew, hence the title of this work.

Situating Du Bois's developing perspective on the color line within the context of western European anti-Semitism has important implications for current and future scholarship. First, the emphasis placed on how the late nineteenth-century German sociopolitical scene affected Du Bois's own theorizing of the color line adds a context that has been missing from our understanding of his intellectual trajectory. To be sure, there have been some considerations of his time spent at the University of Berlin. Yet the focus has been mostly on his academic training as a social scientist; it minimizes the extent to anti-Semitism was a prevailing attitude both in the university and across the larger nation-state. In *The Scholar Denied*, an exceptional contribution to our understanding of Du Bois's role in founding the American sociological tradition, Aldon Morris gives only a brief nod to Du Bois's German adventures and hardly if at all considers the deeply anti-Semitic climate in which Du Bois lived and studied. Seeing this gap, in *The Souls of Jewish Folk* I ask readers to take seriously how our ideas and indeed intellectual work itself are shaped by and embedded in historical and contemporaneous networks of people, places, and prevailing contexts. In Du Bois's case, it means that we must consider whether and how his early thinking on race and racism was shaped by and embedded in the prevailing contexts of late nineteenth-century Germany, in which anti-Semitism was central.[20]

A second implication from the thesis advanced in *The Souls of Jewish Folk* involves the call by sociologist Marcus Anthony Hunter for intellectual reparations owed to marginalized scholars and communities. On a personal note, I saw this need firsthand at a national conference some years ago. I was attending a panel session where a prominent Black scholar was presenting their own work on Du Bois. During the Q&A portion of the panel, a White scholar began to shout down the Black scholar from the back of the room, to the shock and dismay of other attendees. The Black scholar had characterized Du Bois's relationship to a prominent White sociologist as one in which the latter borrowed heavily from the former. Clearly, the White scholar took serious offense to this evidentiary claim. After nearly a full minute of yelling, the White scholar stormed out of the room. To realize that such anger was caused by the simple assertion that Du Bois was a central figure of twentieth-century thought is to realize that, even in the second decade of this new century, the problem of the color line remains as bright as ever and continues to shape the canons of our academic disciplines.[21]

As a sociologist by training, I'm well aware how gatekeepers continue to privilege the early Chicago School of Sociology as central to the founding of the discipline and even the subfield of race and ethnicity. Within many circles, to even mention that many of these early Chicago School social scientists subscribed to and advanced the dominant racialism of their era is to run the risk of an outburst similar to that experienced by the Black scholar during that academic conference. So sociology continues to center the contributions of the Chicago School and often at the expense of Du Bois, Anna Julia Cooper, Ida B. Wells, and others. As we in the humanities and social sciences continue to wrestle with the legacies of our canon and its dominant figureheads, the need only grows for us to put into proper context not only the ideas of those who have long held dominant status within our field but also the ideas of those who have been marginalized.[22]

A third implication from this book's thesis is the enhancement and advancement of a comparative framework through which we may theorize the relationship between what often appear as disconnected racial projects: western European anti-Semitism and American anti-Black racism. Though often treated as separate and unique, anti-Semitism and anti-Black racism share a genealogy. For much of the nineteenth and early twentieth centuries, Jews and Blacks served as the primary vehicles through which science sought to advance the interests of White supremacy; my own previous work documents some of this shared history. While a number of other important scholarly works trace the genealogies of anti-Semitism and anti-Black racism as distinct phenomena, few compare and contrast their simultaneous unfolding or offer insights into their relationship to one another. By examining the roots of western Europe's "Jewish question" in the subsequent routes through which Du Bois considered the Black experience in America, *The Souls of Jewish Folk* can help reveal important points of convergence and divergence between these two racial projects. In turn, this comparison can refine our conceptual repertoire for understanding global racial formations and the persistence of White supremacy across space and time.[23]

Overview of the Argument

As I have stated already, *The Souls of Jewish Folk* considers an important but still-missing subject in the intellectual history of W. E. B. Du Bois: the influence of western European anti-Semitism within his program for the study of race and racism. Whereas previous scholarship examines Du Bois's German adventure for its contribution to his empiricist methods, the shaping of his nimble standing as a humanist, and his identity as a scholar-activist, *The Souls of Jewish Folk* widens the analysis to consider how the intellectual, political, and economic environment of late nineteenth-century Germany—especially its rampant anti-Semitism—influenced Du Bois's theorizing of race and racism. Specifically, *The Souls of Jewish Folk* examines what I refer to as the "specter" of the Jewish question in Du Bois's early thought. I argue that this specter takes shape in two key ways: first, in relation to a nineteenth-century medical model of double consciousness that was part and parcel of a dominant racial discourse on Jews and madness, and second, by way of Du Bois's own experiences with and exposures to anti-Semitism while living and studying in Germany and his subsequent reflections on those experiences and exposures in the decades that followed.

Medical and scientific discourse on Jewish inferiority was common within German higher education, and many of its most influential contributors were trained or taught at German universities. These academicians generally cast Jews as inherently more susceptible to madness and therefore incapable of assimilation. German academic consensus mirrored American racialists regarding African Americans. In *The Souls of Jewish Folk*, I recast racial medicalization as important medical and scientific precursors to double consciousness, one of Du Bois's most significant concepts in his formulation of the race concept and White supremacy. Many nineteenth-century scholars, medical professionals, and laypersons already understood double consciousness as a mental illness. Its etiology and symptoms drew from medical, anthropological, and sociological considerations of Jewish difference and pathology. Du Bois's time at the University of Berlin exposed him to this formulation of double consciousness and the pathologization of Jewish difference. I argue that Du Bois's exposure to western European racism and anti-Semitism influenced his early theorizing on Black Americans' duality as a debilitating condition resulting not from inherent inferiority but from the structural conditions of anti-Black racism.[24]

Moreover, while in Berlin, Du Bois honed a social-scientific lens through which to consider the parallel processes behind anti-Semitism and anti-Black racism. In Germany Du Bois was exposed to an emergent nationalism that defined itself through its intense anxiety, if not outright hatred, toward Germany's Jewish population. This paralleled Du Bois's own observations of how the American narrative at the time defined itself against its Black citizenry. In his notes and in his writings, Du Bois paints us a picture of what we might describe as late nineteenth-century German nationalism's double problem. On the one hand, there existed among late nineteenth-century German intellectuals a desire to see a strong, unified Germany. This would of course both enable and require Jews to function within the nation-state. On the other hand, German nationalism was predicated upon a growing belief in national purity that cast Jews as incompatible with this sentiment. Jews could not be real Germans, because that would dilute the national culture. Du Bois saw in the status of Germany's Jews some of the same political, economic, and social factors he defined as central to the status of Black Americans in the United States in his *Philadelphia Negro* and even later in *Black Reconstruction in America*. Du Bois came to understand anti-Semitism in Germany and anti-Black racism in the United States as two sides of the same coin: central to the construction of the distinction between who is and who is not a member of the body politic.[25]

A few caveats are in order before we proceed. Those versed in the breadth and depth of Du Bois's scholarship know all too well the challenges in presenting, with clarity, the roots and routes of his intellectual thought. If we begin with his 1896 doctoral dissertation, *The Suppression of the African Slave-Trade to the United States of America, 1638–1870* (the first volume of Harvard's Historical Monograph Series), Du Bois's written body of work stretches across eight decades and includes both of the Great Migrations of Black and White Americans from the rural South to the industrialized North; the high tide of lynching; two world wars and the Cold War; the formation of the League of Nations and its later conversion into the United Nations; and seventeen different American presidential administrations (eighteen if we include his posthumous autobiography, published in 1968). Further, Du Bois's writings span a wide range of genres, from traditional academic papers and research monographs; to popular writings for monthly magazines, news-papers, and other periodicals; and even to plays and novels, including *The Black Flame* trilogy.[26]

As would be expected for someone with such a large body of work across such a long period of time, Du Bois's thinking was anything but static. As a young emerging scholar Du Bois showed a particular affinity toward the German imperial aesthetic, but by the 1940s he had denounced the fascist Third Reich and later joined the American Communist Party. While his scholarly concerns at Atlanta University in the early twentieth century were directed almost exclusively toward the conditions of Black American life, by the 1930s those concerns were increasingly turned toward the conditions of non-White people the world over.[27]

The breadth and depth of Du Bois's thought have led some to argue for a kind of periodization in the study of his intellectual history. Periodization strikes me as especially helpful for identifying when, where, and why certain of his ideas emerged and in response to what particular conditions. At the same time, however, Du Bois's ideas have a kind of life cycle. If we are to understand that life cycle, then we need to follow its waves and ripples across the vast ocean of his work. I make no claims about any particular consistency in Du Bois's thought. Instead, my focus is on a specific concept—double consciousness—and the roots and routes of this concept from the late nineteenth-century German scene through mid-twentieth-century America.[28]

I also do not make any claims that the conditions of late nineteenth-century Germany's Jews were identical to those of Black people in early twentieth-century America. Du Bois himself, after returning to the United States from Berlin in 1894, understood that the "national development" of Germany's Jews "is over widely different obstacles than those of my nation."[29] While Germany's Jews had attained both political emancipation and modest economic success by the late nineteenth century, it would be nearly seventy years until, with the passage of the Voting Rights Act, Black Americans would secure their own political emancipation. Meanwhile, the turn of the twentieth century bore witness to the lynching of thousands of Black people in the United States, the codification of Jim Crow throughout the American South, and the institutionalization of convict leasing, which was little more than "slavery by another name."[30] These differences are important.

Yet there are good reasons to examine the German Jewish experience for how it shaped Du Bois's considerations of Black America. In both the German and American scenes, Du Bois recognized how the color line enabled a specific manifestation of nationalism that expressed itself in opposition toward Jews and Blacks, respectively. For these groups, striving to become a part of the very nations that rejected them could only ever produce the condition of "two warring souls within one dark body" that Du Bois so eloquently described in *The Souls of Black Folk*.[31]

The extent to which Du Bois himself expressed or subscribed to the anti-Semitism of his day has been subject to some scholarly debate and public commentary. In the summer of 2022, I found myself rising to Du Bois's defense after witnessing a truly disingenuous effort via social media to paint Du Bois as sympathetic to the Nazis. Having spent a good bit of time reading with a sharp and judicious eye decades' worth of Du Bois's own writings, I can promise my curious readers that Du Bois bore no such sympathies. Indeed, Du Bois was quite clear and forceful in his condemnation of Hitler and the Nazis on several occasions in several different publications. Though I have no interest in centering such absurd and baseless claims about Du Bois in this book or in any other, I do feel some responsibility as a scholar writing a book on his intellectual history to put to rest any unfortunate and ill-founded conclusions regarding Du Bois's position on Jews and anti-Semitism. Some scholars, for example, have suggested that, particularly in his early decades, Du Bois expressed anti-Semitic views, some of which these scholars argue were present in the first editions of *The Souls of Black Folk*. Du Bois himself addressed this criticism directly and, to my mind, satisfactorily in the book's jubilee edition, published in 1953.

More generally, Du Bois maintained close personal relationships with a number of Jews throughout the twentieth century, including those with whom he cofounded the National Association for the Advancement of Colored People (NAACP) and with whom he collaborated for decades: the American Jewish civil rights activist Henry Moskowitz, for example, and brothers and activists Joel and Arthur Spingarn. This of course is not meant to suggest that the company one keeps is evidence of an absence of prejudicial attitudes. We all know far too well that having one or two Jewish or Black friends or even a Jewish or Black spouse does not prohibit a person from harboring hatred or ill will toward the larger group. It is important, however, to locate Du Bois's personal relationships with Jews within their proper social and historical contexts.

The late nineteenth and early twentieth centuries in both Germany and the United States were marked by a virulent anti-Semitism that was meant to maintain social and physical separation between Jews and non-Jews. The late nineteenth-century German scene upon which Du Bois first arrived was, as I describe in chapter 3, marked by virulent anti-Semitism, which was rooted in an emergent German nationalism that, by the mid-twentieth century, would take its most heinous and terrifying form. Meanwhile, Du Bois returned from Germany to an America that was both separate and unequal in form and function. As Du Bois articulated so clearly and concisely in his 1923 essay, "The Superior Race," which was later published in his 1940 *Dusk of Dawn*, "The black man is a person who must ride 'Jim Crow' in Georgia."[32]

Meanwhile, the interwar years in America bore witness to the mainstreaming of anti-immigrant rhetoric and social policy, which often articulated itself through the image of a poor, unclean, and unassimilable European Jew. Schools, colleges, and workplaces imposed restrictions on Jewish participation. Neighborhoods and communities sought to prohibit Jewish settlement. Just one year prior to Du Bois's observation that to be Black in America is to be kept separate, Harvard's then president imposed a 15 percent quota on Jewish student admissions, while major hotels advertised "no Hebrews." Leading American figures such as the automobile company mogul Henry Ford and the widely popular Catholic priest Father Coughlin launched blatant public assaults against Jews. Across the southern United States, the reconstituted Ku Klux Klan targeted Jews for their perceived threat to the rights and claims of the White race.[33]

For Du Bois to maintain close personal relationships with Jews in these circumstances lends credible support to Eric Goldstein's observation that the fervent White nationalism of early twentieth-century America helped foster mutual sympathies and even solidarity among American Jews and Black Americans. Moreover, for Du Bois or his Jewish compatriots to have traversed the physical and social barriers that kept Jews and Blacks apart and distinct not only from White America but also from one another would have required significant personal courage and conviction. In short, there is far more compelling evidence, direct or otherwise, of Du Bois's strong support of Jews as a group than there is for his prejudice toward them.

I do also want to stress early in this book that while I maintain that Du Bois's theorizing of the conditions of Black people in the United States was shaped by his exposure to anti-Semitism in Germany, this in no way suggests that Du Bois's theorizing of anti-Black racism was the repackaging of others' theorizing of anti-Semitism. Du Bois's contributions to our understanding of the color line are novel and important in their own right. A key contribution from the field of Black studies is the acknowledgment that Black epistemologies have their own genealogy and are not dependent upon the intellectual frameworks of Western liberal thought. My claim is, quite simply, that Du Bois, like any other intellectual, was a product of his time and his experiences. Those experiences included, by his own admission, an influential albeit brief period of study in Germany that exposed him to the political and intellectual foundations of western European anti-Semitism. On his own, Du Bois compared and contrasted those experiences with his knowledge and experiences of Black life in America. This, I argue, shapes how he understood and wrote about the color line and in particular his concept of double consciousness.

Finally, there is no so-called smoking gun. I have not found anywhere in the large archive of Du Bois's papers, writings, and other documents any clear statement from him that says, "German anti-Semitism affects how I think about American anti-Black racism." If I had, this would be a short book indeed! Instead, my argument draws from personal letters, writings, and papers, along with a large body of secondary sources, to make inferences connecting Du Bois's thinking while in Germany to his later thinking on the conditions of Black life in America, including anti-Black racism. Put differently, *The Souls of Jewish Folk* is grounded firmly within the difficult field of interpretive work. I have no doubt that some readers will contest my claims. Yet I believe the argument presented here is plausible and well supported by the evidence available. Ultimately, you, dear reader, will be the judge.

The Organization of This Book

My aim here is to examine the influence of western European anti-Semitism within W. E. B. Du Bois's early program for the study of race and racism. Therefore, my focus is on both the roots within his Berlin experience and the routes his intellectual project took after he returned to the United States. The substantive chapters, then, follow somewhat of a chronological narrative structure. The chapters that deal with racialist discourse on both Jews and Blacks expand upon some of my previous scholarship, as does the conclusion, which considers the role of Du Boisian thought in contemporary reflections on the color line.[34]

Chapter 1, "Race, Science, and Madness," traces the roots and routes of one of Du Bois's most significant concepts: Black double consciousness. The term "double consciousness" predates Du Bois's own usage by approximately eighty years. Its origins are in mental health, where the term was used to describe a particular disorder in which the victim presents two versions of a self that are fractured from one another to such a degree that in either state of consciousness each version is unaware of the other. By the mid-nineteenth century, double consciousness was a named pathology with firm roots in the popular imagination, showing up in the popular *Harper's Magazine* and the British *Cornhill Magazine*. Yet by the late nineteenth century, the term had become associated with symptoms such as neurasthenia (emotional disturbance) and hysteria, with some medical practitioners suggesting that double consciousness was the result of inheritable traits. Importantly, however, nearly all of the symptomatic expressions associated with nineteenth-century medical descriptions of double consciousness were disproportionately ascribed to western European Jews. In this chapter, then, I trace the development of the discourse on double consciousness that framed it as a distinct Jewish pathos. I give special consideration of how the image of the Jew figured into this medical and scientific discourse.

In chapter 2, "The Du Boisian Reformulation," I attend to Du Bois's reformulation of double consciousness from a medical description to a figurative one, from a pathos to "a gift and a curse." I consider the extent to which Du Bois explicitly drew from the medical and scientific concept of double consciousness in his own use, as well as the extent to which his use represents a novel conception. I emphasize in this chapter the intellectual climate of German academia and the racialist discourse of the Jew in earlier formulations of double consciousness. For more than a century, scholars have deliberated over the figurative description, social-scientific implications, and theoretical underpinnings of Du Bois's famous passage in *The Souls of Black Folk* where he expressed his reformulation of double consciousness. Du Bois drew upon a wide variety of sources in his formulation of Black Americans' duality. Most scholars agree that Du Bois's use owes a conceptual debt to two discursive strains: a figurative language influenced by European Romanticism and American Transcendentalism, and a medical language carried forward by the emergent field of psychology. In this chapter, I explore how late nineteenth-century Germany's Jewish question within its medical and scientific discourse informed Du Bois's own use of double consciousness within the opening chapter of *Souls*.

Whereas in chapter 2 I emphasize the intellectual climate of German academia and its racialist discourse in the figure of the Jew, in chapter 3, "Germany, Anti-Semitism, and the Problem of the Color Line," the focus turns toward the sociopolitical thought of late nineteenth-century Germany, including its emergent nationalism, in which Du Bois continued to develop his thinking on the race concept. In his autobiography, Du Bois attributed his time spent in Germany to helping him overcome a provincial perspective on race and racism. Late nineteenth-century Germany was both the best and worst of times. On the one hand, Du Bois's arrival in Germany in 1892 coincided with its lengthy and unprecedented economic reform. Like much of western Europe, Germany was also undergoing massive industrialization and urbanization as rural farmworkers from Germany's eastern provinces migrated en masse to urban centers in search of work. On the other hand, political anti-Semitism took hold more strongly in Germany then than during any other period with the exception of the Third Reich. While Germany's Socialist Party had gained a stronger foothold within the Reichstag, the anti-Semitic Christlichsoziale Partei (Christian Social Party) was also solidifying its ranks. By the early 1890s, its party platform had advanced an explicit hatred of Germany's

Jews and promoted the belief in a global Jewish conspiracy to exterminate German *Volk*, or "nation." By 1892 Jews were nearly daily denounced as a menace to German society in public meetings. Jewish religious texts came under increased scrutiny by government officials, and accusations of blood libel made headlines. Despite major reforms to Germany's tax code, the nation experienced a sharp economic recession for which Jews bore the brunt of the blame. Consequently, the 1893 elections resulted in the largest vote for political anti-Semitism in the history of the German Empire. By the beginning of the twentieth century, German notions of a unified *Volk* were increasingly defined through collective hatred of Germany's Jewish population. It is in this context that Du Bois first examined ideas about duality and marginality, but he did so through consideration of the German Jewish experience.

Following the publication of *The Souls of Black Folk*, Du Bois rarely returned to his concept of double consciousness in his academic writings. Yet he continued to theorize the structural features that defined the post-Emancipation condition of Black America: the Veil, or the color line; duality and marginality as both gift and curse; and the collective spirit, or soul, of Black America. Meanwhile, Du Bois's scholarship was marginalized if not ignored outright by his contemporaries, many of whom also employed the figure of the Jew in their own analysis of the American racial system. In chapter 4, "Post-*Souls*, Veiled Mysteries," I compare and contrast Du Bois's post-*Souls* considerations of race, duality, and marginality with those of his contemporaries. I argue that in the post-*Souls* period, Du Bois used the Black American experience to illustrate a racialized social structure that produced a debilitating condition among both African Americans and Whites. Meanwhile, many of his contemporaries used the figure of the Jew to argue that Jews' inability or unwillingness to assimilate into their host societies was evidence of pathos.

The Souls of Jewish Folk is not just a book about intellectual history, nor is it a book that only asks questions important to sociology. In the book's conclusion, I depart from an analysis of the role played by western Europe's Jewish question in Du Bois's intellectual project. Instead, I consider what role, if any, a Du Boisian analysis of race ought to play today in our understanding of ongoing political developments. War, disease, and famine disproportionately ravage Black and Brown people the world over. Those able to flee from their native soils must navigate the shifting sands of race, which recraft and tether religious differences to racial distinctions. Meanwhile, populist movements on both sides of the Atlantic use race as a key vehicle through which to channel widespread outrage into political action that threatens the very foundation of liberal democracy. Despite evidence of the resurgence of anti-Semitism and anti-Black racism across Europe and the United States, many within mainstream media and political punditry insist that our society is a postracial one. This contradiction between the rapid resurgence of anti-Jewish and anti-Black nationalist movements and the continued insistence on the insignificance of race presents an urgent need for a Du Boisian analysis of today's color line and its relationship to the important sociological questions of our time: the problem of the color line in the twenty-first century.

CHAPTER 1

Race, Science, and Madness

It may surprise some readers to learn that Du Bois did not coin the term "double consciousness." The concept's origins are in the psy sciences, and its usage among medical practitioners predates Du Bois's own by roughly eight decades. As a medical term, double consciousness referred to a particular set of observable symptoms: anxiety and hysteria, nervousness, and a split personality whereby neither manifestation was aware of the other.

Double consciousness was far from relegated to the annals of scientific journals. Descriptions of the condition show up in popular literature of the mid-nineteenth century. Moreover, like many other manifestations of mental illness in the nineteenth century, double consciousness and its associated symptoms were depicted as afflicting those groups of people science deemed inferior and thus more susceptible to disease and illness. Across the nineteenth and early twentieth centuries, the Jew served as the archetype for insanity. Nearly all of the associated conditions of double consciousness were ascribed to Jews on account of their perceived susceptibility.

In this chapter, then, my aim is to provide the historical and scientific backdrop for the concept of double consciousness. I do not claim that Du Bois grounded his concept of Black double consciousness in the pseudoscientific rationale that psychologists, psychiatrists, and other medical practitioners used in their theorizing of Jews' predisposition to it and other conditions. Rather, my aim is to show how a general scientific consensus that the Jew was unable to assimilate into Western (read: modern, Christian) society directs our attention toward a Du Boisian reformulation whereby double consciousness is no longer only a debilitating condition for Black Americans and other marginalized groups but a necessary adaptation.

Double Consciousness as a Pathos

In January 1817 American physician Samuel Mitchill wrote with notable enthusiasm to Eliphalet Nott, then president of Union College in Schenectady, New York. Mitchill had been witness to what he described as "an extraordinary case of double consciousness."[1] Mitchill was already a well-regarded medical doctor at the time he penned his letter, having founded the United States' first medical journal, the *Medical Repository*, while holding an academic appointment at the College of Physicians and Surgeons in New York, which he would later leave for an appointment at Columbia College. He was also a former U.S. senator and member of the House of Representatives.

The case Mitchill described to Nott concerned a woman named Mary Reynolds. Mitchill did not witness the events he described to Nott but relayed them as a secondhand account. According to Mitchill, Reynolds began displaying rather odd behaviors, including "unexpectedly, and without any kind of forewarning," falling into a deep sleep. By the time she awakened, Reynolds had, according to Mitchill, lost "every trait of acquired knowledge." These episodes continued for approximately fifteen years, until Reynolds permanently entered the second state of consciousness: "The former condition of her existence she now calls the old state, and the latter the new state; and she is [as] unconscious of her double character as two distinct persons are of their respective separate natures."[2]

From what is known in the historical record, Mitchill's descriptive account of Mary Reynolds's "extraordinary case of double consciousness" marks the first use of the term in Western science. Not only does Mitchill's letter predate Du Bois's 1897 *Atlantic Monthly* essay, " Strivings of the Negro People," by roughly eighty years, but Mitchill's letter marks the origins of the term "double consciousness" as a medical condition, a particular pathos that would garner interest from both scientific and lay audiences across the nineteenth century. Those suffering from double consciousness were said to present two versions of themselves, each fractured from the other to such an extent that, in either state of consciousness, the person was unaware of the other state of being.[3]

Just a year after Mitchill's letter to Nott, the *American Journal of Science* published an article entitled "Facts Illustrative of the Powers and Operations of the Human Mind in a Diseased State." Its author, a physician named Benjamin W. Dwight, prefaced his manuscript by noting that the cases he described were also secondhand accounts provided by men and women who knew the patients and witnessed their behaviors firsthand. "When the facts were communicated to me," Dwight wrote, "I immediately committed them to writing, and to avoid mistakes, read what I had written to the persons communicating them."[4]

Dwight's reporting centered on a case from over a decade prior but roughly corresponding to the timeline in which Mary Reynolds is said to have experienced her own episodes of mental illness. Like Reynolds, Dwight's case was a woman from the northeastern United States. This woman, according to Dwight, was stricken by sudden and violent episodes of delirium. These episodes continued for an indeterminate amount of time and then stopped as quickly as they came on, "leaving her mind perfectly rational."[5]

For those familiar with Du Bois's description of double consciousness as "two warring souls within one dark body," Dwight's description draws eerie parallels. According to Dwight, the woman "appeared as a person might be supposed to do, who had two souls, each occasionally dormant, and occasionally active, and utterly ignorant of what the other was doing." Compare this to Du Bois's account, in which "two souls, two thoughts, two unreconciled strivings" are far from ignorant of one another.[6] Indeed, they are actively warring or competing.

What, if any, connections exist, then, between Dwight's medical usage of double consciousness at the beginning of the nineteenth century and Du Bois's usage toward the end of it? One route between the two usages is the characterization of double consciousness as a kind of pathos. In the medical descriptions of Mitchill, Dwight, and others throughout the nineteenth century, the conditions were brought upon by certain stresses, many of which were associated with a rapidly modernizing society. In Du Bois's rendering, double consciousness is strife: Black Americans long for something impossible to obtain, yet they strive toward it nonetheless. Specifically, it is a responsive condition to a society in which the ideals of modernity are professed, yet the rights and obligations associated with those ideals are withheld. We will return to this point toward the end of this chapter.[7]

By the mid-nineteenth century double consciousness was a named pathos firmly rooted in the popular imagination. Several decades after Mitchill's and Dwight's accounts, an article by physician David Skae appeared in the *Northern Journal of Medicine* in 1845. Skae, a fellow of the Royal College of Surgeons in London, described a professional man "in the prime of his life" yet subject to "an extremely rare form of mental disorder." Among other things, the disorder caused the man to experience a "double existence." The man alternated between states of enjoyment and hopelessness, which Skae described as a mental aberration. "He appears, in short," Skae writes, "to have a double consciousness—a sort of twofold existence."[8]

Fifteen years later, *Harper's* published an essay that revealed how, as double consciousness was absorbed into the popular imaginary, audiences' understanding of its symptomatic expressions shifted. The author referenced the peculiar case of Mary Reynolds from a half-century prior: "[It was as] if her body was the house of two souls, not occupied by both at the same time, but alternately, first by one, then by the other, each in turn ejecting the other until at last the usurper gained and held position."[9] The description provided in this rendering reveals far more alignment with Du Bois's figurative language than with what was originally relayed by Mitchill or Dwight. In comparison, Reynolds's two souls in the *Harper's* essay are not only aware of the other but actively at war with each other, fighting for dominance.

A decade later, the popular British magazine *Cornhill* published an essay entitled "Dual Consciousness" that debated the merits of the theory that humans "have two brains, each perfectly sufficient for the full performance of mental functions." The author argues against the theory of dual brains and in favor of the more general condition of "dual or intermittent consciousness." In considering various cases of dual consciousness, the author does note that they "present characteristic divergencies." One account resembled Mitchill's description, in which "each life was distinct from the other." Another case, however, that of a woman by the name of Felida X, was characterized by "the circumstance that in one state she was conscious of what had passed in the other, but while in this other state was unconscious of what had passed in the former." Put differently, one of the mental states presented by Felida X was the awareness of her state of double consciousness.[10]

Two points need to be made. First, the detailed references in *Harper's* and *Cornhill* to dual and double consciousness reveal that, even as a medical term, the concept of double consciousness was never exclusive to medical audiences. Wider publics, scholars, and laypersons alike were aware of the condition and its associated symptoms. Related to this is my second point. As double consciousness became part of a common language, beyond a scholarly discussion, its meaning transformed: from a twofold existence in which one state of consciousness is unaware of the other to a twofold existence in which each state of consciousness is not only aware of the other but actively at war for dominance over the self.

This shift is important. It reveals the routes from medical to popular usage and the medicalized roots in Du Bois's own figurative language. My claim here is not that Du Bois was well-versed in the medical cases of double consciousness from the early nineteenth century. There is little evidence to support that claim. Rather, my claim is that Du Bois's use of double consciousness was unlikely to be drawn from thin air; instead, it was more likely grounded in the popular transformations of the term that marked the literature of the mid- to late nineteenth century.[11]

Within the medical community, over the course of the nineteenth century the term "double consciousness" would become synonymous with and eventually be replaced by multiple or double personality disorder. This passage from a condition to a named disorder marked a new understanding of double consciousness as a distinct pathos, albeit one with some debate over how it expressed itself. Some scientists and medical specialists linked double consciousness with particular symptoms such as amnesia, somnambulism (sleepwalking), neurasthenia (emotional disturbances), and hysteria. Meanwhile, others differentiated between double consciousness and duplicate consciousness. For example, the physician and superintendent of Bethlem Royal Hospital in London, Daniel Tuke, used the case of a Mr. W. North to distinguish between the two disorders. Mr. North was a lecturer at Westminster Hospital and a former Sharpey Scholar at the University College London. He had undergone hypnosis, after which he relayed his experiences to Tuke. Describing his deep stage of hypnosis, North told Tuke, "I was not unconscious, but I seemed to exist in duplicate. My inner self appeared to be thoroughly alive to all that was going on, but made up its mind not to control or interfere with the acts of the outer self; and the unwillingness or inability of the inner self to control the outer seemed to increase the longer the condition maintained.... I am told I spoke German ... and was not complimentary with my remarks." Based upon Mr. North's account, Tuke concluded, "There may be ... a double or divided consciousness.... This subject of duplicate consciousness (I avoid the term double consciousness, *as it applies to another mental phenomenon*) is one of great interest, and might alone occupy an evening's discussion."[12]

Not only is the shift from a general condition to a named disorder an important turning point in medical and lay understandings of double consciousness, but this passage also marked the point in which double consciousness and other mental disorders became linked to and subsumed by the dominant racialist theories of the era. These racialist theories tied mental illness to supposed biological and physiological markers of race and made claims for their inheritability and prevalence among those races deemed lower or less fit.

As an example, consider physician Theo Hyslop, a protégé of Daniel Tuke and the medical superintendent of Bethlem Royal Hospital. Hyslop's description of double consciousness in the *British Medical Journal* in 1899 revealed it as an "insane type" of mental illness that was born from mental instability, heritable, and ultimately degenerative:

> In mental disease, there is apt to be first a change in the vital feelings, the sequence of fundamental inner experience is broken, and the patient feels not quite himself, complete estrangement being prevented by the processes of experience which enable him to form a bridge between the old and the new feelings.... When the conscious memory connection is lost periodically, then we have double conscious-

ness, and lastly, when the brain is incapable of forming or reviving a sequence, then the final stage of mental dissolution is reached.[13]

Given the reputation of both Hyslop and the *British Medical Journal* at the turn of the nineteenth century, his account of double consciousness marked another important development in medical and popular understandings. Hyslop presented double consciousness as degenerative—from "a change in the vital feelings," to an eventual estrangement as the person became less able to "bridge between the old and the new feelings," to eventual "mental dissolution." This evaluation, as well as his overall presentation of double consciousness as hereditary, fits well within the emergent consensus of mental disease on the whole. Hyslop himself was among the better-known eugenicists of the late nineteenth century. He frequently lectured on the topic of moral insanity, which he described as an inheritable type of degeneracy prevalent among both the poor and the "lower races." In addition, and most important for the larger thesis of this particular chapter, by the end of the nineteenth century nearly all of the symptomatic expressions Hyslop and others associated with degenerative descriptions of double consciousness were also more commonly ascribed to western European Jews.[14]

Writing in the *Journal of Mental Science* in 1908, for example, physician Harvey Baird claimed that Jewish women were "of a more neurotic temperament" and that as a whole Jews were more susceptible to general paralysis on account of their Jewishness.[15] At the annual meeting of the Medico-Psychological Association in London, physician Cecil F. Beadles presented a paper entitled "The Insane Jew." In it, Beadles argued:

> By those who come in contact with the race in hospital and private practice, the men are looked upon as neurotic, the women as hysterical. Neurasthenia, and all that term implies, would seem to be a common complaint amongst those seeking medical aid. Hereditary insanity probably figures high in the race. . . . The mental strain resulting from excessive zeal in acquiring riches, and the worry and annoyance which must invariably accompany this greed for worldly goods, doubtless play no small part in the mental breakdown of these people.[16]

The recorded discussion following Beadles's presentation is illuminating. A Dr. Savage replied to Beadles's paper by stating, "The forms of moral depravity common among Jews are very marked and disproportionate, and perhaps that is not altogether surprising, considering the history of the race." A Dr. Shuttleworth remarked that "the parents, among the upper classes, are exceedingly neurotic" and that Jewish children in particular are "all highly nervous, and require very careful training by teachers before they make very much progress." A Dr. Mickle aimed his remarks at the recovery rate for Jews suffering from mental illness, noting that Jews are "essentially marked by hereditary mental degeneration." A Dr. MacDonald from New York noted that "our experience in America is very much that which has been detailed," that American hospitals were largely occupied by Jews, and that he could "corroborate what has been stated by the reader of the paper as being in accordance with our own observations." Finally, the president of the Medico-Psychological Association closed the discussion by stating, "My more recent hospital experience has convinced me that nervous diseases, especially epilepsy, are very common among [Jews]. I have also seen a good many Polish Jews, who work in close rooms as tailors in London, and who suffer from neurasthenia."[17]

These comments reveal the near consensus in the dominant racialist discourse of the nineteenth century on Jews and madness. When taken as a whole, these accounts show that the associated symptoms of double consciousness—nervousness and emotional disturbances—were also understood as markers of Jews themselves. That is, Jewishness was understood as a harbinger of these associated symptoms. Their association with double consciousness marked a significant shift in how double consciousness was understood among late nineteenth- and early twentieth-century medical practitioners as an illness especially commonplace among Jews.

The Specter of the Jew in Medical Constructions of Madness

Now is a good time to review where, thus far, my argument stands. First, double consciousness was for over eighty years prior to Du Bois's usage broadly understood as a mental affliction—first a general malaise and then a named mental illness with specific, associated symptoms. Amnesia, sleepwalking, emotional disturbances, and hysteria were the most common identified expressions.

Second, double consciousness's passage from a general malaise to a named mental illness coincided with a larger shift within the psy sciences: many mental illnesses became subsumed within and identified through dominant racialist theories of the nineteenth century. These racialist theories explained mental illness as the by-product of inheritability through so-called racial lineage. Men and women belonging to the so-called lower races were characterized as more susceptible to certain mental illnesses on account of their perceived biological and genealogical inferiority.[18]

Third, by the late nineteenth century double consciousness had been subsumed within these dominant racialist theories, which depicted the condition as both an inheritable and a degenerative disorder. Importantly, the associated symptoms that informed diagnoses of double consciousness were broadly understood as more prevalent among western European Jews. The near consensus among nineteenth-century medical practitioners on the linkages between Jews and the associated symptoms of double consciousness meant that, in practice, double consciousness was understood as a Jewish ailment.

How was it that Western science came to associate race with mental illness? How did race become configured as a precursor to mental illness? These questions have been the subject of serious scholarly treatment, so I will only summarize the key points for consideration.

The great majority of scholarship points to the age of Enlightenment and capitalist expansion as the period in which modern understandings of race and racism emerged. Some of the most significant works in the field of race scholarship argue, for example, that race "took on most of its importance as a result of the creation of the modern world." This conclusion has had the effect of rendering everything before this time as unimportant or insignificant to contemporary matters. Though some scholars have sought to better understand the roots of modern racism through premodern ethnic conflicts, they nevertheless still argue that our modern understandings of race and racism are cut entirely from a different epistemological cloth. An odd assertion, to be sure, if premodern ethnic conflicts are indeed where the roots lie.[19]

In previous work I've challenged these claims, as have others, by pointing to the fact that the possession of a concept can, for a group of people, predate the possession of a corresponding word. In the case of the concept of race, the active work to distinguish groups of people based upon perceived physical differences is rooted in medieval Christianity's efforts to mark Jews as inferior to and in need of separation from Christians. This active work and its effects antedate the sociopolitical categories of race developed across the eighteenth, nineteenth, and twentieth centuries. As historian Sander Gilman notes, it was ultimately Christianity that provided the vocabularies of difference for much of the modern Western world, including science and medicine.[20]

This point is especially important when considering the centrality of anti-Semitism and anti-Black racism within the project of modernity itself. Even in its post-Enlightenment secularized form, the rhetoric of Western culture remains deeply permeated by Christian thought, including its imagery of the debased and debauched Jew. Eighteenth- and nineteenth-century medicine, for example, drew upon medieval representations of the cloven-footed "devil-Jew." Likewise, Hitler's own *Mein Kampf* traces the roots of syphilis as a Jewish disease to the 1492 "Peste of the Marranos" declaration of Charles VIII of France. Whereas the Jew's inherent inferiority was once thought curable through conversion, later depictions and representations portrayed the Jew as ultimately irredeemable and in need of containment or, worse, elimination.[21]

The eighteenth and nineteenth centuries are significant to the history of the race concept because this was the period that bore witness to the biologization of difference, which became cataloged and categorized as race. In many ways, this new language of race transmuted assumptions of racial difference from being located in the soul to being located within the mind and body. This era marked the emergence of biologically driven conceptions of mental illness. It is therefore not surprising that madness during this era was ascribed to particular so-called racial groups. As early as the Enlightenment, race was believed to be a causal factor for mental illness, but almost exclusively for those deemed racially inferior: Blacks in the United States, the Irish in Great Britain, and Jews in western and central Europe. Colonial and imperial conquests in Latin America and parts of Africa paved the way for similar attributions of mental illness to subjugated natives once they were under colonial rule.

This point is important. The frequency with which Black people in the United States were diagnosed with certain mental illnesses coincided with that point in American history in which Blacks were emancipated. Likewise, the attribution of insanity to indigenous peoples in Latin America and parts of Africa coincided with their subjugation under colonial regimes. In both instances, Western (read: White) liberalism was the primary mechanism through which racial subjectivity and mental illness were conjoined. Free society was seen as too complex for the minds of the newly emancipated to readily adapt. Likewise, colonial rule was believed to provide the necessary structure to prevent the natives from going insane. The solution put forward for both emancipated Black Americans and colonial subjects abroad was a bifurcated and repressive regime that, not inconsequentially, was also economically exploitative.[22]

Meanwhile racialism, the so-called scientific perspective on the veracity of racial differences, became hegemonic across the nineteenth and early twentieth centuries. It was both cause and consequence of the epistemological shift within European society from religious doctrine to scientific rationale. The Enlightenment and subsequent emergence of scientific knowledge as the mode of authoritative truth helped crystallize beliefs in clearly defined biological categories of humans. Because scientific authority was considered independent of political authority, these emergent categories of difference were understood as free from political influence. Nevertheless, these categories were used by both scientists and political figures to reinforce political boundaries between groups—enslaved and free, citizen and noncitizen, and what we might call the category of not-quite-citizen, or those who reside between.[23]

By 1775 the scientific study of races was commonplace. German researcher Johann Friedrich Blumenbach, in his *De Generis Humani Varietate Nativa*, described race as "more or less formal systems of classification: any of the major groupings of mankind, having in common distinct physical features or having a similar ethnic background." In 1795 *The Oxford English Dictionary* noted the popular acceptance of this view: "These Tartar tribes, which he supposes to be of the Red Race, [are] distinct from the European White Race." By the end of the eighteenth century, then, race was not merely "pseudoscience" but both reaction to and catalyst of the increasingly authoritative position of the biosciences in Western knowledge regimes. In this first age of positivistic and empirical science, racialism became so widespread, so thoroughly woven into the human and medical sciences, that to contest its veracity was to challenge scientific authority itself. As pragmatist philosopher George Herbert Mead wrote, "Knowledge is never a mere contact of our organisms with other objects. It always takes on a universal character. If we know a thing, explain it, we always put it into a texture of uniformities. There must be some reason for it, some law expressed in it. That is the fundamental assumption of science." By the nineteenth century, Mead's view on science as a systematized form of knowledge held for racialism as well.[24]

The role the Jewish archetype played in systematizing and legitimating racialism across the biosciences during this era cannot be understated. Beginning in the eighteenth century and with increasing legitimacy throughout the nineteenth and twentieth centuries, Western science and medicine institutionalized the relationship between Jews and madness. As early as 1791, anti-Semitic pamphlets stressing the immutability of the Jewish mind and alleging that stubbornness and corruption were psychopathic qualities associated with Jews circulated among both medical professionals and laypersons. The debates about outlawing slavery in Great Britain and the civil emancipation of European Jews beginning in the late eighteenth century were paralleled by the growth in the rhetoric of scientific racism throughout western Europe.

The nineteenth century was for European Jews, especially for German Jews, a period that brought both hope and despair. Civil emancipation, increased economic and social mobility, and access to secular education were slowly acquired by European Jews throughout the nineteenth century. Yet these gains were counterbalanced by the rise of political anti-Semitism, which sought to reverse civil emancipation, and the reappearance in altered form of medieval forms of anti-Semitism, including "blood libel" accusations. Meanwhile, political realities within the Russian Empire led to massive pogroms and the flight of millions of eastern and mainly unacculturated Jews to the cities of western Europe and beyond.

How Jews themselves responded to these events ranged widely. Some assimilated and converted. Others developed a political consciousness that served as prototype to Zionism. Still others sought to navigate the institutions of their host societies while maintaining their distinct cultural identities, establishing secular Jewish political parties (at least in the Austro-Hungarian Empire). Of course, this snapshot is reductive. But it is broadly accurate and corresponds to the range of scholarship on the matter.[25]

Across western Europe the gradual integration of Jews into the body politic was understood as both the cause of Jewish psychopathology and a source of danger to the purity of the national spirit. Scientists believed that acculturation had triggered a racial predisposition to madness among Jews. For example, German neurologist Wilhelm Erb, at a birthday celebration for the king of Baden in 1893, commented on the increased nervousness among the "Semites, who already are a neurotically predisposed race. Their untamed desire for profit and their nervousness, caused by centuries of imposed life style, as well as their inbreeding and marriage within families, predisposes them to nervousness." Jews' political emancipation was also understood as the source of their susceptibility to madness. The dean of fin-de-siècle German psychiatrists, Emil Kraepelin, professor of psychiatry at the University of Munich and founder of the Institute for Psychiatry there, spoke with authority about the "domestication" of the Jews, their isolation from nature, and their exposure to the stresses of modern life. For Kraepelin and others, it was the Jews' inherent biological weakness that determined their susceptibility.[26]

Even nineteenth-century liberal views of Jews shared a similar notion of a Jewish predisposition to madness. In Paris, the most important neurologist of the time, Jean-Martin Charcot, lectured on the stated presumption that "nervous illnesses of all types are innumerably more frequent among Jews than among other groups." Charcot described Jews as "the best source of material for nervous illness." He also described the predisposition of Jews to specific forms of illness as the result of the biological consequences of their religious practice rather than as a result of their racial makeup. Jews were mad because of their rates of endogamous marriage, which, in terms of nineteenth-century thought, was a form of incest. Religious practice, to Charcot, a radical opponent of all organized religion, was as much a sign of the primitive nature of the Jewish psyche as it was of Catholic sophistication. According to Charcot, acculturation could ameliorate but never eliminate this tendency.[27]

Meanwhile, in the United States, the premise that immigrant Jews were more susceptible to mental illness was a matter of great debate at the New York Neurological Society's annual meeting in April 1914. There, a presentation was given by Jewish psychiatrists A. A. Brill (who was also trained as a psychoanalyst) and Morris J. Karpas. Brill and Karpas stressed that the differences among the statistics reflected the national status of American Jews. According to Brill and Karpas, though "the Jewish race contributes a rather high percentage to the so-called functional form of insanity . . . the Jew is not disproportionately insane." Functional psychopathologies, such as hysteria, were more evident among Jews even in New York City, where they supposedly were freed from the state oppression of the Russian Empire. Brill and Karpas focused on newly arrived Eastern European Jews who were admitted to the public mental hospitals from which they gathered their sampling of cases.[28]

The debate following Brill and Karpas's presentation was intense, according to the meeting records. A George H. Kirby argued that it was important to understand the frequency of diseases such as dementia praecox (precocious madness) in order to better treat various immigrant groups who were more likely to suffer from these ailments. The president of the society, Smith Ely Jelliffe, reportedly threw up his hands and stated that statisticians could make what they wanted out of the figures and could make the superficial important. Physician-anthropologist Maurice Fishberg, a public health official in New York City who was present by invitation, then presented his argument of the contextual cause of higher incidences of mental illness.[29]

According to Fishberg, American Jews were urban dwellers who engaged in "financial and commercial pursuits" more than others. Jews' proclivity for mental illness seemed to change based on where they lived and the local conditions. Indeed, elsewhere Fishberg had argued that new Jewish immigrants from eastern Europe, who were the focus of the debate at the society's meeting, were actually of a racial stock different from that of the older German immigrants, who seemed to be less at risk and more at home in the world of American capitalism: "The Jews in Russia are not Semites at all . . . and actually belong to an entirely different race." In sum, whether viewed as a collective, a race, or a social group, Jews could be defined by a higher risk for insanity.[30]

By the beginning of the twentieth century, the image of the Jew as inherently predisposed to specific forms of insanity with multiple etiologies was commonplace. In his widely read and translated *General Psychopathology*, Karl Jaspers, a psychiatrist in Heidelberg and one of the major innovators of clinical psychiatry of his day, as well as one of the creators of a systematic existentialist philosophy, argued for the close relationship of race and mental illness. Within his two-volume work, Jaspers cited in great detail what were then commonplace claims of the Jews' general predisposition for mental illness. Jaspers was a member of sociologist Max

Weber's Heidelberg circle, a group of German intellectuals, many of whom were Weber's students. Jaspers's politics were certainly liberal, if not nationalistic, although they were far less overtly racist for his time than the views of his more conservative compatriots.[31]

Among nineteenth- and early twentieth-century psychiatrists and medical professionals, including more liberal ones like Jaspers, the Jew was the ideal type for representing a variety of psychopathological conditions, including double consciousness and its associated symptoms. Various theories were put forth to explain the nature of Jewish madness. All of these explanations functioned to produce a uniform biological category: the Jew. Thus, Georg Burgl's 1912 handbook of forensic medicine states quite clearly, "The Jewish race has a special predisposition for hysteria." For Burgl, this was a result of the degenerate nature of the Jew, marked by "physical signs of degeneration such as asymmetry and malocclusion of the skull, malocclusion of the teeth, etc." The visibility of the Jew was identical to the visibility of the degenerate, with signs and symptoms pointing to Jews' susceptibility.[32]

Given that the biology of race stood at the center of the nineteenth-century sciences of human beings—biology, medicine, and anthropology—it would have been extraordinary for anyone who thought of themselves as a scientist during this period to have avoided confronting the dominant racialist paradigm of their day. Jewish scientists bore witness to how their religious and cultural identities were rendered as precursors for diseases of the mind and body by the very knowledge regime that credentialed them as scientists. Yet this same regime, which conferred upon them the title of scientist, also demanded they confront the regime's assertion that they, Jews, were from a biologically inferior stock of humans. Jewish scientists and medical practitioners had little choice but to acknowledge, if not accept, what was then scientific consensus on their predisposition to madness, as this consensus was part of what defined clinical medicine. For Jewish doctors to refuse to acknowledge this claim, including even challenging its scientific basis, could have reflected poorly on their own mental stability! Thus, the standard Jewish medical rationale for supposed higher incidences of Jewish psychopathology was that mental illness was the expression of a collective deficit caused by Jews' centuries-long diasporic condition and subsequent struggle to survive. It was the Jews' struggle for political recognition, for full citizenship, that made it especially difficult for them to acclimate to emancipation once granted. The shift here is notable. Whereas much of the scientific consensus centered on Jewishness as a precursor to madness, Jewish doctors of this era were offering a different diagnosis: anti-Semitism was to blame.[33]

The Coconstruction of Jewish
and Black Insanity

As I have shown, by the mid-nineteenth century the linkage between Jews and madness was commonplace within the scientific and medical communities. Rates of mental illness were often cited and functioned as a kind of circular reasoning: Jews were understood as more likely to suffer from various psychopathologies, and evidence of Jews suffering from some psychopathologies was seen as demonstrating that these psychopathologies were so-called Jewish diseases.

Key to establishing this circular reasoning was the emergence of and subsequent belief in the authority of statistical knowledge. Indeed, the frequency in statistical findings of idiocy and mental illness among Jews coincided with the expansion of statistics as a kind of technical and legitimating form of support for the scientific enterprise. Statistics was the new science of measurement, and the associations it claimed to reveal between madness and racial categories served to validate racialist theories of the nineteenth century.[34]

Jews were not the only targets of statistical claims, however. Both Jews and Black people had for more than a century been portrayed by Western science and medicine as inferior, as folk people bound to customs and traditions perceived as antithetical to western European civilization. The field of statistics helped buttress these claims. Rates of mental illness among Jews and Black Americans were frequently cited within mid- to late nineteenth-century medical and anthropological journals as empirical evidence of both groups' inabilities to deal with modernity's complexities.[35]

It is worth mentioning that despite the prevalence of these claims within the medical and scientific literature, statistical findings on the inheritable inferiority of Blacks and Jews did not go unchallenged. One of the more notable challenges was issued by a Black physician and statistician by the name of Edward Jarvis. Jarvis's contention was aimed toward the 1840 U.S. Census, which had mistakenly (or fraudulently, depending upon the interpretation) reported the incidence of insanity among Blacks in northern states as roughly seven times greater than among northern Whites and nearly eleven times greater than among southern Blacks. Having looked closely at summary reports from each state, Jarvis found "the secret of error."[36]

In its counting of public charges, the census had reported many as "coloured insane" despite the fact that they were White patients. In fact, Jarvis found that within many towns where the census had reported the presence of Black public charges, there were actually no Black inhabitants. Having discovered this error, Jarvis cut straight to the matter: "The same carelessness, which gave insanity without subjects in some places, may have given none in others, where it actually existed."[37]

Jarvis was not the only one to catch this error. The American Statistical Association sent a letter to Congress notifying it of the mistake, as did former president John Quincy Adams. Despite these well-documented criticisms, the census did not issue any corrections to its count. The real lesson from this ordeal, then, was that beliefs in the power of statistical evidence were stronger than even the methodology itself.[38]

While statistics were frequently used to lend scientific credibility to claims of Jews' predisposition to madness, the commentary on its etiology was more diffuse in comparison to that of Black Americans. On the one hand, nineteenth-century science and medicine relied heavily upon visual categories as markers of racial pathology for Jews. Rather than external markers such as style of dress, occupation, and geographic location, specific biological and thus physical markers were used to identify Jewish pathology. Jews' noses and eyes, for example, were broadly understood as physical markers of degeneration and subsequently linked to a wide range of diagnoses of mental illnesses. On the other hand, some pointed toward distinct Jewish customs and traditions as the roots of Jews' madness.

A debate within the Parisian Anthropological Society's bulletin in 1884, for example, reveals that some participants located Jews' susceptibility to madness in their perceived preoccupation with mysticism and the supernatural. Others, however, drew upon statistical evidence that "hysteria and neurasthenia are more frequent among the Jewish races than all other races."[39]

The latter claim on the supposed frequency of hysteria and emotional disturbances among Jews refers back to a point made earlier: by the late nineteenth century, both of these disorders were more commonly ascribed to Jews and understood as symptomatic expressions of double consciousness. Both hysteria and emotional disturbances were understood as conditions that were caused by the stresses of civilized society. The scientific and medical consensus on Jews was that their backward customs and traditions were incompatible with modernity. Moreover, their inferior racial stock made assimilation more difficult. These conditions and, by extension, double consciousness were understood as inevitable outcomes of trying to adjust to a society too advanced and too different from Jews' own. Neurasthenia, for example, was understood among medical practitioners as resulting from an exhaustion of the central nervous system, "most frequently met with in civilized, intellectual communities . . . a part of the compensation for our progress and refinement."[40]

Meanwhile, hysteria, originally defined as a physical ailment primarily afflicting women, would by the end of the nineteenth century take on new psychopathological meaning. In his 1888 textbook, Charcot drew upon the case study of a Jewish woman's hysterical condition to argue that all forms of nervous illnesses are more frequent among Jews than other racial groups. By 1890 the view of hysteria as a Jewish disease was commonplace in psychiatry. Alfred Binet's *On Double Consciousness* (1905) went one step further in cementing hysteria's relationship to double consciousness: "In possession of precise observations drawn from experiments and second hand accounts we know that in hysterical individuals there exist phenomena of double consciousness." If Charcot popularized the belief that Jewishness was a precipitating factor for hysteria, and if Binet's observation affixed hysterical individuals to the condition of double consciousness, then by the early twentieth century the medical imagery of a patient suffering from double consciousness was likely that of the Jew.[41]

It should be noted that while claims for double consciousness's associated symptoms as Jewish diseases are key to making connections between Jews and double consciousness, these associated symptoms were also commonly ascribed to women, irrespective of their religious identification. Indeed, from antiquity through the nineteenth century hysteria was a condition only ascribed to women. It was not until the late nineteenth century that hysteria was reimagined as an affliction more frequent among Jewish women and then Jewish men. What accounts for this shift?

Hysteria's redefinition from a disease associated with women's physiology to a disease associated with Jews' mental unfitness exemplifies a broader trend across the nineteenth and early twentieth centuries whereby Jewish degeneracy was fashioned upon the feminization of Jewish men. So commonplace was this feminization and then pathologization of Jewish masculinity that it eventually led to the emergence of a popular counternarrative among Jews: *Muskeljudentum*, or "muscular Judaism." This counternarrative was made popular by the physician and cofounder of the Zionist Organization (later renamed the World Zionist Organization), Max Nordau. In his 1898 speech to the Second Zionist Congress in Basel, Switzerland, Nordau offered muscular Judaism as a sharp contrast to popular portrayals of Jewish men as physically and mentally weak. Jewish suffering—mental, physical, and spiritual—was the result of widespread anti-Semitism, which prevented the Jews' acceptance within their home nation. The cure, according to Nordau, was a moral and physical regeneration only possible through national consciousness and eventually the Jews' own nationality—Zionism.[42]

Jews, like women, were widely believed to have an inherent susceptibility to mental illnesses on account of their weakened physical and mental states. Just as Western democracies used Western scientific and medical accounts of inferiority to dismiss women's claims for political inclusion in the late nineteenth century,

those same democracies dismissed Jews as unworthy of full citizenship for similar reasons. Likewise, just as Western science and medicine labeled as mad an enslaved Black population in America on account of their refusal to accept slavery as
their natural condition, western European Jews proved their madness by demanding their political emancipation.[43]

As mentioned previously, one of the great ironies of this period of Western science and medicine is that imagery of Jewish pathology and degeneracy emerged
and became dominant as Jews were making great inroads within the medical and
scientific professions. Yet despite these important inroads, the image of Jewish
madness persisted even among Jewish scientific and medical experts. Importantly,
however, while the dominant racialist theories of this period posited Jewish madness as hereditary and therefore unavoidable, many Jewish scientists rejected these
biological explanations in favor of social ones. Italian Jewish forensic psychiatrist
Cesare Lombroso argued that the roots of Jewish madness were in the centuries-
long persecution of the Jews. Viennese Jewish physician Martin Englander made a
similar claim, arguing that the prevalence of Jewish rates of insanity was the result
of "overexertion and exhaustion of the brain" brought upon by "a two-thousand
year Diaspora" and the "struggle for mere existence up to emancipation."[44]

Literary critic Robert Byrnes notes that at the turn of the twentieth century,
"within both the pseudo-science of anti-Semitism and the psychiatric explanations accepted by Jewish physicians themselves, the Jewish race bore a stigma of
degeneration that could be interpreted, but not interpreted away." For those scientists and physicians who subscribed wholesale to the dominant racialist paradigm of this era, Jewish degeneracy, because it was believed to be hereditary, "was
ineradicable—another of the signs of Cain—making the Jew a permanent *Unter-
mensch* as well as an eternal wanderer." Meanwhile, for those sympathetic to the
Jewish condition, including Jewish scientists and medical doctors themselves, Jewish pathology "simply rehearsed the Jew's tragic destiny again in the new arena of
the urban wilderness." Both the demand that Jews repress their Jewishness in order to assimilate into the body politic and their subsequent inability to do so because of prevalent anti-Semitism produced among them a range of mental afflic-
tions, including double consciousness. Double consciousness, then, emerged as a
mental illness brought upon the Jew by modernity, which included modern anti-
Semitism. And modern anti-Semitism, politically grounded in a way that previous
forms had not been, marked the Jew as incompatible with the ideals and values of
modernity and with it the modern nation-state.[45]

The Jewish response to the mental strains associated with this political form of
anti-Semitism is exemplified in proto-Zionist physician Leon Pinsker's pamphlet
Auto-Emancipation! In it, Pinsker locates the roots of Jewish madness in the En-

lightenment demand that Jews become "like everyone else" and the fact that to do that, Jews must repress all that makes them Jewish. Pinsker's claim is not incongruent with the scientific consensus of his day on Jews' predisposition to madness. Rather, like Jewish scientists and doctors before him, Pinsker sees Jews' endless torment from the pressure to acculturate as the cause of their mental strain. Where Pinsker goes further, however, is in his consideration of the Jews' tormentors. For Pinsker, Judeophobia—fear and hatred of Jews—is an obsession among European Christians, one that conjures a serious aversion not at all dissimilar from the aversion of "the living [to] a corpse ... the native [to] a foreigner ... the homesteader [to] a vagrant ... the patriot a man without a country, for all a hated rival. ... Judeophobia is a psychic aberration." Anti-Semitism itself is product and producer of mental illness.[46]

Ultimately, Pinsker argues, Judeophobia leads to self-hatred. Unable to assimilate into their host nations on account of their Jewishness, Jews will only continue to suffer. Nothing can cure the obsessive anti-Semitism of the world that the Jew must confront. However, like Nordau and other Zionists of the era, Pinsker locates the cure for this self-hatred in the development of a Jewish national consciousness and a physical nation-state.[47]

The power of Pinsker's argument resides in describing Jews' lack of national consciousness through the imagery of psychopathology: "In the case of a sick man, the absence of desire for food is a very serious symptom. ... Not only do they feel no need for it, but they go so far as to deny the reasonableness of such a need. ... Jews are in the unhappy condition of such a patient." The Jewish nation-state, for Pinsker, would serve as catalyst for the moral, mental, and physical regeneration of European Jewry.[48]

This appeal for a Jewish nation-state complemented that of Nordau, who was a contemporary of Pinsker. The Diaspora, especially its rampant anti-Semitism, had weakened the Jew mentally, physically, and spiritually. The only cure was a new ideal of self-consciousness rooted in nationhood. Reclaiming muscular Judaism—a tradition Nordau traced to the ancient Maccabees and the Jewish insurgent Simon bar Kokhba—would lead to a new nation of Jews, "deep chested, sturdy and sharp-eyed."[49]

Pinsker's pamphlet was first published more than two decades prior to *The Souls of Black Folk*. While Pinsker's calls for a national consciousness were clearly grounded in the specific experiences of the Jewish Diaspora and anti-Semitism, his thinking nevertheless presented important parallels to Du Bois's own theorizing of Black double consciousness. Broadly, Pinsker's writings leading up to *Auto-Emancipation!* present a complex call for Jewish sovereignty rooted in criticism of the modern social contract. This contract, which from the French Revolution forward had slowly been transforming across western Europe, demanded from Jews nothing short of their complete, collective abandonment of a national Jewish character in return for full membership in the body politic.[50]

In his editorials for the Russian weekly *Sion* (1861–62), however, Pinsker forcefully argued that Jews ought to be able to have their cake and eat it, too. Jews could be loyal patriots to their host nation without compromising their own ethnohistorical traditions. As historian Dimitry Shumsky shows, within the specific context of Russia, Pinsker believed that while Jews ought to assimilate to some degree, "the Russian state, for its part, should not regard Russianization as a means of assimilating non-Russian groups or of converting non-Pravoslavic peoples to Christianity."[51]

Yet the years between these editorials and *Auto-Emancipation!* proved instructive for Pinsker. He had witnessed mob-based terrorism against Jews in Russia and the slow erosion of Jews' hard-gained political and civil rights elsewhere. As a consequence, his views on nationalism shifted. Emancipation was no longer a matter of assimilation into host nations, with Jews retaining their ethnonational character. Emancipation was only possible through the formation of a Jewish nation-state:

> Since the Jew is nowhere at home, nowhere regarded as a native, he remains an alien everywhere. That he himself and his forefathers as well are born in the country does not alter this fact in the least. . . . [N]ever is he considered a legitimate child of the fatherland. . . . [The] legal emancipation [of the Jews] is not social emancipation, and with the proclamation of the former the Jews are still far from being emancipated from their exceptional social position. . . . The stigma attached to this people, which forces it into an unenviable isolation among the nations, cannot be removed by any sort of official emancipation, as long as this people produces in accordance with its nature vagrant nomads, as long as it cannot give a satisfactory account of whence it comes and whither it goes.[52]

Pinsker's new views on Jewish nationalism were rooted in his experiences with the modern European nation-state, which he now understood as incompatible with a collective Jewish consciousness. The demands from European nation-states for the repression of all that was Jewish as precursor for full citizenship produced among the Jews an "irreconcilable condition"—two warring ideals within one Jewish body. Obtaining recognition within the modern nation-state as Jews was impossible because the modern nation-state defined itself against the Jew. And without a Jewish national consciousness, the collective Jewish psyche suffered.

For Du Bois, the "two warring souls" represented incompatible forms of national consciousness: Blackness and Americanness. Blacks strive for full recognition as political subjects but can never obtain complete recognition because America continues to define itself against all that is Black. Both Pinsker and Du Bois, then, understood the duality of Jews and Black Americans, respectively, as rooted in their futile efforts to belong to the body politic while retaining their own collective consciousness or recognition of their collective identity and its importance on its own terms. To use the German word, their two warring souls are competing *Volk*.

Moreover, whereas the general scientific and medical consensus was that Jews and Blacks were predisposed to duality on account of their perceived racial inferiority, Pinsker and Du Bois understood that the problem of duality arose from external forces—group-based oppression that expressed itself as anti-Semitism and anti-Black racism.

Finally, both Pinsker and Du Bois recognized that though this condition of two warring souls arises from external forces, it manifests within Jews and Blacks as trauma. Neither Jews nor Black Americans can resolve this condition of twoness, of striving yet failing to fully belong to their host nation, because neither group's respective host nation will allow incorporation into the body politic under any other terms than that impossible resolution.[53]

CHAPTER 2

The Du Boisian Reformulation

Nineteenth-century science and medicine crystallized race as a precursor or marker of mental illness. The medicalization of double consciousness leaned heavily upon the figure of the Jew, including a general scientific consensus that the Jew was particularly susceptible to manifest symptoms of double consciousness. But what, if any, relationship existed between this medicalized and racially charged account of double consciousness at the turn of the twentieth century and W. E. B. Du Bois's own formulation? Du Bois used double consciousness as a means to account for the social and psychological affects resulting from two incompatible systems of belonging, one as part of a Black collective living in the United States and the other as American defining itself against that Black collective. Was Du Bois aware of how double consciousness was used within psychopathological accounts of Jewish madness?

Admittedly, there is reason to doubt that any relationship exists. The evidence is circumstantial, and, as I noted at the beginning of this book, there is no smoking gun of which I am aware. I spent nearly two months in the Du Bois archive at the University of Massachusetts at Amherst combing through Du Bois's correspondence, notes, papers, and other writings. I failed to unearth any clear evidence Du Bois had read such accounts of Jewish psychopathology. Nor did I discover any testimony from Du Bois that his use of double consciousness was inspired by these accounts. How, then, can I argue convincingly that Du Bois's use of double consciousness was, indeed, informed by this image of the Jew?[1]

That question is the wrong one to ask. It does not matter whether or not Du Bois was directly inspired by the figure of the Jew suffering from double consciousness. Rather, the questions are, How does Du Bois's own formulation compare? And if there are parallels, what accounts for them?

German intellectual Karl Mannheim encouraged a sociology of knowledge that eschewed biographies of intellectual figures. Instead, Mannheim argued for social histories that situated those figures within the times and events in which they lived. By shifting the questions, then, my aim is to move toward an analysis of the social, political, and intellectual contexts in which Du Bois was situated as he was actively developing his own formulation. These contexts shape the concepts we use to explain them; focusing on how these contexts inform Du Bois's own thought will prove instructive.[2]

Elsewhere, sociologist Rutledge Dennis has written extensively on Du Bois's intellectual contributions to sociological thought. In those writings, Dennis has argued that "Du Bois had a minimal understanding of psychology." I do not believe that this claim holds up well against the historical record.

Du Bois was Harvard trained. While there and under the tutelage of professors like William James, he would have undoubtedly been exposed to and aware of the emergent field of psychology. Moreover, the parallels between nineteenth-century medicalized accounts of double consciousness and Du Bois's own are, prima facie, too significant to dismiss outright. These parallels, at minimum, reveal that even if Du Bois had no direct knowledge of previous medicalized versions (a dubious claim itself), his knowledge of and proximity to psychology would have indirectly exposed him to the general racialist frameworks of Jews' and Blacks' susceptibility to mental illness. Finally, Du Bois's awareness of and proximity to the dominant racialist discourse at the University of Berlin is difficult, if not impossible, to ignore.[3]

William James, Fractured Selves, and Du Bois's Double Consciousness

While at Harvard, Du Bois was mentored by American pragmatist and psychologist William James. James's mentorship of Du Bois overlapped with the 1890 publication of James's own highly influential text, *The Principles of Psychology*. In it, James posited that the two-part structure of the human brain allowed for one form of consciousness to emerge in one part while a simultaneous consciousness could emerge, even coexist, in the other. Elsewhere in the text, James attempted to account for a "social self" as the product of ongoing social relationships. James's version of this social self would, of course, serve as precursor to different iterations from pragmatist and philosopher George Herbert Mead and social psychologist Charles Horton Cooley.[4]

James theorized the social self as "the recognition [one] gets from [one's] mates":

> We are not only gregarious animals, liking to be in sight of our fellows, but we have an innate propensity to get ourselves noticed, and noticed favorably, by our kind. No more fiendish punishment could be devised, were such a thing physically possible, than that one should be turned loose in society and remain absolutely unnoticed by all the members thereof. If no one turned round when we entered, answered when we spoke, or minded what we did, but if every person we met "cut us dead" and acted as if we were non-existing things, a kind of rage and impotent despair would ere long well up in us, from which the cruelest bodily tortures would be a relief; for these would make us feel that, however bad might be our plight, we had not sunk to such a depth as to be unworthy of attention at all.[5]

Decades later, in *Dusk of Dawn*, Du Bois would take up this unimaginable "fiendish punishment," but from the perspective of a Black collective forced to live their lives according to the color line, behind "the Veil," rendered near invisible by their White counterparts:

> It is difficult to let others see the full psychological meaning of caste segregation. It is as though one, looking out from a dark cave in a side of an impending mountain, sees the world passing and speaks to it; speaks courteously and persuasively, showing them how these entombed souls are hindered in their natural movements, expression, and development; and how their loosening from prison would be a matter not simply of courtesy ... but aid to the world. ... It gradually penetrates the minds of the prisoners that the people passing do not hear; that some thick sheet of invisible but horribly tangible plate glass is between them and the world. They get excited; they talk louder; they gesticulate. ... Then the people within may become hysterical. They may scream and hurl themselves against the barriers, hardly realizing in their bewilderment that they are screaming in a vacuum unheard and that their antics may actually seem funny to those outside looking in.[6]

Here, to the extent that Black Americans are noticed at all, they are noticed as "non-existing things." Imprisoned with voices unheard, they are rendered as objects, even humorous ones, to White passersby. Like the more general figure in James's account, the image provided by Du Bois is empathetic to the pain and suffering Black Americans experience as they strive toward, yet ultimately fail to achieve, full recognition from an America that "cuts them dead" upon sight.

James, meanwhile, continued his treatment of the social self by elaborating on the multiple iterations within a given individual. How many iterations there are, according to James, depends upon the number of "distinct groups of persons about whose opinion [the individual] cares." Recognizing that our presentation to each of these groups is accomplished in such a way as to prevent drawing negative attention toward ourselves, James writes, "From this there results what practically is a division of the man into several selves; and this may be a discordant splitting." The individual, for James, strives for recognition from those groups the individual deems important. These groups may and often do have incompatible values, ideas, and beliefs. Yet for the individual, each group remains important for the individual's own formation of a self. Therefore, in striving toward recognition from these groups, the individual experiences incongruence between the versions of his or her social selves.[7]

To be clear, I do not believe Du Bois's formulation of double consciousness mirrors James's psychological account of multiple social selves. My point, rather, is that at the time Du Bois was James's protégé, James was actively writing about the concept of duality. There is no world in which Du Bois would not have been aware of James's thinking on this subject, especially given their close, even personal, relationship. Simply put, there are parallels between James's version of fractured selves and Du Bois's imagery of "two warring souls" in one Black body that we cannot so easily dismiss. And given these parallels, we ought to at least reject the claim that Du Bois had only a "minimal understanding of psychology."[8]

Returning to James, in *The Principles of Psychology* he takes up the phenomenon of "alterations in the present self," which James divides into three types: insane delusions, alternating selves, and mediumship or possessions. In the first type, the manifestations are varied:

> One patient has another self that repeats all his thoughts for him. Others, among whom are some of the first characters in history, have familiar demons who speak with them, and are replied too. In another someone "makes" his thought for him. Another has two bodies, lying in different beds. . . . Occasionally, parts of the body lose their connection for consciousness with the rest, and are treated as belonging to another person and moved by a hostile will. Thus the right hand may fight with the left as with an enemy.[9]

It is in the second type, however, that James comes closest to the medicalized concept of double consciousness:

> In the pathological cases known as those of double or alternate personality the lapse of memory is abrupt, and is usually preceded by a period of unconsciousness or syncope lasting a variable length of time. . . . The most famous case, perhaps, on record is that of Félida X., reported by Dr. Azam of Bordeaux. At the age of four-

teen this woman began to pass into a "secondary" state characterized by a change
in her general disposition and character, as if certain "inhibitions," previously existing, were suddenly removed. During the secondary state she remembered the
first state, but on emerging from it into the first state she remembered nothing of
the second.[10]

James then quotes at length another case, that of the infamous Mary Reynolds,
before moving on to the case that James had "become quite recently acquainted
with": the Reverend Ansel Bourne of Green, Rhode Island.

Described by James as a man whose "health is good," Bourne had, in January
1887, withdrawn the equivalent of nearly $15,000 in today's dollars from a Prov-
idence bank, with which he bought "a certain lot of land in Greene, paid certain
bills, and got into a Pawtucket horse-car."[11] This is, according to James, the last
incident that Bourne remembered before disappearing for two months. In mid-
March of that year, however,

> a man calling himself A. J. Brown, who had rented a small shop six weeks previ-
> ously, stocked it with stationery, confectionery, fruit, and small articles, and car-
> ried on his quiet trade without seeming to anyone unnatural or eccentric, woke
> up in a fright and called in the people of the house to tell him where he was. He
> said that his name was Ansel Bourne, that he was entirely ignorant of Norristown,
> that he knew nothing of shop-keeping, and that the last thing he remembered—it
> seemed only yesterday—was drawing the money from the bank.[12]

James discovered, after subjecting Bourne to hypnotism, that Bourne's memory of
himself as A. J. Brown came back so much that "it proved quite impossible to make
him whilst in the hypnosis remember any of the facts" of his life as Ansel Bourne.
Despite James's efforts, Bourne continued to display "two distinct personal selves,"
neither fully aware of the other while in their own state of consciousness.[13]

These accounts from James are in no small part fascinating because Ansel
Bourne's case served as inspiration for the popular *Bourne Trilogy* film series star-
ring Matt Damon. For the purposes of my argument, however, they matter most
for their timing. James's consideration of double consciousness and his conceptual
development of the "divided self," "alternating selves," and "primary selves"—all detailed in his two-volume *Principles of Psychology*—were published while Du Bois
studied at Harvard and worked closely under James.[14]

Whether Du Bois and James discussed these concepts explicitly together is
difficult to prove. As I stated earlier, I could not identify any notes or records in
which Du Bois detailed such a conversation taking place. But it would have been
unlikely that Du Bois and James would not have shared their thoughts on any

number of subjects, given what Du Bois describes as their close intellectual and personal relationship. Du Bois himself acknowledged that James provided a level of mentorship to him far and above that of any of his other instructors. Reflecting in 1960 upon his time at Harvard nearly seven decades prior, Du Bois wrote: "I became a devoted follower of James at the time he was developing his pragmatic philosophy. . . . James guided me out of the sterilities of scholastic philosophy to realist pragmatism. . . . I was repeatedly a guest in the home of William James; he was my friend and guide to clear thinking."[15]

Indeed, in the preface to the jubilee edition of *Souls* in 1953, Du Bois wrote that, having been a student of William James and others, he was "therefore not unprepared for the revolution in psychology which the twentieth century has brought." Du Bois acknowledged his familiarity with the psychological sciences of his mentor yet also made clear in his reflection upon his time under the tutelage of James that his own treatment of the psychology of race prejudice within *Souls* was inadequate because he did not give enough attention to the role of social structure, including how it shapes unconscious action and ritualistic behaviors.[16]

Beyond James's *Principles of Psychology*, we find important parallels between Du Bois's use of double consciousness and James's concept of the divided self from James's Edinburgh lectures of 1901–2. These parallels are not just in the psychological material but also in both Du Bois's and James's figurative language.

In his Edinburgh lectures, James described the divided self as an interior battleground for what the person "feels to be two deadly, hostile selves, one actual, the other ideal." Compare this with Du Bois's own formulation of double consciousness as "two souls, two thoughts, two unreconciled strivings; two warring souls in one dark body." In Du Bois's own description, the two warring ideals within the Black psyche "long to attain self-conscious manhood, to merge [their] double self into a better and truer self." Yet while for James the divided self is split between a concrete, objective self and an ideal self at odds with one another, Du Bois's formulation depicts two souls as two warring ideals. In fact, if not for the Black American's "dogged strength alone," the irreconcilability of these two selves might tear the host apart. Du Bois's reformulation here is important because it reflects a shift from double consciousness as an aberration of the self to double consciousness as a condition of a collective.[17]

So far, I have shown clear parallels between Du Bois's own formulation of double consciousness and the concept of multiple, fractured selves from Du Bois's Harvard mentor, William James. Yet even if these parallels reveal that Du Bois was somewhat versed and modestly influenced by the field of psychology, how does James's influence on Du Bois somehow serve as a bridge between dominant racialist frameworks regarding Jews' and Blacks' susceptibility to mental illness and Du

Bois's formulation of Black double consciousness? How does the specter of the Jew reveal itself?

Nowhere in *The Principles of Psychology* or anywhere else, for that matter, did James assert that a fractured or divided self is more prevalent among Jews. Yet James would not need to say this explicitly, given the general scientific and medical consensus of his day. At the time of the publication of *The Principles of Psychology*, it was already a taken-for-granted assumption among scientists and medical practitioners that Jews were more susceptible to mental illnesses, including double consciousness, and that Blacks were mentally inferior to those socially defined as White. Du Bois had clear familiarity with the basic principles of late nineteenth-century psychology, and William James had helped define the field.

As I argued in the previous chapter, given that the biology of race stood at the center of nineteenth-century psychology, it would have been extraordinary for anyone who thought of themselves as part of this scientific enterprise to have avoided confronting the racialist frameworks that shaped it. Scientific consensus on Jewish madness and Black inferiority was part of what defined nineteenth-century clinical psychology and medicine.

The point here is that the parallels matter, as do the intellectual, political, and historical contexts in which ideas about Jewish pathology and Du Bois's own ideas about double consciousness emerged. The specter of the Jewish figure haunts Du Bois's concept vis-à-vis the emergent field of psychology and its general consensus on Jewish psychopathology. This haunting is important for properly historicizing Du Bois and his key ideas in the environments in which they were seeded and took root. Du Bois's passage through the figure of the Jew on his journey toward theorizing Black double consciousness is not so much a journey along a clear-lit pathway. Rather, it is akin to walking through a thick fog. The evidence is reflected in the droplets of condensation left upon your skin.

Having made our way through this fog, we now turn toward the other significant intellectual context in Du Bois's formulation of Black double consciousness: his German adventure from 1892 to 1894. In Germany, Du Bois was provided with two key conditions necessary for his formulation of Black double consciousness: critical distance from America's racial caste system and direct exposure to nineteenth-century German anti-Semitism. These key conditions not only significantly shaped Du Bois's thinking on Black double consciousness but also contributed to his developing understanding of the relationship between race, nation, and the color line.

Germany and Berlin

Shortly after William James published *The Principles of Psychology*, in 1891 Du Bois completed his master's degree in history at Harvard University. Du Bois's study had received support by way of two years of funding from the prestigious Henry Bromfield Rogers Memorial Scholarship. Along with William James, Du Bois was mentored by Albert Bushnell Hart, whom many regard as the founder of modern historical studies. Driven by an unrelenting intellectual curiosity, Du Bois set his sights on further study in Germany at the Friedrich-Wilhelms-Universität, then known as the University of Berlin (and renamed Humboldt University after World War II).

At the time, the University of Berlin was the largest institution of higher education in the German system. There was general consensus that the German system had refined academia through its invention of modern graduate education. As a result, as many as nine thousand American students and scholars, including William James and Albert Bushnell Hart, became part of a transatlantic academic migration between 1820 and 1920 that studied abroad within the German system. Other Harvard professors under whom Du Bois studied, including George Santayana and Josiah Royce, also studied abroad in Germany, including at the University of Berlin. Du Bois's quest to live and train within this system, then, must be seen within this context. For aspiring academics, Germany and the University of Berlin were something of a badge of honor, a measuring stick for intellectual potential. Du Bois wrote, "The German universities were at the top of their reputation. Any American scholar who wanted preferment went to Germany for study."[18]

The University of Berlin's impact on Du Bois's intellectual development has been the subject of other scholarly works. Few, however, center the climate of the university and Germany more broadly within the context of widespread intellectual and political anti-Semitism. In chapter 3, I discuss in detail the political climate of nineteenth-century Germany. In this chapter, however, my focus is on the intellectual anti-Semitism that was seeded and nurtured within German higher education. However, in both this chapter and the next, I want to explore how the "Jewish question" shaped German conceptions of nationhood, seeding the development of what I term "racialized nationalism." Racialized nationalism describes the process through which the race concept becomes a necessary ingredient in the active formation of nationhood, where racial ideology and racial purity become wedded to nationalist discourse and movements. I will save a more complete discussion of racialized nationalism and its relationship to Du Boisian thought for this book's conclusion.[19]

German academia, including the University of Berlin, was ground zero for the development and proliferation of dominant racialist discourses on Jewish inferiority. Almost from the beginning of the European Enlightenment, many of the Continent's most prominent thinkers gave great consideration toward what to do with western Europe's Jewish population—a population whose customs and traditions appeared to these thinkers as juxtaposed to and at odds with the ideals of modernity. Many questioned whether such a "backward people" could ever be incorporated into the body politic of a modern nation-state. If there was any hope for the redemption and inclusion of this group, it was believed to reside in their emancipation.

German intellectual Christian Wilhelm von Dohm, for example, argued that the Jews' supposed corrupt spirit was the result of the centuries of oppression under which they lived. Once that oppression was eliminated, Jews would shed all of their negative traits and become morally fit for inclusion into the nation-state. Elsewhere, Montesquieu argued that Jews' backward, negative customs were the result of their segregated environments. Once Jews were included within larger (and less Jewish) communal life, their characters would positively adjust. Voltaire was the exception. The essential qualities of the Jew were, for Voltaire, baked in. There was no hope for changing what he saw as their natural dispositions. In Germany, Judaism was condemned by the Young Hegelians as outdated and rooted in traditionalist beliefs and practices that were antithetical to the progressive nation-state. Jews could only be granted emancipation, the Young Hegelians argued, when they abandoned their particularism, which meant abandoning their Jewishness.[20]

By the late eighteenth century, western European intellectuals had begun to employ the organic analogy. Society was, for them, akin to a living organism. Like any organism, its system was comprised of a set of parts mutually dependent upon one another. If any part was diseased or suffering, the entire system was put at risk.

This analogy was quite easily adaptable for those who viewed the Jews as morally corrupt, inferior, and therefore posing great dangers to the vitality of the modern nation-state. National (and nationalist) consciousness throughout the nineteenth century became increasingly tethered to and even defined by anti-Semitism. Much of this anti-Semitism was influenced by science and medicine, which were rapidly becoming the dominant epistemological framework of these modern societies. These nations emphasized the need for and development of a common history, a shared language, and even shared sentiments, such as love toward the nation itself as the great unifier, especially in societies seeking national unification. At the same time, science and medicine were put into service on behalf of nationalist movements and discourse that increasingly framed national belonging through biological terms and stressed purity as a condition of belonging. Nationalism, when taken to these extremes, readily became racialized and subsequently weaponized against those deemed impure or inferior.[21]

In Germany, philosopher and poet Johann Gottfried von Herder carried the mantle of national development and unification, particularly through his writings on what he identified as the "inner spirit," or *Volksgeist*, of the German people, expressed through shared culture and shared language. As William Brustein notes in *Roots of Hate: Anti-Semitism in Europe before the Holocaust*, Herder's writings influenced a generation of other German intellectuals who searched for the "origins" of German culture, which for many was located in an almost mythical ancient past. In time, the genealogy of language and culture identified by these figures became the chief markers of both nationhood and racial purity, with the two so tightly wedded to one another that they were, in practice, indistinguishable.[22]

By the time Du Bois made his trip across the Atlantic, the seeds of German intellectuals' anti-Semitism were well sown and the roots of racialized nationalism established. Many of the most prominent racialists of the era were located within German academia or products of its system. These racialists advanced a variety of explanations whose purpose was to characterize the Jew in opposition to the German national project.

German historian and philosopher Julius Langbehn's *Rembrandt als Erzieher* (*Rembrandt as Educator*) was published in Germany in 1890, and by the time Du Bois arrived just two years later, the book had gone through dozens of editions, each taking on increasingly anti-Semitic and nationalist overtones. Elsewhere, Orientalist professor Paul de Lagarde, who had studied at the University of Berlin prior to his academic post at the University of Göttingen, had already published a series of essays on Germany's Jews that made frequent reference to their supposed biological inferiority and compared their threat to German society with that of "pests and parasites" that required extermination.[23]

Not only were these intellectual figures present within the institution, but also they and their intellectual contributions were given great weight and consideration. Within the University of Berlin's Department of Medicine, for example, physician Emanuel Mendel offered several courses on psychiatry, neurology, and pathology between 1892 and 1893. Mendel would later publish his *Leitfaden der Psychiatrie für Studirende der Medizin* (1902, *Text-Book of Psychiatry: A Psychological Study of Insanity for Practitioners and Students*) to widespread acclaim. In it, Mendel casually observed, "Undoubtedly there appears to be a greater disposition to insanity and diseases of the nervous system among the Jews." Importantly, among the conditions of insanity Mendel identified in his textbook is none other than double consciousness: "In those instances in which these twilight states appear generally at night with wandering about, as is especially observed in epilepsy and hystero-epilepsy, the term somnambulism (sleep-walking) has been used. Sometimes in these states the dominant ideas of the normal waking condition are forgotten, but return to the patient as soon as the attack recurs. From this, the patient has a double mental life, a condition which has been designated by the name of double consciousness or alternating consciousness."[24]

Even those professors perceived as progressive could not help but draw upon the racialist consensus of their day. At the University of Berlin, Rudolf Virchow served as rector. Virchow was regarded by many as a progressive reformer, having served in the Reichstag for over a decade and even helping to found the German Progressive Party (Deutsche Fortschrittspartei). As an elected member of the German parliament, Virchow advanced several public health initiatives, including regular examinations for German children.

In his reflections on his University of Berlin experiences, Du Bois described an occasion that reveals the pressures faced by reformers such as Virchow when it came to Germany's Jewish question: "I was met by a handbill urging me: 'Go by all means to the second voting District, and help the warmly patriotic Professor Wagner to beat the cold stony rector of the University, Professor Virchow; pay the rector back for saying that the German youth of today have little idealism because they do not rally to the standard of (Jewish!) liberalism.'" The handbill Du Bois mentioned was part of a larger campaign to elect Virchow's colleague Adolph Wagner to the Reichstag in Virchow's stead. Wagner was running as a member of the openly anti-Semitic Christian Social Party, which had added "Christian" to its name and charter only recently in order to signal that Jews were not welcome in it or the German nation-state. Wagner's campaign focused, in part, on what he and others considered to be Virchow's Jewish sympathies, or philo-Semitism.[25]

Wagner's criticism of Virchow not only reveals the growing political anti-Semitism within late nineteenth-century Germany but also indicates how the Overton window for anti-Semitism was shifting dramatically to the right. Just a few decades prior, Virchow had directed a study of physiology among more than six million German children. In the study, Virchow and his colleagues made physiological distinctions between Jewish and German children, which, as I have shown elsewhere, was quite standard within science and medicine of that period.

To my own surprise, many historians have wrongly asserted that Virchow's study disproved widely held beliefs in racial differences. Their error seems to be driven by a general confusion and conflation of political anti-Semitism and scientific anti-Semitism. There is little doubt about Virchow's personal sympathies toward Jews. Some have even pointed to Virchow's tutelage of German Jewish anthropologist Franz Boas as evidence of his sympathetic personal politics. Boas had studied under Virchow in 1885 and 1886, and according to George W. Stocking Jr., Boas's eulogy of Virchow "leave no doubt of Virchow's influence."[26]

Elsewhere, however, Andrew Zimmerman correctly notes that in marking Jews and Germans as racially different, Virchow's study helped train an entire generation of German scholars to perceive these racial differences as both real and of political importance. Similarly, German historian Werner Kümmel took issue with the characterization of Virchow as intensely anti-Semitic, demonstrating that his attitudes toward Germany's Jews were fairly typically liberal in their tone but far from generous. Virchow believed Jews could assimilate, which went of course against the grain of many of his colleagues. But Virchow also believed that for Jews to succeed, they must assimilate. That is, Virchow's position did not tolerate cultural and religious differences between Jews and non-Jews, in part because Virchow's position was quite similar to that of most of his scientific and political contemporaries: Germany must be one nation, undivided; it must be one *Volk*.[27]

These points notwithstanding, Virchow was regarded as a friend to the Jews, as were other German professors during Du Bois's stay. Yet like Virchow, those academics who expressed sympathies toward Germany's Jews did so through appeals to a unified German culture that required the suppression of all that was Jewish in order for Germany to reach its full potential.

Emil Du Bois-Reymond, whom Du Bois described as "perhaps the most widely known professor today in Berlin," was professor of physiology at the University of Berlin from 1858 until his death in 1896. Du Bois-Reymond had made his opposition to anti-Semitism known as far back as 1880 in response to an essay by his colleague (and one of Du Bois's own professors) Heinrich von Treitschke. Treitschke, in this essay, had famously proclaimed that the Jews were Germany's national misfortune, a claim that would be resuscitated under Hitler's Third Reich. In November 1880 fellow University of Berlin classics scholar Theodor Mommsen had circulated a written defense of Germany's Jews, describing them as an essential part of the national culture. Du Bois-Reymond added his name to the defense, though he expressed misgivings upon seeing the defense published in the *National-Zeitung*, a liberal German newspaper (and not to be confused with the Far Right publication of the same name founded after World War II).[28]

Nevertheless, Treitschke's condemnation coincided with a series of escalating incidents of anti-Semitism. An 1881 petition to exclude Jews from public life gained more than 250,000 signatures. Attacks were launched against Jews in Pomerania and West Prussia. In Vienna an arsonist set fire to a theater that killed hundreds of Jewish attendees. Meanwhile, at the University of Berlin, students openly heckled Jewish instructors. Du Bois-Reymond responded with force. In

a March 1882 lecture, he compared rising anti-Semitism to a "hydra of pathologi-
cally inflamed nationalism" and argued that "racial wars" threatened the very foundation of European civilization. In August 1883, in a memorial to Alexander von
Humboldt, Du Bois-Reymond asked his audience, "How would we stand up to
Humboldt now if he knew about the recent persecution of the Jews?"[29]

Du Bois-Reymond was only one among the "83 full professors, 87 assistant professors, and 186 instructors" teaching at the University of Berlin during Du Bois's
stay. Also among the more than 350 faculty was jurist, political scientist, and politician Rudolph von Gneist. In 1872 Gneist had spoken against the dominant racialist position in racial purity. He argued that language, customs, legal systems, and
religion—not folk mythologies about blood—are the foundation of national culture. Yet, as we have seen with other so-called progressives like Virchow, Gneist's
consideration of Germany's Jewish question maintained that the only solution for
both Jews and Germany was the complete erasure of Jewish differences through
assimilation. In his 1881 speech against political anti-Semitism, Gneist declared,
"When the Jews give up their distinctiveness, we shall witness the final consumma-
tion of the emancipation [of the Jews]."[30]

Intellectuals such as Du Bois-Reymond, Virchow, and Gneist defended Jews'
place in German society. Yet those defenses were conditioned upon Jews abandoning their religious, cultural, and ethnic identity in favor of complete and total assimilation into German society. Others, including those under whom Du
Bois studied while at the University of Berlin, were far less civil. Among them was
Treitschke, who had been admonished by Du Bois-Raymond in 1880 for his anti-
Semitic proclamations. In his autobiography, Du Bois described Treitschke as "by
far the most interesting of the professors" he encountered while in Germany. Indeed, by the time of Du Bois's trip across the Atlantic in 1892, Treitschke was already somewhat of a German institution. His lectures frequently drew the largest
audiences of any course taught at the university.[31]

Yet Treitschke's views on Germany's Jewish question, which he made known on
many occasions, contained a distinct proto-Aryan nationalist bent. Treitschke had
been a strong supporter of the formation of the anti-Semitic Christian Social Party
and by the 1870s was referring to Germany's Jews in his speeches and writings as
"an element of national decomposition," a global conspiratorial regime that cor-
roded and corrupted German bonds of national unity.[32]

In his classroom, Treitschke frequently professed a set of nationalist views that
espoused hatred for nearly anything defined as non-German, including Jews. More
than one historian has gone so far as to argue that Treitschke, who along with
other University of Berlin professors of his day served within the German Reichstag, was partly responsible for the brand of German nationalism that drove Ger-

many into World War I and subsequently paved the way for the rise of the Third Reich. In his 1879 political pamphlet, which was widely circulated among German audiences, Treitschke famously quipped, "In the circles of educated Germans, who would protest indignantly against the charge of religious and national intolerance, one single cry is heard, 'The Jews are our misfortune.'" Treitschke's firm belief in the institution of the military as key for preserving national unity would echo in Du Bois's own writings on German politics. In 1893 Du Bois wrote, "Strong military monarchy is indispensable" to Germany's integrity as a German nation.[33]

In his notes and papers from Germany, Du Bois did not describe ever having been the target of Treitschke's classroom outbursts. He did, however, recall an episode when, standing in front of a large lecture hall of students, Treitschke loudly declared, "Mulattos are inferior! They feel themselves inferior!" As one Du Bois biographer stated, "It is a measure of [Treitschke's] magnetism that Jewish students could not help being fascinated by the forcefulness of his oratory despite his antisemitic outbursts."[34]

This statement reveals much. Given Treitschke's tendency for such outbursts and his reputation both in the classroom and in parliament, it's quite likely that the political fever of late nineteenth-century anti-Semitism was commonplace within the University of Berlin. Even at the university of his dreams, then, Du Bois could have no illusions that it or he was free from race prejudice and discrimination, even if in the German context Du Bois was not the explicit target of that prejudice and discrimination.

Among Du Bois's most memorable and influential courses, for example, was his political economy seminar, which was cotaught by Gustav von Schmoller and Adolph Wagner. Kwame Anthony Appiah and others have noted the deep influence of Schmoller on Du Bois's own development of an empirical social-scientific research agenda. Yet little has been said of Wagner, who, like Treitschke, was widely known (and highly regarded) for his political opposition to the incorporation of Jews into German society. Wagner was, like Treitschke, a member of the Christian Social Party and as part of his calls for German national unity "insisted upon the forcible Germanization of inferior cultures," including Jews.[35]

A review of the private letters and notes in the Du Bois archives revealed significant commentary on the rampant anti-Semitism within the university. In a draft of what later became his posthumous autobiography, Du Bois described in detail one particular incident:

> The Independent Student Association has been holding a number of meetings lately in the auditorium of the University. The Jews, who are not admitted into the Verbindungen [social clubs], and the socialist students, captured one of the

meetings and had things their own way. This aroused a perfect furor among the
German nationalist students, among whom a strong and even bitter anti-Semitic
feeling is developing. They called a meeting in the same hall, but Rector Virchow refused to allow it, fearing that the breach among the students would become too great. Whereupon the honored professor received some disrespectful
manifestations in his recitation room and the meeting was called in an outside
hall. . . . There were upwards of 700 students present, seated along rows of tables,
smoking and drinking beer. The meeting opened with a "Hoch" to the Emperor,
and then the assembly disported itself in condemning Jews in no uncertain terms,
even showing marked discourtesy to several speakers who sought to defend them.
The meeting ended in smoke and song and afterward I went to a Socialist meeting
as a fit conclusion to the day.[36]

What is striking about this account is the mundanity with which Du Bois remem-
bers it. An uprising of no fewer than seven hundred students ended with singing,
smoking, and, for Du Bois, a socialist meeting, as if the events of the day were entirely routine.

The reality is that anti-Semitism was at such a fever pitch across late nineteenth-
century Germany that not to denounce German Jewry in no uncertain terms invited a public questioning of one's own patriotism, as Virchow could well attest.
This context, both in and outside of the university, was of particular interest to
the young Du Bois. In his letter to the Slater Fund, the organization paying for his
study abroad, Du Bois provided an update on his academic progress: "Besides my
regular work I have been following the political movements of the country, the rise
of anti-semitism, which has much in common with our own race question and is
of considerable interest to me."[37]

If the Jewish question was beginning to weigh upon Du Bois's mind, it was at
least partly due to how heavily it weighed on the minds of Du Bois's professors—
from the staunchly vocal anti-Semitic nationalism of Treitschke and Wagner to the
cultural chauvinism of Virchow, Gneist, and economist Max Sering, with whom
Du Bois took a seminar during his first semester entitled "The Labor Question in
England and Germany." Yet this set of facts on its own is still not sufficient proof
that Germany's Jewish question shaped Du Bois's own formulation of America's
Negro question: what to do with its emancipated Black men and women. This set
of facts, thus far, only allows us to see that Du Bois was well aware of the debates
surrounding Germany's ongoing Jewish question. We will save the discussion of
whether and how this German nationalist discourse informed Du Bois's consideration of Black double consciousness for the next chapter.

Germany and the University of Berlin as
Critical Distance from the Color Line

The impact of the University of Berlin and its professoriate on Du Bois's intellectual development has been the subject of several scholarly examinations. Du Bois wrote glowingly of his two-year study: "I am here free from most of those iron bands that bound me at home [away] from the physical provincialism of America and the psychological provincialism of my rather narrow race problem into which I was born and which seemed to me the essence of life. . . . [T]his momentary escape from my own social problems [is] an introduction to new cultural patterns."[38] Yet except for a few singular works, scholars have given the rampant anti-Semitism within the University of Berlin or even in Germany at large short shrift, often only as the backdrop to other, supposedly more significant moments and events.

Kenneth Barkin, for example, questions whether Du Bois's thinking on race, let alone double consciousness, significantly advanced at all while he was in Germany. Barkin's assertion seems to rest on the influence of Schmoller, who had little to say about Germany's Jews, considering them far less serious a threat than did his contemporaries, given that they were less than 1 percent of the nation's total population at the time. Likewise, Sieglinde Lemke confines the German influence to Herder's consideration of a German *Volk* and its parallels to Du Bois's use of "souls" in his 1903 classic of the same name. Appiah provides a similar, if not more detailed, analysis. It is as if the cries for national unity, nearly always accompanied by proclamations against Germany's Jews, were either inaudible or insignificant.[39]

As any graduate student will attest, your studies consume you. Beyond the pursuit of knowledge, the reading of books upon books, the drafting and redrafting of papers, and the vibrant discussions with your professors and peers about the world around you as you are coming to understand it, there is little time for anything else. This time of intense study is one where your activities and your inspirations exist in an ongoing, circular movement. Sparks truly fly during this time!

It is an unfortunate circumstance that appreciation for this period often only comes the greater your distance from it, when you have finally emerged from the piles of papers, exams, and deadlines, ready to confront the world in a way you never imagined before in no small part because you no longer see the world as you once did.

How bizarre, then, would it be to think that Du Bois's own experiences might be so wildly different? That Du Bois would have given only brief attention to the events happening around him at the university and in the streets of Berlin?

If there was anything unusual for Du Bois, it would have been the sharp contrast between his experiences as a Black man studying abroad in Germany and his experiences as a Black man living in America. Du Bois had left perhaps the most prestigious institution of higher education in the United States to continue his studies at perhaps the most prestigious institution of higher education in the world, a place where many of his Harvard professors had received their own training. In his autobiography, Du Bois recalled deriving "a certain satisfaction in learning that the University of Berlin did not recognize a degree even from Harvard University, no more than Harvard did from Fisk." For Du Bois, "The German Universities were at the top of their reputation. Any American scholar who wanted preferment went to Germany for study. The faculties of Johns Hopkins, and the new University of Chicago, were beginning to be filled with German Ph.D.'s, and even Harvard had imported [Hugo] Muensterberg for the new experimental psychology, and Kuno Fran[c]k[e] had long taught there." Add to this the fact that Du Bois arrived at the University of Berlin at the end of the very century in which the slave trade ended, emancipation was fought for and won, and political citizenship for Germany's Jews as well as Black Americans was codified into their respective nation's laws.[40]

In Berlin, Du Bois wrote, "We studied history and politics almost exclusively from the point of view of ancient German freedom, English and New England democracy, and the development of the White United States. Here, however, I could bring criticism from what I knew and saw touching the Negro." What Du Bois seemed to indicate in his recollection of his Berlin days was a kind of critical distance from the color line not possible for him in late nineteenth-century America. As he noted in his autobiography, though he fondly recalled some of his professors, he had little kindness to extend to the institution of Harvard. History and politics at Harvard were, as we would expect, whitewashed. But for Du Bois, studying abroad in Germany gave him a reprieve from the daily confrontations of race prejudice that defined what it meant then and still means today to be a Black man in America. The University of Berlin allowed Du Bois to pour himself into his studies, not unlike what we would expect from any serious student.[41]

This sense of reprieve from daily encounters with the color line is evident in Du Bois's personal correspondence. Shortly after arriving in Germany in 1892 Du Bois wrote to the students of his former Sunday school in Great Barrington, Massachusetts, and their teacher, a Mrs. Van Lennep. His letter details his travels across the German state to this point. At the time of the letter, he was staying in the town of Eisenach, "one of the most beautiful spots of a beautiful region," on the northwest edge of the Thuringian Forest and the place where Martin Luther lived while he attended school. Du Bois wrote to the children and his former teacher, "It is ever a strange experience for an American to walk for the first time in a land, the natural beauty of which is surrounded and enhanced by the thought, legends, and deeds of a thousand years." Beautiful as it is in its description, this letter is also revealing. Du Bois did not describe himself as Black or Negro, as that would have been the more common descriptor. Rather, Du Bois referred to himself as an American.[42]

Elsewhere, writing again to the Slater fund in 1893, Du Bois expressed his enthusiasm in completing his first full semester of study abroad. He proudly informed his funders of the paper he completed under the direction of Schmoller in which he compared and contrasted the peasant and plantation systems in the U.S. South from 1840 to 1890. Du Bois informed his audience that Schmoller was so pleased with the paper that he promised Du Bois that he would publish part of it in his forthcoming volume, subject to revisions. In this same letter, Du Bois described Treitschke as the most interesting of his professors; he revealed that he had begun to follow with interest the rise of anti-Semitism, which, Du Bois noted, "has much in common with our own race question and is of considerable interest to me." Du Bois also expressed his desire to not only finish his degree in Berlin in just three semesters—what would have been an unusually short period—but also, upon completion, "go to Paris and enter the Ecole Libre de Science Politique where I shall spend as much time as my [illegible] allows." Then Du Bois intended "to get a place in a Negro university and build up a department for two purposes: 1, empirically study the Negro question . . . with a [illegible] to its best solution." Shortly before leaving Berlin, Du Bois reflected on the kind of critical distance from the race problem provided by the University of Berlin: "I am here free from most of those iron bands that bound me at home [away] from the physical provincialism of America and the psychological provincialism of my rather narrow race problem into which I was born and which seemed to me the essence of life. . . . [T]his momentary escape from my own social problems [is] an introduction to new cultural patterns."[43] Even decades later, Du Bois framed his German adventures through this same kind of critical distance that allowed him to better understand the color line and its global importance. In his autobiography, he wrote, "In Germany I turned still further from religious dogma and began to grasp the idea of the world of human beings whose actions, like those of the physical world, were subject to law." And in *Dusk of Dawn*, Du Bois wrote that while at the University of Berlin, "I began to see the race problem in America, the problem of the peoples of Africa and Asia, and the political development of Europe as one."[44] These reflections show that Germany and the University of Berlin were far more influential in the development of Du Bois's considerations of the color line than previous studies have allowed.

Parsing Du Bois's language, we can interpret it in the following way: Du Bois entered Germany and German higher education at a time of rampant political anti-Semitism, in which Germany's Jewish population was increasingly scrutinized for their inability and unwillingness to fully assimilate into the German *Volk*, although this assimilation was a condition of their racialization within the German and, more broadly, the western European scene. Germany's "Jewish question" was, in fact, its very own "race problem."

It should not come as a surprise to students and scholars of race and racism that German academia figured so prominently in the proliferation of late nineteenth-century anti-Semitism. After all, the roots of contemporary racism are found in the laboratories of nineteenth-century medical, psychological, and social scientists. Likewise, we find that the roots of late nineteenth-century German anti-Semitism were not seeded in the anxieties of its newly industrialized proletariat or in the antipathies of its waning aristocracy. Instead, anti-Semitism was seeded and nurtured within German higher education among professors of literature, medicine, and anthropology and among the classicists and the psychiatrists.[45]

The "political development of Europe as one" was also a matter of western European nationalism, which in Germany, France, and other western European nations could not be separated from their ongoing "Jewish question." Du Bois would have confronted these political and moral questions in the classrooms and among the faculty of the university of his dreams. Both inside and outside of his German classrooms, Du Bois learned to recognize that to be Jewish and German was nearly incompatible without the subduction of one to the other. His observations of the larger Berlin and German scenes only helped confirm this lesson. It is to these larger contexts and Du Bois's reflections on the German political environment that we now turn.

CHAPTER 3

Germany, Anti-Semitism, and the Problem of the Color Line

The previous chapter centered the intellectual contexts in which Du Bois studied, first at Harvard and under the mentorship of William James and then at the University of Berlin. In both the American and German intellectual scenes, the dominant racialist frameworks of that era ascribed to both Jews and Blacks an innate inferiority and a predisposition to insanity on account of their perceived inability to assimilate into Western (read: White, Christian) society. These racialist frameworks became tethered to ongoing nationalist movements in Germany, marking the Jew as biologically and mentally unfit and therefore incompatible with the German state. Meanwhile, in the United States a much lengthier history of anti-Black racism stretching back to the nation's founding was being recast by scientific rationale in the late nineteenth and early twentieth centuries, but with similar effects as its antebellum antecedent. Yet this is only the half of it.

The relationship between science and society is dialectical. It is certainly true that during the Enlightenment period and beyond, Western science and medicine led the charge in defining both Jews and Blacks as antithetical to the ideals of "civilized society." However, Jews had been considered a backward and morally bankrupt people long before the Enlightenment. These ideas of Jewish impurity, rooted in Christian beliefs and the authority of church figures, did not disappear with the Enlightenment, even as religious orthodoxy was usurped by scientific reason. Instead, they were recrafted to fit the ideas and values of the emergent scientific enterprise. As in the premodern era, beliefs about Jewish inferiority both shaped and were shaped by the political machinations of nation-states wrestling with what became commonly described as their Jewish question: What to do with the Jews?[1]

This dialectical relationship is important for properly understanding the German scene onto which Du Bois arrived in 1892. Germany, by 1892, was on the tail end of unprecedented reforms to its political, economic, and social landscapes. At the same time, the nation suffered a virulent wave of anti-Semitism that would remain unparalleled until the rise of the Third Reich some four decades later. Finally, Germany had helped accelerate the "scramble for Africa" just eight years prior by hosting the West Africa Conference (Berlin Conference) of 1884–85. There is a scholarly debate on whether the Berlin Conference initiated widespread Western colonialism of the African continent or simply accelerated it. Nevertheless, the effects of partitioning African nations and peoples by way of arbitrary boundaries and without their express participation or consent certainly eroded African self-autonomy and existing cultural and political norms. Importantly, the new restrictions on African people's movements and economic opportunities became important mechanisms for reducing for most of the Western world the most ethnically, culturally, religiously, and politically diverse geographic region of the world into a monolithic, artificial racial category—Black. This reduction has had lasting and reverberating effects through the present day.[2]

Our systems of knowledge, our ideas and beliefs, are rooted in the social, political, and economic circumstances of our day. The major events and episodes that we live through greatly influence how we think about the world around us. The German scene of the late nineteenth century was no different. Its transformation—from a mid-nineteenth-century loose confederation of states to a late nineteenth-century centralized, albeit contentious, parliamentary system—had an enormous effect on how German academics, political actors, and laypersons alike understood both themselves and the society in which they were living. Yet, to date, despite a large body of scholarship on these economic, political, and social transformations, Du Boisian scholars have given little consideration to how these shifts may have affected Du Bois's own intellectual development and trajectory.[3]

There are exceptions, of course: Kenneth Barkin's analysis of Du Bois's Berlin days; Kwame Anthony Appiah's exploration of German empiricism and romanticism in Du Bois's writings; and Shamoon Zamir's consideration of the Hegelian influence in Du Bois's theorizing of Black duality. But even within these important works, little if any attention is given to the political strain of anti-Semitism that was birthed by nineteenth-century Germany's great transformation.[4]

How, then, did the emergent German nationalism of this period, a racialized nationalism motivated by Germany's increasing hatred of its Jews, affect the young Du Bois's understanding of the color line?

Germany in Transition

The mid- to late nineteenth-century transformation of a loose confederation of German states into a unified empire resulted in significant political gains for Germany's Jews. The 1848 revolutions could not conceal the prominent role that Jews played in this moment. And for a brief time, up until the revolution's collapse, Jews made inroads into German politics, including holding high-profile positions within the German government. As historian Peter Pulzer shows, at least five Jews were elected to the Frankfurt parliament. A year after the 1848 revolution, only Bavaria had thus far failed to grant political equality to its Jewish citizens.[5]

By 1867 the transformation of the German Empire was nearing completion and would involve the expulsion of Austria from its confederation, Jewish emancipation, and the revival of a liberal political philosophy that subsequently shaped the new empire. In comparison to that of other central and eastern European nation-states, the German strain of liberalism had both firmer footing and greater influence. Yet it was far more conservative and authoritarian than either the French or British version. Historian Donald Niewyk reasons that this is not surprising, given that both France and England had more stable economic systems and more robust political and revolutionary traditions. This German tendency toward conservatism would fully reveal itself through the German response to its Jewish question.[6]

Following the developments of 1867, German liberalism increasingly began to emphasize the need for a national culture, or *Volk*. Calls for a national culture went hand in hand with those for a strong, centralized state that could provide structure for a common language and a set of "real" German values. To facilitate the development of a centralized state apparatus that could meet the demand for national unity, a slew of political reforms were enacted: universal suffrage, the repeal of debt and usury laws, the adoption of the metric system, the transfer of postal communications to the Reich, the establishment of the gold mark as the national currency, the enabling of free trade and movement of both individuals and merchandise, the abolishment of any remaining privileges for guilds, a progressive lowering of import duties on corn and manufactures, and by 1877 the total eradication of all import duties on iron and steel goods. In the decade prior to Du Bois's arrival, the Reichstag passed more regulations and policies guaranteeing worker protections than in any other period. Nearly all of these reforms would remain intact well after Du Bois's return to the United States.[7]

Much like the rest of western Europe, Germany was also undergoing rapid industrialization. Germany's economic transition was concurrent with and driven by major population shifts, including mass urbanization. While Du Bois studied at the University of Berlin, Germany passed from a predominantly rural to a mostly urban demographic base. Farmworkers from poor eastern territories flooded German cities, including Berlin, seeking better pay and living conditions. As a whole, these massive social and economic transformations had a tremendous effect on the German political system. By 1890 'the Sozialdemokratische Partei Deutschlands (Social Democratic Party of Germany) had more power and support than in any previous period. Finally, and as briefly mentioned above, Germany, along with the dominant western European nation-states and the United States, had set its sights on the African continent and its rich human and natural resources as an important site for continued capitalist expansion and development.[8]

For Germany's Jews, these truly were the best of times. Now for the worst. In response to Germany's abolishment of import duties, cheaper English iron flooded Germany's market. Likewise did Russian grain. France's own mills were already more mechanized, making it difficult for Germany to compete. As a result, in 1873 Germany's market crashed. Investment continued, however, and the rapid industrialization of the German Empire unfolded on a scale previously unseen. Yet how Germans experienced these transformations was uneven.

For those whose lives were most unsettled by economic transformations and population shifts, unrest and strife were commonplace. Recall the relative youth of German liberalism, as well as its conservative bent. German farmers and workers had not yet adapted to or incorporated the liberal tradition at the pace in which these economic and social shifts unfolded. The strife and unrest that resulted from such rapid change produced an odd alliance between Germany's merchant class and its ruling class. This became the basis for a "coalition of extremes against the common enemy"—the Jew.[9]

Broadly, the Western liberal philosophical tradition that shaped much of nineteenth-century political thought contained the following key tenets: the promotion of representative government, the rule of law, a supposed desire for a society free from caste or class privileges, the privileging of a free market economy, and active support for free speech and free association. The historical record, of course, shows that quite often when push came to shove, political actors were willing to abandon many, if not all, of these ideals. But the general tendency toward these principles remained true, even if they were not realized nearly as often as they were professed.

I mention this because some have argued that the "coalition of extremes" formed in the aftermath of major German reforms was in many ways a backlash against this emergent liberal tradition, as well as against the systems of rationalism and humanism that undergirded it. Yet whatever aspirations the liberal philosophical tradition held, it was never—even in its idealized version—inclusive of all political subjects. The supposed social contract—whether we refer to the conjectural historical account or some more historically grounded version—was a contract only for and among those socially defined as White, Christian men.[10]

It is not a coincidence that the development of the Western liberal philosophical tradition coincided with the rise and subsequent dominance of scientific reason. Nor is it a coincidence that the rise of scientific reason as a dominant epistemology occurred alongside the emergence of race as a scientific category of human difference. Race set the terms through which individuals were understood and classified as human subjects capable of participating in civil society, as actors who could legitimately enter into formal and informal agreements with one another to form something above and beyond themselves. This emergent scientific enterprise identified Jews, Blacks, and some other groups as belonging to the "lower races" or as "subhuman." Science understood them as not fully formed, morally and spiritually lacking, and thus unable to participate as political subjects.[11]

Although Germany's Jews had received emancipation in 1867, their status as Jews continued to run counter to the conservative liberal tradition, which desired a strong and unified national consciousness in which all group differences would be subsumed in a national culture. Consider, for example, German philosopher and politician Constantin Frantz, whose 1874 work, *Der Nationalliberalismus und die Judenherrschaft* (National liberalism and the rule of the Jews), fit squarely within the conservative backlash to the mid-nineteenth-century German reforms. Frantz saw these reforms of the newly formed empire as harmful to "those elements who form the stable basis of a nation"—German farmers and the working class. Only "the mobile section of the population is at all interested in it, i.e. those who have no fixed abode, or who travel frequently, or whose business activities result in far-flung connections." And who, according to Frantz, were these mobile populations? The Jews: "It need hardly be said that nothing suits the Jewish point of view better than the idea of the so-called constitutional state, in which no more [attention] is paid to men's religion than to their real conditions of life and to the historical facts on which the character and political position of individual states is founded." In "providing elbow-room for this mobile element," reformers were guilty of having "shaken the solid foundations" of the German nation-state.[12]

The insider/outsider status of the Jews was not antithetical to the German liberal tradition, then. It was there from its birth, legitimated first by science and then further buttressed by German intellectuals across the nineteenth century. Jews labored on behalf of the emergent German nation-state in an effort to create a strong, unified collective. Yet they could never belong to the nation-state because of the threat their status as Jews posed to that unified collective.

This same condition also characterized the Black experience in postemancipation America, an experience Du Bois understood long before his German adventures. Yet the social, political, and economic contexts of late nineteenth-century Germany proved instructive for Du Bois. It was in Germany where Du Bois "began to feel the dichotomy which all my life has characterized my thought: how far can love for my oppressed race accord with love for the oppressing country? And when these loyalties diverge, where shall my soul find refuge?"[13]

It is instructive that the political scene of a German nation under enormous transformation—one that would thrust Germany's Jews into its narrative not as coauthors but as conspirators—is also where Du Bois "began to see the race problem in America, the problem of the peoples of Africa and Asia, and the political development of Europe as one." Here, personally free from the "physical provincialism of America and the psychological provincialism of my rather narrow race problem into which I was born and which seemed to me the essence of life" yet submerged in the rapid rise of political and intellectual anti-Semitism, in addition to increased colonial expansion, Du Bois would develop lines of inquiry that would shape his thinking and scholarship for decades to come.[14]

German Nationalism and Its Jews

I have neither the desire nor the range to provide a full account of German Jewish history. Nor is my aim to narrate German anti-Semitism as some sort of slow buildup to the atrocities committed under the Third Reich. There is danger in depicting German history as simply awash in anti-Semitism. First, that portrayal mistakenly reads German history backward, "especially the history of anti-Jewish sentiments and activities in Germany so that events and developments point to a culmination in the Third Reich." The available historical evidence shows that anti-Semitism across the modern era was far from consistent in its scale and scope and lacked any clear, linear progression in its movement. Moreover, Jewish experiences within the emergent German nation-state were far from uniform, despite the gravity of the political anti-Semitism many were forced to confront. Monika Richarz's collection of German Jewish memoirs spans nearly two centuries and is quite helpful in demonstrating this latter point.[15]

The second danger in rendering Germany as thoroughly immersed in hatred of its Jews is that it implies a Western exceptionalism while positioning Germany as the exception to that exceptionalism for its extreme anti-Semitism. Yet at no time in western Europe—from the medieval to the modern period—were Jews free from anti-Semitism and violence. After World War II it became commonplace among both scholars and laypersons to place the blame for the atrocities committed under the Third Reich upon some aberration of the German collective psyche. Even today, explanations for genocide and other collective harms that center or suggest insanity and madness remain popular. But insanity and madness are, by definition, abnormal conditions affecting only a small percentage of any given population. They cannot explain the dominant political and social behaviors of groups of people. German anti-Semitism is no more an aberration of the tradition of Western liberalism than American chattel slavery and Jim Crow.[16]

Most importantly, perhaps, we ought to be mindful that using nineteenth- and even twentieth-century models of anti-Semitism and anti-Black racism as the gold standard for judging all subsequent models limits our ability to understand whether and what connections exist between then and now. Anti-Semitism is not distinctly modern in thought or practice, though certainly its modern articulations are qualitatively different from its premodern versions. If continuity exists between premodern and modern forms of anti-Semitism, then the common bond is Christianity, which provided the vocabularies of difference for the Western world, including secularized science and its liberal philosophical tradition.[17]

On the one hand, violence against Jews was commonplace across the eighteenth and nineteenth centuries. It was often tied to Jews' increasing demands for civil and political rights, as was the case for German Jews in 1819. Their calls for political equality, combined with widespread famine, which left many indebted to bankers and moneylenders, professions in which Jews were disproportionately concentrated, spurred what were known as the Hep-Hep riots. These riots began in Würzburg and soon spread to Bamberg, Bayreuth, Frankfurt, Leipzig, Dresden, and Heidelberg, among other locales. Ultimately, military troops were called in to suppress the rioters.[18]

Later, in 1840, the disappearance of an Italian friar in Damascus led to accusations of blood libel against its Jewish community. News of the friar's disappearance and the accusations against Jews quickly spread to continental Europe, sparking international outrage and galvanizing anti-Semitic attacks against western Europe's Jews. Influential newspapers such as *The Times* of London and the German *Leipziger Allgemeine Zeitung* were quick to reproduce polemics that were hardly different in tone or content from their medieval predecessors. One editorial from *The Times*, published in June 1840, opined, "[The affair is] one of the most important cases ever submitted to the notice of the civilized world. . . . Admitting for the moment [the accusation to be true] . . . then the Jewish religion must at once disappear from the face of the earth."[19]

On the other hand, the same eighteenth and nineteenth centuries that bore witness to such violent outbursts were also marked by rising toleration and significant political gains for Jews across continental Europe. Obstacles to professional development were lessened and in some cases disappeared altogether. Rules and norms governing where Jews could and could not live were changed or eliminated. Some Jews rose to prominence in economic, social, and even political life. When taken as a whole, then, the violent outbursts of anti-Semitism coupled with significant Jewish advancements demonstrate a qualitative shift in the character and bent of western European anti-Semitism across the nineteenth century. Whereas prior to the nineteenth century Jewish hatred was largely rooted in religious intolerance and perceptions of Jews' exploitative economic practices (e.g., usury), by the late nineteenth century these forms of anti-Semitism had been joined by a rising tide of racial and political hatred of Jews.[20]

What makes this qualitative shift in German anti-Semitism quite remarkable is that racial and political hatred toward Jews failed to coincide with any major demographic dominance among German Jewry. German Jews never even obtained a strong minority position within late nineteenth-century Germany. Census records of this era are notoriously deceptive but nevertheless serve as a useful proxy of Jews' demographic representation. In 1871 there were barely half a million Jews living in Germany, roughly 1.25 percent of the nation's entire population. Four decades later, the number of German Jews had slightly increased, to around 615,000 in 1910. But this increase was not proportional to Germany's overall population increase. Though greater in number, by 1910 Jews were less than 1 percent of the nation's population.

The increase, albeit slight, was largely the result of eastern European Jewish migration, which some sources suggest rose from roughly sixteen thousand to seventy thousand between 1880 and 1910. Many of these immigrant Jews settled in Germany's urban centers. Berlin's Jewish population, for example, grew by roughly 380 percent between 1881 and 1925. The larger point here, however, is that had it not been for this wave of Jewish migration, intermarriage and less-than-average birthrates would have led to a significant decline in the already small number of Jews living in Germany.[21]

The settlement of Germany's Jews in its urban centers put them in direct contact with the growing system of higher education. Jewish men enrolled in the Austrian and German university systems in large numbers and soon came to dominate the professional classes. By 1890 Jews accounted for roughly one-third of enrollments in Vienna and Prague and nearly 40 percent of Vienna's medical faculty. Their dominance was most evident, however, within the profession of journalism. Throughout the late nineteenth century, Jews were at the helm of many of the leading German publications, including Berlin's well-regarded *National-Zeitung*.

Of the more than twenty daily papers published in Berlin throughout the 1870s, more than half were owned or managed by Jews.[22]

Among those who have written extensively on the rise of anti-Semitism across western Europe, historian Albert Lindemann's work stands out for its scope and balance. In *Esau's Tears: Modern Anti-Semitism and the Rise of the Jews* (1997), Lindemann forcefully argues for situating the rise of anti-Semitism across western Europe against the backdrop of Jews' dominance in the professional classes. Lindemann, however, mistakes the direction of the relationship. Jews' dominance in the professional classes may indeed have led to increased anti-Semitic sentiments among the German people. Yet Jews' concentration in these occupations was itself a product of anti-Semitism, not happenstance. Other avenues for social and economic mobility were closed, if not de jure, then de facto. The large-scale economic restructuring of the late nineteenth century made Jews' successes within these fields unbearable for many German laborers and members of the ruling classes, whose own fortunes fell while those of Germany's Jews rose.[23]

Along with migration shifts and economic restructuring, political strife helped to seed and grow the rising tide of anti-Semitism in the post-1870 German Empire. Two assassination attempts against Chancellor Otto von Bismarck led him to dissolve the Reichstag in order to eliminate what he characterized as a communist scourge. Following the election of a new parliamentary body, Bismarck introduced an anticommunist bill that received the assent of liberal party members who had campaigned on promises to support it. As historian Peter Pulzer notes, these developments helped to shift the balance of political power and further strengthened a growing nationalist fever by forcing members of the more liberal wing of the Reichstag to choose patriotism over their own political leanings. But this patriotism was always indebted to an active suspicion of and nearly conspiratorial attitude toward Germany's Jews. The National Liberal Party (Nationalliberale Partei), for example, began demanding that German Jews prove themselves worthy of citizenship by abandoning their membership in the German Progressive Party and forgoing activities in support of Zionism. Party members also demanded that Jews cease traditional Jewish religious practices such as the observance of the Sabbath, dietary laws, and circumcision because these practices made Jews appear to be separate from their German compatriots.[24]

It was against the backdrop of this political shift and the economic restructuring of the 1870s that the Christian Social Party appeared on the scene. Cofounded in 1878 as the Christian Social Workers' Party by Lutheran clergyman Adolf Stöcker and German economist and politician (and later a professor of Du Bois) Adolph Wagner, the CSP was a response to the rise of what was considered the

more radical Social Democratic Party. Yet in just one year the CSP, whose original platform included progressive measures such as support for cooperatives, social
insurance, eight-hour workdays, and more regulations over factory labor, largely
abandoned its prolabor platform in favor of Christian nationalism.

On September 19, 1879, Stöcker gave a speech entitled "Our Demands on Modern Judaism." He made the party's new position on Christian nationalism and its
view of German Jews' future within the nation-state clear: "We respect the Jews
as fellow citizens and honor Judaism as the lower step of divine revelation. But we
firmly believe that no Jew can be leader of Christian workers in either a religious
or an economic capacity. The Christian Social Party inscribes Christianity on its
banner."[25]

One year later, Wilhelm Marr's *Der Sieg des Judentums über das Germanen-
tum* (*The Victory of Judaism over Germanism*) appeared in print. The significance
of Marr's diatribe cannot be overstated. His book went through twelve editions in
just its first six years. Marr was clear in his message to German citizens of what was
on the horizon should they fail to heed his warning: "[We] cannot count on the
help of the 'Christian' state," Marr wrote. "The Jews are the 'best citizens' of this
modern, Christian state, as it is in perfect harmony with their interests. . . . German culture has proved itself ineffective and powerless against this foreign power."
Marr argued that the Jews had triumphed over the centuries not through their
military might but through their unique spirit, or *Volk*. Meanwhile, Marr accused
Germans of, through their own negligence, having become "Jewified." There was
only one solution: the forced separation of Germans and Jews. In making this demand, Marr overtly racialized Germany's Jews far beyond any of his contemporaries or any who came before him, the vast majority of whom had attributed the
problem of the Jews to one of religious differences that were solved through assimilation, intermarriage, and the like. The title of Marr's text demonstrates that the
real contrast—and conflict—was not between the Jew and the Christian but between the Jew and the German. For Marr, "there must be no question here of pa-
rading religious prejudices when it is a question of race and when the difference
lies in the 'blood.'" Marr also in this text coined the term "anti-Semitism," giving it
a kind of positive connotation aligned with a defense of the national spirit, or *Volk*.
In doing so, Marr popularized racial hatred of the Jews as an expression of German
patriotism.[26]

The same year *The Victory of Judaism over Germanism* was published, Marr also
founded the Antisemiten-Liga (League of Anti-Semites), the first organization to
bear such a title. The purpose of the league was to "bring together non-Jewish Germans of all denominations, all parties and all walks of life into a common, fervent
union which will strive, by setting aside all special interests and all political differ-

ences, and with the greatest energy, earnestness and industry, towards the one aim of saving our German fatherland from complete Judaisation and to make life tolerable there for the descendants of the original inhabitants."[27]

Marr's anti-Semitic populism paved the way for a modern, nationalist fever of anti-Semitism that was qualitatively different from its predecessors. Max Liebermann von Sonnenberg, a former military officer and ally of Stöcker, proclaimed, for example, that the only hope for a resurgent German nation was nothing less than the "material and moral rebirth of German Volkstun, intensification of German being, [and] stimulation of the practical application of the Christian Doctrine." Two years removed from Stöcker's proclamation of the new Christian Social Party's platform as the future of the German nation, a grammar school teacher and aspiring intellectual by the name of Ernst Henrici founded the Soziale Reichspartei (Social Reich Party). If Stöcker's platform centered loyalty to a pure, Christian nation, Henrici's platform appealed to even more radical and nationalist sectors within the nation-state.[28]

Henrici's Social Reich Party demanded an end to all Jewish immigration into Germany, the exclusion of Jews from any public office, and the administering of a special census for Jews living in the German nation-state. For Henrici and his political allies, Germany's Jewish question was a racial one: "If [the Jewish question] is a question of racial characteristics, then both body and spirit must be kept in mind." The use of the term "spirit" here, in keeping with its late nineteenth-century meaning, is a matter of national culture or identity. Not only are the Jews racially distinct from Germany because of their cultural practices, but those racial differences ultimately collapse into biological differences ostensible through Jews' physiology.[29]

Henrici's position, then, though arising just a few years removed from the CSP platform, was a significant departure from it in that the CSP maintained that Jews were assimilable as long as they cut their religious ties and subsumed themselves to the German national culture. German Orientalist Paul de Lagarde, for example, argued that "friendship is possible with individual Jews, but only on one condition, that he ceases to be a Jew. Jewishness as such must disappear." But whereas the Christian Social Party thought the answer to Germany's Jewish question was in the active conversion of Jews to Christianity, for Henrici, racial differences were understood as immutable and tied to biology. Henrici's Social Reich Party rejected conversion as both impractical and undesirable, for "the religion of the Jews is a *racial religion*." One year later, Henrici would help jointly organize an anti-Semitic petition laying out the demands of the party. By April, when it was presented to Bismarck, it had already obtained 225,000 signatories.[30]

Elsewhere, University of Berlin economist Eugen Dühring made his own contribution to this new nationalist parlance with his 1881 text, *Die Judenfrage als Racen-, Sitten- und Culturfrage* (*The Jewish Question as a Racial, Moral and Cultural Question*). The title conveys Dühring's main thesis, that Germany's Jewish question requires a discussion to take place on levels beyond simply religious differences. Dühring's faculty appointment, along with his prominent position within the Social Democratic Party, carried significant weight within this ongoing national (and nationalist) debate. The kind of "national" socialism for which he advocated was increasingly becoming tethered to political anti-Semitism, so much so that to rid spheres of influence—public office, business, and finance—of the Jews was understood by Dühring as a patriotic duty.[31]

The 1880s, then, marked two important moments in the development of German anti-Semitism. First, there was a noticeable shift in the degree or intensity of anti-Semitism. This intensification occurred in tandem with violence against Jews, which was becoming increasingly routine throughout Europe. Pogroms in czarist Russia, for example, led to rapid western migration of millions of eastern European Jews. Blood libel accusations reemerged in parts of central Europe, stoking further flames. In Austria, France, Hungary, and Germany, anti-Semitic parties were founded, and many saw surprising electoral success. In 1886 French journalist Édouard Drumont published *La France juive* (*Jewish France*), a massive, two-volume, twelve-hundred-page condemnation of French Jewry. Despite or perhaps because of its size, Drumont's tome quickly became a best seller. Among other claims, Drumont's work asserted that Jews—in particular, those new arrivals from eastern Europe—were prone to mental illness, sickness, and disease. These sickly Jews, then, presented a clear and present danger to the strength and vitality of the French body politic. Then, in 1894, the court-martial for treason of Alfred Dreyfus, a French captain and the first Jew to rise to the General Staff in the French military, grabbed the world's attention, including that of a young W. E. B. Du Bois, who claimed to have followed the trial and its ugly fallout quite closely.[32]

Along with the intensification of anti-Semitism, the second development of the 1880s was the continued, qualitative shift from an anti-Semitism with roots in general religious intolerance to a political anti-Semitism that articulated German national unity as distinct from and in opposition to Germany's Jews, even as it continued to draw inspiration from religious bigotry. By this decade, Henrici's efforts through the Social Reich Party had helped to bridge significant divides between the larger, more dominant Conservative Party and the presumed fringe anti-Semitic efforts of Henrici and company. In 1892, motivated in part by a feud with the newly appointed German chancellor, Leo, Graf von Caprivi, Conservative Party members called for a public conference to be held in Berlin. There they set out to define a political program of broad, national appeal. By the end of their conference, it had become clear that anti-Semitism would not only play a role in this program but also need to be at the center of the entire effort. Following their conference, the first paragraph of their new platform plainly stated, "We combat the widely obtruding and decomposing Jewish influence on our popular life. We demand a Christian authority for the Christian people and Christian teachers for Christian youth." Note that while the appeals to Christianity are explicit, they are coupled with a nationalist appeal against the "decomposing Jewish influence" on national culture.[33]

With this platform, the field was set for the 1893 elections. Though absent any official cooperation, the ideological alliance between the traditional Conservatives and the new anti-Semites was enough to obtain a joint victory. On their own, anti-Semitic candidates won 263,000 votes, or just under 3 percent of the total votes cast. Given that the views of many Conservative candidates following the Tivoli conference were undifferentiated from those of anti-Semites, some historians argue that the total votes cast for anti-Semitic candidates may have been closer to 400,000. Importantly, anti-Semitic candidates from a number of independent German parties that formed a loose coalition for this election gained sixteen seats in the Reichstag. Though on their own a small minority within the 397-member body, when combined with the 69 seats won by the German Conservative Party, their bloc was second only to the Centre Party's 96 seats. Moreover, it was far larger than the 44 seats won by the liberal Social Democratic Party, which had, ironically, won a plurality of the popular vote.[34]

By the turn of the twentieth century, German nationalism was tethered to anti-Semitism, with the latter serving as the former's primary driving force. The unity of this emergent racialized nationalism, though it had been determined by the intellectual preferences and demands of particular German figures, was accomplished through an emphasis on a common German *Volk*, or national culture, and coupled with a growing desire for German superiority by way of national purity. The desire for purity was not an entirely German development, as Joseph de Gobineau's French racialism was influential in the German strain. Gobineau was an aristocrat whose 1853 essay, "The Inequality of the Human Races," advanced a pseudoscientific theory of an Aryan master race that was praised and adopted by a range of academics and politicians in both Europe and the United States. Gobineau, of course, had denounced Jews not for their religion but for something they could not change: their supposed race. Both in France and in Germany, then, the Jew was not only on the outside looking in but also a barrier to be overcome by the ascending nation-state. German nationalism was, at this moment, a reaction against the dominant Western liberal tradition, with which Jews had been made synonymous. By the end of the nineteenth century, including during Du Bois's two-year Berlin adventure, Germany's Jewish question had become its Jewish problem.[35]

Returning to Du Bois, his recollection of this period of great transition is instructive. In his autobiography, Du Bois expressed an ambivalence toward the rising fever of German nationalism:

> The pageantry and patriotism of Germany in 1892 astonished me. In New England our patriotism was cool and intellectual.... When I heard my German companions sing "Deutschland, Deutschland ueber Alles, ueber Alles in der Welt" [Germany, Germany above all else, above all else in the world] I realized that they felt something I had never felt and perhaps never would.... I began to feel the dichotomy which all my life has characterized my thought: how far can love for my oppressed race accord with love for the oppressing country? And when these loyalties diverge, where shall my soul find refuge?[36]

The national pride of Du Bois's German peers was, in contrast to his New England upbringing, a matter of the gut and not the brain. It was rooted in sentiment, not just ideology. Importantly, Du Bois recognized in Germany's racialized nationalism the problem of its American version: racialized nationalism differentiates and distinguishes as much as, if not more than, it unifies. To be Black in postemancipation America was, like Germany's Jews, to ever feel one's twoness. That Du Bois saw this through the lens of his German compatriots is key. Du Bois came to understand this sense of twoness not only by what he felt as a Black man living in a country that defined itself against him but also by way of a German nationalism that defined itself against its Jews.[37]

Du Bois on German Anti-Semitism

Some of Du Bois's early writings while in Germany serve as groundwork for the conceptual material that would frame the question that opens *Souls*: "How does it feel to be a problem?" Among those writings, the most significant is his 1893 unpublished essay entitled "The Present Condition of German Politics," penned while he was working on a political campaign for that year's parliamentary elections.

In this essay, Du Bois intended to examine "the political machinery by which such a government as Germany's is maintained" and compare it with that of the United States. He began with a "basic paradox": Germany's "geographical situation in the very midst" of potentially hostile European powers required it to have a strong military monarchy. Yet "the extraordinarily developed intellectual activity" of Germans, coupled with a growing industry, had "set in motion a demo-cratic movement" that ran counter to "monarchy and militarism alike." While the United States could "afford to tumble in the sloughs of democracy for the sake of that individual liberty so prized by us," Germans had concluded that only an "un-bending Prussian militarism" could maintain national unity and lead to "sturdy na-tional development."[38]

Still only a young man, Du Bois demonstrated a keen awareness of the fact that German national unity rested, in no small part, upon the resurgence of German anti-Semitism:

> It may surprise one at first to see a recrudescence of anti-Jewish feeling in a civi-lized state at this late day. One must learn however that the basis of the neo-anti-Semitism is economic and its end socialism. Only its present motive force is ra-cial hatred. It must be ever remembered that the great capitalists of Germany, the great leaders of industry are Jews; moreover, banded together by oppression in the past, they work for each other, and aided by the vast power of their wealth, and their great natural abilities, they have forced citadel after citadel. . . . This of course is a menace to the newly nationalized country.[39]

Despite the prevalent attitudes rampant within his academic institution and the intellectual climate of Germany writ large, Du Bois rejected the anti-Semitism of his day, which posited that Jews are unassimilable due to their racial inferiority. In-stead, he situated it squarely within the large-scale economic restructuring of the late nineteenth century and the resulting class antipathies. In Germany's Jews, Du Bois recognized resistance—even modest success—as rooted in Jews having been "banded together by oppression in the past." Put differently, the strivings of Ger-many's Jews were conditioned by German anti-Semitism. In this passage, then, we can see Du Bois working through some of the intellectual material that would later develop his conceptual framework for *The Souls of Black Folk*, including his con-cepts of the Veil and double consciousness.[40]

Jewish emancipation came in 1871 with the unification of Germany. In Prus-sia it had come much earlier, in 1812. The extension of political and civil rights to Germany's Jews facilitated their economic and cultural ascension. While anti-Semitism may have separated Germany's Jews from the rest of the polity due to "the cake of custom," it also cemented within Germany's Jews their collective sense of spiritual striving. They "work for each other" rather than for the nation-state. As a result, they have forced open one German institution after another, becoming "the great leaders of industry."[41]

Yet despite these strivings, Du Bois wrote, "all that Marx, Blanc, or Bellamy ever laid at the door of capitalism is, by the German Antisemitic Party, charged

upon the Jew because the Jew happens to be the great capitalist of Germany." German Jewry's spiritual strivings, as both Jews and Germans, are products of the Veil.
Du Bois saw Jews' economic success as an obstacle to the untested nationalism of
a new Germany. Their ability to "force citadel upon citadel" in spite of intense political anti-Semitism caused even more anti-Semitic German nationalist feelings.
Du Bois recognized in the status of German Jews the political, social, and even
economic factors he would come to define as central to the status of Black Americans. Jews in Germany, like Black Americans in the United States, strove toward
a higher national ideal despite knowing this ideal rested upon the rejection of all
that they represented. Thus the Jew, like the Black American, remained the focus
of a collective nationalist character that articulated itself through racism.[42]

German nationalism, then, presented a kind of double problem that was not at
all dissimilar to the double problem of American nationalism. On the one hand,
German nationalism enabled its Jews to get along within German society as part of
a desire to see a strong, unified nation-state. Jews were prohibited by law and custom from certain professions, but they were allowed entry into and came to dominate medicine, journalism, and even the professoriate. Yet at the same time, the
"recrudescence of anti-Jewish feeling" Du Bois described was baked into how Germans thought of themselves as "good Germans." This sentiment prevented Jews
from attaining recognition as good Germans or even "real" Germans. Against this
backdrop of widespread Jewish hatred, their success had become the source and
strength of a Jewish *Volksgeist*. Yet at the same time, their success fueled Germans'
growing resentment, which increasingly defined itself against Jews and with which
Germany's Jews had to always contend.[43]

Let me be clear here. Du Bois was not claiming a direct parallel between the
Jewish experience in Germany and the Black experience in America. After his two
years of study in Berlin, Du Bois readily admitted that "the Jew remains a half-
Veiled mystery to me" and that "their national development is over widely different obstacles than those of my nation." Jews were not fully assimilated into German society by the late nineteenth century. As the political movements analyzed
above show quite clearly, there was significant resistance to including Jews within
the German body politic. Nevertheless, Jews had achieved a modicum of economic success, albeit concentrated within the few professions that remained open
to them. Their political emancipation, including suffrage, had been attained nearly
three decades prior to Du Bois's arrival. While Black suffrage was theoretically obtained through the 1870 ratification of the Fifteenth Amendment to the U.S. Constitution, the historical record is quite clear that Black Americans' right to vote was
significantly infringed upon throughout most of the twentieth century, often by
way of violence. Finally, in his personal writings and notes, Du Bois pointed to in-

termarriage among Jews and Christians during the late nineteenth century as more evidence of Jews' successful assimilation in comparison to Blacks in America.[44]

In his 1893 essay on German politics, Du Bois went as far as to express optimism toward the abatement of German anti-Semitism. This optimism toward the overcoming of group-based prejudice was not expressed by Du Bois toward the condition of Black people in America. Indeed, legal political emancipation for Black people in the United States did not come until the passage of the 1964 Civil Rights Act, which was one year after Du Bois's death. Meanwhile, Du Bois could not help but think about the state of affairs he was returning to when he left Germany in 1894. It was not at all different from what he had left just two years prior. Reconstruction was over, Jim Crow was well under way, and lynchings of Black people were becoming a regular occurrence. The distinction Du Bois made between a German nationalism rooted in the resentment of Jews' success in spite of Germany's best efforts to interfere and an American nationalism rooted in the denial of opportunity—social, political, or economic—to Black Americans should not be overlooked. Yet the differences also should not be overstated.

While the evidence strongly shows that late nineteenth-century German nationalism arose from a collective resentment of Jews' success, Germany's racialized nationalism nevertheless rested upon an underlying assumption that Jews' success was undeserved because Jews were not really German. Du Bois understood this point quite well. During Du Bois's stay in Berlin, Germany's racialized nationalism was becoming increasingly mainstream and competing for hegemony over the German masses. Two of his professors, Treitschke and Wagner, were leading intellectual and political figures in the rising tide of German conservative nationalism, and both were supporters of the anti-Semitic Christian Social Party. As mentioned in the previous chapter, Du Bois's 1893 essay on German politics shared at least some affinity for Treitschke's nationalist politics. In the essay, Du Bois stressed the importance of a strong military monarchy for maintaining national unity, using nearly identical language to that found in Treitschke's lectures on the matter. Meanwhile, as he had in his recollection of the rally against Professor Virchow that took place while Du Bois was a student at the University of Berlin, Du Bois noted the shared affinities many of his classmates at the University of Berlin had toward this new German nationalism.[45]

At minimum, we ought not to dismiss the subtlety so quickly in Du Bois's characterization of Germany's Jews as "half-Veiled." For Germany's Jews, German nationalism was expressed as antagonistic to their own ethnoreligious culture. To be Jewish was to be in constant conflict with what it meant to be German. This is a kind of Du Boisian double consciousness, even if Du Bois did not name it as such. Jews strove toward success and achieved it to some degree. Yet their striving

and their successes made them, as Jews, less accepted. Likewise, America's denial of
full citizenship to Black Americans in the post-Reconstruction era was rooted in
Whites' collective understanding and practical actions, that America is a White racial state. Black people were denied incorporation, then, because they were Black.
Or, as James Baldwin stated so painfully clearly in 1962, "The social treatment ac-
corded even the most successful Negroes proved that one needed, in order to be
free, something more than a bank account." So despite the important distinctions
we might make between Germany's Jews and Black Americans at the end of the
nineteenth century, they shared a common experience by way of the Veil. For both
Jews and Blacks, the Veil enabled nationalism to express itself in such a way that
double consciousness was an inevitable by-product. The "souls" of both Jews and
Blacks proved incompatible with the "soul" of the nation-states within which they
resided but to which they could never truly belong. Arguably, Du Bois understood
these parallels at a visceral level even before his time in Germany, given he lived his
life as a Black man in America. Germany and its Jews simply provided an opportunity for Du Bois to stand, some distance apart, as a critical observer in a foreign
land.[46]

In his autobiography, written some seventy years after his return from Berlin,
Du Bois would again consider the extent to which full incorporation into the
body politic was possible within the German and American racial state. Within
each, an irreconcilable antagonism existed: in Germany, it was the antagonism between a late nineteenth-century German *Volksgeist* that rested upon ethnic and racial purity and a Jewish *Volksgeist* fashioned from the experiences of always striving
toward yet failing to fully obtain recognition as part of Germany's national culture.
Likewise, the strivings of Black Americans were in large part defined through the
sacrifices they made on behalf of the nation in which they sought membership. Yet
the color line was so baked in through law and "the cake of custom" that those sacrifices were in vain.

Germany's late nineteenth-century liberal economic and political reforms
could not be separated from its growing anti-Semitism at home nor its colonial
and imperial expansion abroad. And both developments were significant to the
kind of German nationalism that emerged in the late nineteenth and early twentieth centuries and ultimately took their most violent form in the rise of the Third
Reich.

Writing for *Foreign Affairs* in 1942–43, Du Bois argued that Germany's hosting of the Berlin conference in 1884–85 "brought colonial imperialism to flower,"
substituting the previous African trade in men and women with trade in raw materials, only now maintaining "the exploitation of African labor inside the continent." Just a few years later, and writing near the end of World War II for the

Black-owned and Black-operated daily the *Chicago Defender*, Du Bois captured the essence of Black double consciousness as he had first theorized it in his *Atlantic* essay some fifty years prior. Black American servicemen abroad "force[d] citadel upon citadel" in service to American democracy. Likewise, Black men and women within the United States were enrolling in colleges and universities, creating their own businesses, and striving toward some version of the American dream. However, "when with joyful faces we turn from this, we turn to a world still persisting in the discrimination we know all too well."[47] The spread of democracy both at home and abroad remained in the service of White supremacy.

CHAPTER 4

Post-*Souls*, Veiled Mysteries

Du Bois's intellectual project took on a wide range of topics, interests, and themes in the years following the publication of *Souls* in 1903. He had already published *The Philadelphia Negro* and established the Atlanta Sociological Laboratory at Atlanta University. Here, he would train the next generation of Black social scientists and advance the study of Black American social and cultural life through the laboratory's annual conferences and reports. Over the next several decades, Du Bois's writing and thinking shifted frequently and seemingly effortlessly between the academy and public scholarship. Along with editing *The Crisis* magazine, he published a semiregular column through the *Chicago Defender*. Du Bois also tried his hand at playwriting and penned the three-part *Black Flame* trilogy. It is not hyperbole to state that Du Bois's range as a public intellectual was unparalleled among his contemporaries.[1]

By the mid- to late 1930s and with the publication of *Black Reconstruction in America*, Du Bois had introduced a unique form of dialectical materialism that was both critical of and an extension of the Marxist tradition. His analysis of how post-Reconstruction racism and class relations shaped the nation redefined classical Marxism and advanced one of the most important theses on Black agency of the entire twentieth century. According to Du Bois, emancipation was not the result of a benevolent Lincoln or the heroics of any number of Union soldiers and generals, including Grant. Rather, emancipation was due to Black men and Black women who, through their own Herculean efforts, broke the fetters that bound them and freed themselves.[2]

Du Bois's thesis shaped an entire line of inquiry for Black intellectuals in the decades that followed. Though C. L. R. James's *The Black Jacobins* was published just a few years after Du Bois's *Black Reconstruction*, James acknowledged the intellectual debt he owed to Du Bois's provocative and original thesis. In a lecture given at the Institute of the Black World in Atlanta in 1971 entitled "*The Black Jacobins* and *Black Reconstruction*: A Comparative Analysis," James stated:

> He had opened out the historical perspectives in a manner I didn't know. He had been at it for many years. He was a very profound and learned historian.... I have to ask you the question, though I don't expect answers. Did you ever think that the attempt of the black people in the Civil War to attempt democracy was the finest effort to achieve democracy that the world had ever seen? Don't answer, I know you have it. You have to grapple with that.... Du Bois knew about it, and he said the tragedy of these millions from Africa was a tragedy that "beggared the Greek." ... Du Bois taught me to think in those terms.... That was a tremendous thing for Du Bois to say![3]

Indeed, James argued that Black Reconstruction was a necessary blueprint for understanding the arc of revolutionary action, including the revolutionary action he himself analyzed in *The Black Jacobins*:

> Without the blacks the war would not have been won. What I want to emphasize is that it was not only that the blacks brought their forces into the Northern army and gave labour. It was that the policies that they followed instinctively were the policies ultimately that Abraham Lincoln and his cabinet had to use in order to win the war. That is something entirely new in historical writing.... The policy by which Abraham Lincoln mobilized the blacks and the way in which they were mobilized against the South came from the instinctive action of the masses of the slaves. The only men I know, two men, have written about politics in that way. They are Marx and Lenin.[4]

Du Bois's thinking continued to evolve considerably even beyond his intellectual interventions within *Black Reconstruction*. In the post–World War II era, Du Bois continued his engagement with the tradition of historical materialism and in the process reshaped it through his deep consideration of European colonialism, imperialism, capitalism, and the role these forces played in the underdevelopment of Africa, Asia, and Latin America. In many ways, Du Bois's analysis of the color line had come full circle since his youthful studies in Berlin, where he first "began to see the race problem in America, the problem of the peoples of Africa and Asia, and the political development of Europe as one."

In his 1945 *Color and Democracy*, for example, Du Bois addressed the new configuration of global geopolitical hegemony: unless and until all people—regardless of race, color, or creed—are afforded the basic principles of democracy, then de-

mocracy can only ever fail, and the world will find itself yet again in global war-
fare, the results of which would be far worse than that from which we had just
emerged. Just one year later, in *The World and Africa*, Du Bois repositioned African history as central both to global history and to the capitalist development of
western Europe.[5]

Of course, these later works were subject to criticism among historians and others for loose speculations and broad generalizations. And though *Black Reconstruction* is now seen as a field-defining text, it was not nearly as well received among
mainstream historians at the time of its publication. Yet among his Black intellectual peers Du Bois received significant praise for his vision, which one contemporary noted "easily transcends that of any colored leader that has yet appeared." This
same contemporary also exalted Du Bois for demonstrating a voice that "has appealed through the darkness of prejudice and inhumanity to man with a tardy triumph in spite of concerted efforts to suppress stinging truths always anathema to
the white world." And no less than the renowned African American historian Carter G. Woodson praised Du Bois for providing in *Color and Democracy* an "outstanding example of this forceful appeal" to basic human rights for Black people
the world over.[6]

On the face of it, the Du Bois who wrote *Black Reconstruction* and became
more expressively anti-imperialist in the decades after its publication appeared
far removed, intellectually speaking, from the Du Bois who penned *The Souls of
Black Folk*. He wrote so much and so broadly post-*Souls*. This has led many academics who study Du Bois to assert matter-of-factly that the conceptual apparatus across that rogue set of early twentieth-century essays is one to which Du Bois
rarely, if ever, returned. By Du Bois's own admission, he had not meaningfully encountered, much less engaged with, Karl Marx's writings until well after *Souls* was
published. Nor had Du Bois given full consideration to Pan-Africanism, socialism,
or imperialism, which would increasingly become of interest to him after World
War I. These clear truths notwithstanding, it strikes me as a significant oversight to
claim that Du Bois abandoned the concepts and analytical tools developed across
the essays within *The Souls of Black Folk* in his subsequent decades of work.[7]

It is true that double consciousness was hardly ever explicitly mentioned by Du
Bois after the publication of *Souls* in 1903. Yet Du Bois routinely returned to the
structural features of double consciousness that defined Black American life in
the twentieth century: the Veil, duality, and second sight. Indeed, his more popular writings regularly noted the challenges associated with having to navigate the
American social and cultural milieu as a Black person. At the same time, Du Bois
barely said anything at all about anti-Semitism post-*Souls*.

Combing through his papers and writings, I found myself at first surprised at

Du Bois's apparent silence. After all, there was a rapid resurgence of violent anti-Semitism in the aftermath of Germany's defeat in World War I. Du Bois was far too well read and traveled to have been unaware of these developments and their relationship to the subsequent ascendance of Hitler and his Nazi Party and the eventual attempted genocide of the German Jewish people that played across the world's stage. It was not until after his own visit to Nazi Germany in 1936 that Du Bois offered any written criticism of the "vindictive cruelty and public insult" of the Nazi regime, to which he compared other atrocities in human history.[8]

How, then, should we understand the figure of the Jew in Du Bois's post-*Souls* scholarship? How do we account for what appears as an absence? In his shift in focus on the conditions of the Black diaspora to the forces of imperialism and colonialism, did the figure of the Jew become, for Du Bois, obsolete?

In the previous chapters, I have drawn attention to the parallels between the nineteenth-century German Jew and the post-Reconstruction Black American. These two archetypes, despite important differences, share the status of second-class citizens with little in the way of formal recourse for the injustices they faced at the hands of their host nations. What, if any, parallels remained by the mid-twentieth century, especially with regard to a comparison of the Black American experience with that of the American Jewish experience? These questions are admittedly distinct and on separate planes. Nevertheless, my aim in this chapter is to trace the routes of Du Bois's intervention in *Souls* in order to see what, if any, light might be shed on both experiences.

Interrogating the Racialized Social Structure Post-*Souls*

To answer these questions, I want to turn our attention to Du Bois's post-*Souls* considerations of Black Americans' duality and marginality. In doing so, I want to also compare those considerations with his twentieth-century contemporaries' considerations of Jewish duality in both western Europe and the United States.

As a whole, Du Bois's post-*Souls* body of scholarship centers what sociologists José Itzigsohn and Karrida Brown refer to as the racialized social structure. Briefly, this racialized social structure both organizes and is organized by the economy, law, and politics and by a variety of civil institutions. For Du Bois, the racialized social structure fosters among both Black and White Americans an increasing inability to recognize their full humanity. That is, America's racialized social structure is retrogressive for all its citizens. Meanwhile, among those intellectuals wrestling with the Jewish question in the early to mid-twentieth century, the Jews' continued struggles to assimilate into Western Christian society produced the effects, not the cause, of a unique kind of pathology. Du Bois's intervention, then, is an important one for the social sciences. Even while his contemporaries continued to understand Jewish duality as resulting from inherent pathological tendencies among Jews, Du Bois posited that the negative conditions of Black American life were external to Black Americans and fundamentally social and economic in nature.[9]

As I argued in chapter 3, Du Bois's German adventures seeded in him a global perspective of the color line. Du Bois continued to develop this perspective across his life's works. Germany and the University of Berlin changed Du Bois. In part, his German experiences provided Du Bois with a kind of critical distance from America's so-called Negro question, allowing him some reprieve from the structure of the color line, which was ingrained within America's racial caste system. At the same time, Du Bois's time in Berlin exposed him to Germany's own, ongoing Jewish question.

In the national and local debates and politics surrounding the matter of what to do with German Jews, Du Bois saw important parallels to his own experience as a Black person living in America. Du Bois was well aware of these parallels upon his return journey from Berlin. As he noted in his diary during his passage back to the United States, he was returning to a land in which Jim Crow was codified into the state constitutions of most of the American South. The political and economic rights of those White men who fought on behalf of a treasonous separatist movement had been fully restored. Meanwhile, northern states were not much better off socially, economically, or culturally. Black people were still unable to live next to, work alongside of, or worship with White people for fear of rebuke or much worse. And though he could not have concretely known that this would be the case, the boundaries of the racial caste system in the United States would only get brighter during his lifetime. American cities were even more segregated by the turn of the twentieth century than they were at the end of the nineteenth century. Reconstruction had, by the time of Du Bois's return to the United States, objectively failed. With its failure, the hopes of more than four million formerly enslaved, along with their children, were crushed.[10]

By the end of the nineteenth century, Germany's Jews were undergoing a similar resurgence of anti-Semitism in law, politics, and the public domain. Despite or perhaps because of the inroads Jews had made collectively within particular professions such as medicine, journalism, and finance, they were increasingly becoming the targets of an odd alliance between the German proletariat and the German elite. Jews' collective strivings, as Du Bois noted in his 1893 essay, "forced citadel upon citadel, until now they practically control the stock-market, own the press, fill the bar and bench, are crowding the professions—indeed there seems to be no limit to the increase of their power." To the German proletariat and representative organizations such as the Christian Social Workers' Party, the Jew was Germany's misfortune. Among the elites and intellectuals, including economist Eugen Dühring and former military officer Max Liebermann von Sonnenberg, as well as representative organizations such as the Social Democratic Party, it was understood that a central duty of every patriotic German was to advocate for the complete removal of all Jews from public office, business, and finance.[11]

Throughout western Europe, the figure of the Jew had long been depicted in a constant state of wandering, of statelessness, as perpetual strangers in the land of others. This image is not all that different from how Du Bois wrote about and understood the Black experience in the United States, including in the opening lines to *The Souls of Black Folk*:

> Between me and the other world there is ever an unasked question: unasked by some through feelings of delicacy; by others through the difficulty of rightly framing it. . . . How does it feel to be a problem? . . . It is in the early days of rollicking boyhood that the revelation first bursts upon one, all in a day, as it were. I remember well when the shadow swept across me. I was a little thing, away up in the hills of New England, where the dark Housatonic winds between Hoosac and Taghkanic to the sea. In a wee wooden schoolhouse, something put it into the boys' and girls' heads to buy gorgeous visiting-cards—ten cents a package— and exchange. The exchange was merry, till one girl, a tall newcomer, refused my card,—refused it peremptorily, with a glance. Then it dawned upon me with a certain suddenness that I was different from the others; or like, mayhap, in heart and life and longing, but shut out from their world by a vast veil.[12]

It is revealing that Du Bois described this experience of being a problem, of being shut out from the world of his White peers, as "strange" and "peculiar"; one can imagine it feels foreign, even alien. This feeling for Du Bois was not because he was Black but rather because he was a Black person living in America. The experience was dependent upon that external, relational condition. This revelation is ultimately where Du Bois's own thinking took a turn from that of his contemporaries. The early twentieth century marked, for Du Bois, a period in which his thinking on the color line would increasingly incorporate his critiques of imperialism, colonialism, and capitalist exploitation. This allowed Du Bois to pivot from asking, like so many of his peers, what is wrong with Black America to the more fundamental question, what is wrong with American empire?[13]

While a student in Germany, Du Bois had argued that the resurgence of German anti-Semitism was the by-product of class antagonism. An economic crash had resulted in widespread unemployment and underemployment, and the elite

had taken a significant hit to their collective wealth. Economic anxieties mani-
fested themselves as racial hatred against what was seen as the common enemy of
Germany's working class and its capitalist class: the Jews. According to Du Bois,
Jews were a menace to the emergent nationalist sentiment because of their collective economic success, their willingness and ability to band together and work toward collective uplift. This theory of economic anxiety undergirding racial antip-
athy is one Du Bois developed considerably over the next several decades but by
way of an analysis of the class antagonisms between Black and White labor in the
United States. Most notably, of course, he accomplished this in *Black Reconstruction*, first published in 1935. Recently, Du Boisian scholar Michael Saman argues
quite convincingly that Du Bois's Marxist turn, though unfolding over a period
of several decades, had not been completed until the 1930s. Politically speaking,
Du Bois had joined the American Socialist Party in 1911, but he promptly left it
the following year to endorse Woodrow Wilson. Saman shows that it was only
after having traveled to the newly revolutionized Soviet Union in the mid-1920s
that Du Bois was ready to declare, with some trepidation, "I am a Bolshevik." Du
Bois's Harvard professors had paid very little attention to Marx, and in Germany,
he wrote, "we only studied the criticisms."[14] As Saman so astutely observes, "It is
only when Marxism would become a matter of political fact rather than of theory
that Du Bois finally arrived at Marx's books; it is not the theory that led him to the
politics, but the politics that would lead him to the theory."[15]

It's worth considering an earlier text, Du Bois's contribution to the 1923 volume *These United States*, edited by American journalist and later U.S. senator Ernest Gruening.[16] Du Bois titled his essay "From Georgia: Invisible Empire State."
In it, Du Bois described Georgia's post-Reconstruction scene as one where economic competition between White and Black labor fueled an ambient racial hatred: "In order to secure output and profits, the one essential was to bring race hatred and economic competition into such juxtaposition that they looked like two
sides of the same thing. This is what Georgia did and did first. She did it so success-
fully that the whole South has followed her although few other States have been so
clear and single-minded." Race hatred works in part to mask or hide the true purpose of the economic empire, which is the exploitation of cheap labor, be it Black
or White: "This doctrine of the economic utility of race hate is never stated as a
fact in Georgia or in the South. It is here that the secrecy of the economic empire
of Georgia enters. Two other facts are continually stated. The first is the eternal
subordination and inequality of the Negro. The second is the efficiency and necessity of Negro labor, provided the subjection of the Negro is maintained."[17]

Paralleling his position on anti-Semitism in late nineteenth-century Germany,
Du Bois also saw anti-Black racism in Georgia as a kind of distraction, one that

further drove a wedge between Black and White labor to the great benefit of the Georgian capitalist class:

> [It] is usual for the stranger in Georgia to think of race prejudice and race hatred as being the central, inalterable fact and to go off into general considerations as to race differences and the eternal likes and dislikes of mankind. . . . The central thing is not race hatred in Georgia; it is successful industry and commercial investment in race hatred for the purpose of profit. All the time behind the scenes in whispered tones and in secret conference, Georgia is feeding the flame of race hatred with economic fuel.[18]

Reflections on American Empire and the Color Line Post-*Souls*

"From Georgia" is far from the only piece of writing in which Du Bois demonstrated how the racialized structure of society produced anti-Black racism. Three years prior, Du Bois had published another collection of essays entitled *Darkwater: Voices from within the Veil*. In this volume, Du Bois revealed his evolving thinking on the color line, situating its production and maintenance squarely in the colonialist and imperialist projects of European powers in Africa, Asia, and Latin America.

Darkwater was actually completed near Du Bois's fiftieth birthday in 1918. It was not published for another two years, however, due to revisions Du Bois continued to make to several of the essays. The essays themselves were the product of more than a decade of intellectual growth coupled with significant changes in Du Bois's life. By 1910 Du Bois had left Atlanta University, where he "grew to fear lest my radical beliefs should so hurt the college that either my silence or the institution's ruin would result." As far back as his days as an undergraduate at Fisk University in Nashville, Tennessee, Du Bois had possessed a desire to form "a strong organization to fight the battles of the Negro race." Having grown tired of the politics behind his appointment at Atlanta University, he resigned from his teaching position to work for the NAACP, an organization he helped found. He became its new director of publications and research and served as the founding editor of the NAACP's magazine, *The Crisis*. The first issue of the new magazine had a circulation of just over a thousand copies. Yet by the time *Darkwater* was published just a decade later, Du Bois had helped increase the circulation of the magazine to well over one hundred thousand copies for some of its most popular issues.[19]

Du Bois's second essay in *Darkwater*, entitled "The Souls of White Folk," was originally published by the Boston-based abolitionist magazine *The Independent* in 1910. Between its original publication and the revision for 1920's *Darkwater*, Du Bois wrestled with the juxtaposition of America's imperialist efforts to spread democracy abroad and its abject failure to provide democracy at home to its Black citizenry. Du Bois was quite critical of imperialism in the main, but he had also actively participated in the weeklong United War Work Campaign, touring the American South to drum up support among predominantly Black communities for America's World War I efforts. Yet by 1919, Du Bois was involved in organizing the First Pan-African Congress, to be held in Paris. There, he and others presented a collective case against colonialism, including making demands for liberty and the right to self-determination on behalf of colonized people the world over.[20]

In what is considered the definitive biography of Du Bois, historian David Levering Lewis writes that the revised "Souls of White Folk" appeared to "belch fire." When Du Bois, for example, wrote, "Merciful God! In these wild days and in the name of Civilization, Justice and Motherhood," it was in response to the "orgy, cruelty, barbarism, and murder" that Black people had been subject to since the arrival of the first slave ships to the eastern shores. Moreover, his revised essay makes clear that Du Bois viewed the failure of American racial democracy—the failure of America to provide the principles and practices of democracy to its non-White peoples—as fundamental to the emergent European world order of the early twentieth century. The Great War, which Du Bois had gone so far as to support through his United War Work efforts, was not a historical aberration, nor was it "Europe gone mad." Instead, he wrote, "This is Europe; this seeming Terrible is the real soul of white culture—back of all culture,—stripped and visible today. This is where the world has arrived,—these dark and awful depths and not the shining and ineffable heights of which it boasted. Here is whither the might and energy of modern humanity has really gone." It was not just Europe, either, where Du Bois directed his scathing critique. He juxtaposed, for example, America's campaign during the Great War to "make the 'World Safe for Democracy'" with the "orgy" of mob violence against Black people across the United States. Du Bois referenced the May 1917 lynching of Ell Persons in Memphis, Tennessee. Persons, who was Black, had been arrested and accused of murdering a White girl. Persons was forcibly taken from local deputies by a mob, tortured, and burned at the stake in front of a crowd estimated at least ten thousand in number.[21]

Du Bois also made reference to the attacks on Black workers by White mobs in East Saint Louis, Illinois, that same May 1917. Frustrated with having to compete with Black workers migrating to Saint Louis from Mississippi, Alabama, and other southern states, over three thousand White workers gathered in downtown East Saint Louis and began attacking Black people. Local police refused to interfere on behalf of Black residents, and there is some evidence that local police participated in the attacks. The governor of Illinois eventually called in the National Guard.

Shortly thereafter, a car driving through the area in which the attacks occurred was mistaken for one carrying White instigators. Black residents shot at the vehicle, killing two police officers who happened to be riding in the car. Thousands of Whites returned, marching through the Black neighborhoods of East Saint Louis, setting fire to entire sections, and then shooting residents as they attempted to escape the blaze. White rioters also lynched several Black people, declaring to the local press that "Southern negroes deserve a genuine lynching." More National Guardsmen were called in to squash the riot, yet some ended up participating in it. The *Chicago Defender*, which at the time was helmed by Du Bois's contemporary Ida B. Wells, estimated that between 40 and 150 Black people were killed and another 6,000 left homeless.[22]

The quotes Du Bois placed around the phrase "make the 'World Safe for Democracy,'" then, reflect what he viewed as the height of American hypocrisy, as well as its true legacy. Liberty, freedom, and democracy were and remain little more than philosophical cover for American empire to advance its imperialist and colonialist mission abroad, all while denying those same values at home to the poor and to people of color. This is why, for instance, Du Bois described whiteness in this essay as a subjective experience whereby White men and women learn to see and understand themselves as unbounded, without restriction in thought or movement. Whiteness is, he so sharply quipped, "the ownership of the earth forever and ever, Amen!"[23]

This description of whiteness as a kind of global ownership reveals its deep imbrication in the imperialist expansions of Europe taking place prior to, as well as after, the Great War. Du Bois captured this moment when he wrote, "Wave on wave, each with increasing virulence, is dashing this new religion of whiteness on the shores of our time." So long as non-White peoples and nations accept this new religion with grace and mercy, all is well. However, if African, Asian, and Latin American nations and peoples "dispute the white man's title to certain alleged bequests of the Fathers in wage and position, authority and training," if they treat White benevolence with "sullen anger rather than humble jollity" or insist on their "human right to swagger and swear and waste,—then the spell is suddenly broken and the philanthropist is ready to believe that Negroes are impudent, that the South is right, and that Japan wants to fight America. After this the descent to Hell is easy."[24]

Political theorist Lawrie Balfour brilliantly traces the "roots" and "routes" between Du Bois's 1903 *Souls of Black Folk* and *Darkwater*. Balfour notes that in Du

Bois's 1940 *Dusk of Dawn*, he had described *Darkwater* as the second, following *Souls*, of "three sets of thought centering around the hurts and hesitancies that hem the Black in America." Balfour then argues that Du Bois carried forward "the work of interpreting the experiences of African America inaugurated" nearly two decades prior. Certainly, Du Bois's scathing criticism in "The Souls of White Folk" suggests a kind of bitterness to his writing and analysis. Yet Balfour argues that beyond simply diagnosing the danger of global White supremacy and American empire, Du Bois was also widening his readers' democratic imagination "through focused engagement with the condition of Black lives."[25]

Part of this condition includes "second sight," which in *Souls* Du Bois described as both gift and curse and which is present from the opening of the essay. Recall that in *Souls* Du Bois described double consciousness as the condition through which Black people come to know themselves both through their own eyes and through the eyes of White people. Double consciousness is not something innate; instead, it is an effect of Black people living within a racialized social structure.[26]

In "The Souls of White Folk," however, Du Bois reworked the concept and reversed the relationship between White and Black people. "I know their thoughts, and they know that I know," Du Bois wrote. The knowledge that White people's thoughts expose them to the gaze of Black people makes White men and women "now embarrassed, now furious. . . . [C]rouching as they clutch at rags of facts and fancies to hide their nakedness, they go twisting, flying by my tired eyes and I see them ever stripped, —ugly, human."[27]

Du Bois's reworking of his description of "second sight" is important for what it reveals about the racialized social structure, both its present form and its future demise. The racialized social structure provides durable, material advantages for those racialized as White. This was true in the early twentieth century and remains true today. For example, the racial wealth gap—the difference in wealth holdings between typical White households and typical Black households—is larger today than it was even just twenty years ago. The racialized social structure also affords greater political power, as well as access to political power, to those racialized as White. From school boards, municipal wards, and state houses to courtrooms, commissions, and executive offices, White people—and, to be clear, predominantly White men—hold a disproportionate share of local, state, and federal elected and appointed offices. Moreover, the access to the ballot—the primary method through which everyday people exercise their political power in a democracy—remains uneven and across many states is becoming even more unequal. Finally, the racialized social structure affords those racialized as White far greater social status than their non-White counterparts. This is, of course, not separate from the material and political power provided to them through this same social structure. Whether in education, health care, or commerce, White people enjoy better access to and treatment within these institutions.[28]

Yet at the same time, Du Bois understood that advantages afforded to White people through this racialized social structure inevitably produced, among Black people, the necessary consciousness for its dismantling. This critical consciousness comes to Black people in the form of second sight, a kind of superpower that helps render for those who possess it the true purpose of the color line. Black people know and understand, by way of second sight, that the color line does far more than just relegate them to inferior status within American society. They also know and understand that the color line's true purpose is to hide the simple yet powerful fact that White people everywhere are ordinary.

The Superpower of Second Sight

It's worth taking a detour here to reflect on the idea of second sight as a superpower, one developed under conditions of systemic racism that both strips Black people of their humanity and ultimately renders their humanity, as well as the humanity of White people, more intelligible. This reading of double consciousness, or second sight, is shared by several scholars, though few if any characterize it as a superpower. Cultural theorist Paul Gilroy, for example, understands second sight as a mechanism for accessing the shared experiences of a Black diaspora. Meanwhile, religious studies scholar Craig Forney discusses double consciousness as both gift and curse. Likewise does scholar James W. Perkinson, who theorizes double consciousness as "shamanic combat" against White supremacy. These interpretations complement my own, not just Du Bois's original use in *Souls* but also Du Bois's reformulation of second sight in the decades after its 1903 publication. Post-*Souls*, all efforts to strip Black people of their agency and their humanity give rise to the superpower of second sight, which is entirely agentic and humane.[29]

Thirty-five years after *Souls* announced Du Bois's intellectual genius to a wide public audience, he was invited to give the commencement address to the graduating class of his undergraduate alma mater, Fisk University, in Nashville, Tennessee. Du Bois entitled his address to this 1938 class "The Revelations of Saint Orgne the Damned." Like many of his works, including *Souls*, Du Bois made extensive use of religious allegory in his address. In this speech, the use of allegory served to convey to his audience higher education's importance to the collective uplift of Black people in the United States.

Du Bois's speech focused on his protagonist, Saint Orgne, who finds himself one morning questioning whether the color line is destiny and what might lie beyond it: "What is this life I see? Is the dark damnation of color, real? Or simply

mine own imagining? Can it be true that souls wrapped in black velvet have a destiny different from those swathed in white satin or yellow silk, when all these cov-
ering are fruit of the same worm, and threaded by the same hands? Or must I, ig-
noring all seeming difference, rise to some upper realm where there is no color nor
race, sex, wealth nor age, but all men stand equal in the Sun?" Orgne's questions
are answered by a "great Voice," who instructs Orgne to overcome his fear and to
make sense of "the mystery of the seven stars and the seven golden candlesticks"
from which the Voice resonates. And so "Orgne turned and climbed the Seven
Heights of Hell to view the Seven Stars of Heaven. The seven heights are Birth and
Family; School and Learning; the University and Wisdom; the great snow-capped
peak of Work; the naked crag of Right and Wrong; the rolling hills of the Freedom
of Art and Beauty; and at last, the plateau that is the Democracy of Race; beyond
this there are no vales of Gloom—for the star above is the sun itself and all shadows fall straight before it."[30]

Du Bois then took his captive audience on the years-long journey of Saint
Orgne as he makes his way through the "Seven Heights of Hell," "up and down,
around and through seven groups of seven years until in the end he came back
to the beginning, world-weary but staunch." Du Bois's telling of Orgne's journey
was meant to reveal how and why the color line remained the central question
for Black people to grapple with across the twentieth century. While, for instance,
one's life "depends on [a strong family] and not on color or unchangeable and un-
fathomable compulsions before births," Orgne realizes that even those Black boys
and girls born to loving and nurturing families eventually had to leave their parents' care and enter into an American educational system that was anything but
loving and nurturing: "the elementary schools of the South; in schools with short
terms; with teachers inadequate both as to numbers and training; with quarters ill-
suited physically and morally to the work in hand; with colored principals chosen
not for executive ability but for their agility in avoiding race problems; and with
white superintendents who try to see how large a statistical showing can be made
without expenditure of funds, thought nor effort." The echoes of "From Georgia" and its critique of what Cedric Robinson later termed "racial capitalism" ring
loudly in Du Bois's storytelling. For Du Bois, the blame lies with White America,
"which does not thoroughly believe in the education of Negroes," as well as "the
South, which still to a large extent does not believe in any training for Black folk
which is not of direct commercial profit to those who dominate the state."[31]

The journey of Saint Orgne continues, with him absorbing lessons on the importance of knowledge and wisdom, of working toward collective Black uplift
while resisting the reproduction of capital for capital's sake, and of understanding
that living a free life is the true "expression of art." At last, Saint Orgne arrives "at

an old forest amid falling leaves with the starry heavens above him." Though he is surrounded by death, "somehow somewhere beneath lies some Tone too deep for sound—a silent chord of infinite harmony." Having borne witness to the extent to which the racial caste system constrains and restricts Black people's liberty and freedom, Saint Orgne, in a moment of doubt, asks the Voice, who has accompanied him the entire way, "Is not our dream of Democracy done?" The Voice does not answer. Instead, "in his own heart Saint Orgne's answer comes."[32]

Democracy, Du Bois told his audience of new college graduates, does not mean freedom. Democracy, rather, means the submission of the individual to the general will of the people. This submission, according to Du Bois, is justified so long as the will of the people is general and not the will of just a privileged few. Yet as Saint Orgne learns, the color line makes it all but impossible for the collective will of Black people to express itself through the general will of American democracy.[33]

It is worth quoting at length Du Bois's central lesson to his audience that day, one that is clearly a version of the argument he made in *Black Reconstruction*, published just three years prior to this address:

> We American Negroes form and will long form a perfectly definite group, not entirely segregated and isolated from our surroundings, but differentiated to such a degree that we have very largely a life and thought of our own.... We Black folk have striven to be Americans. And like all other Americans, we have longed to become rich Americans. Wealth comes easiest today through the exploitation of labor and by paying low wages; and if we have not widely exploited our own and other labor the praise belongs not to us, but to those whites whose monopoly of wealth and ruthless methods have out-run our tardy and feeble efforts. This is the place to pause and look about, as well, backward as forward. The leaders of the labor movement in America as in Europe, deceived us just as they deceived themselves. They left us out. They paid no attention to us, whether we were drudging in colonies or slaving in cotton fields or pleading in vain at the door of union labor factories. The object of white labor was not the uplift of all labor; it was to join capital in sharing the loot from exploited colored labor. So, we too, only half emancipated, hurled ourselves forward too willing if it had but been possible, to climb up a bourgeois heaven on the prone bodies of our fellows. But white folk occupied and crowded these stairs. And white labor loved the white exploiters of black folk far more than it loved its fellow black proletarian.[34]

As to where this left Black people in the United States, Du Bois's words cut like a hot knife through butter: "With few exceptions we are all today 'white folks' niggers.'"[35]

Without consideration of tone, the substance of Du Bois's remarks here may strike some as overly harsh, especially so given the context in which they were made. Certainly his comments are provocative. Yet underneath his provocation is a remarkable consistency with regard to Du Bois's conceptualization of color line and how it affects Black people in the United States. In his 1897 essay for *The Atlantic* and in his revised version for *Souls*, Du Bois argued that the color line incapacitates Black people from recognizing themselves except through the eyes of others. Their conceptualization of themselves, then, is through how White folks see them, think about them, and fundamentally interact with them. White people, because of the color line, cannot see Black people as fully human, even those Black people—like these recent college graduates—who might think of themselves as having achieved or as being on their way to achieving some modicum of the American dream. White people only ever saw Black people, even so-called middle-class Black people, as less than themselves because of the racialized social structure. It is why, according to Du Bois, leaders of the labor movement in both Europe and the United States left Black people entirely out of their conceptualization of a revolutionary proletariat. And it is why in 1938, with few exceptions, Black people's futures remained determined by White people and their unwillingness to share in "ownership over the Earth."[36]

Yet in this commencement speech, Du Bois extended his original thesis on the Veil by considering its deleterious effects on other groups, including White people. To those Fisk University graduates, he stated:

> Very, very many colored folk: Japanese, Chinese, Indians, Negroes; and, of course, the vast majority of white folk; have been so enthused, oppressed, and surpassed by current white civilization that they think and judge everything by its terms. They have no norms that are not set in the 19th and 20th centuries. They can conceive of no future world which is not dominated by present white nations and thoroughly shot through with their ideals, their method of government, their economic organization, their literature, their art; or in other words their throttling of democracy, their exploitation of labor, their industrial imperialism and their color hate.[37]

Yes, the color line structures how Black people are perceived and subsequently treated. This produces among Black people the condition of second sight, or double consciousness. Yet the color line and its effects are internalized and acted upon not only by Black people but also by all who live under it, including White people. This latter point constitutes a significant reformulation. Du Bois stated: "If, however, the effect of the racial caste system on the North American Negro has been both good and bad, its effect on white America has been disastrous. It has repeatedly led the greatest modern attempt at democratic government to deny its political ideals, to falsify its philanthropic assertions and to make its religion to a great extent hypocritical."[38]

The color line is debilitating for its perpetrators. The very racialized social structure that affords to White people both psychological and social wages also creates among them an irreconcilable condition. So long as American racism is maintained, the ideals of American democracy cannot be achieved. The color line both prevents Black people from fully participating in the American narrative and strips White people of their abilities to recognize this as fact. Because White people cannot recognize how this system advantages them based upon no more than their skin color, the color line also robs them of that which makes all of us human—our empathy. For what is more human than to see oneself in a fellow person? To empathize with the plight and suffering of others? And to direct one's complete and total efforts toward their immediate relief and ultimate liberation?[39]

On his sixtieth birthday, Du Bois penned a letter to himself that would ultimately serve as the postlude to his posthumous autobiography, *A Soliloquy on Viewing My Life from the Last Decade of Its First Century*. In it he wrote:

> And yet it hangs there, this Veil, between then and now, between Pale and Colored and Black and White—between You and Me. Surely it is but a thought-thing, tenuous, intangible; yet just as surely it is true and terrible and not in our little day may you and I lift it. We may feverishly unravel its edges and even climb slow with giant shears to where its ringed and gilded top nestles close to the throne of Eternity. But as we work and climb we shall see through streaming eyes and hear with aching ears, lynching and murder, cheating and despising, degrading and lying, so flashed and fleshed through this vast hanging darkness that the Doer never sees the Deed and the Victim knows not the Victor and Each hate All in wild and bitter ignorance.[40]

This passage, written some five years prior to his Fisk University commencement address and during the time he would have been researching and writing *Black Reconstruction*, reveals Du Bois wrestling with what seems like the inevitability of the color line. Dismantling it forces us to encounter its violent legacy, along with the reverberations of that legacy into our present day. Even then, we are unlikely to complete the task in our own lifetime. Then what of the next generation? The color line is so vast, our world so steeped within it, that those who suffer rightfully direct their rage at those who benefit; yet those who benefit from the structure of the Veil fail to see their advantages as deriving from anything else but merit, divine providence, or a combination of the two.

Some two decades later, in his draft of a manuscript on the study of Black Americans, Du Bois provided insight into a debate within Black American communities on how to best respond to the color line and its structural conditioning of their lives:

> [Black America] has long been internally divided by dilemma as to whether its striving upward should be aimed at strengthening its inner cultural and group bonds, both for intrinsic progress and for offensive power against caste; or whether it should seek escape wherever and however possible into the surrounding American culture. Decision in this matter has been lately determined by outer compulsion rather than inner plan; for prolonged policies of segregation and discrimination have involuntarily welded the mass almost into a nation within a nation with its own schools, churches, hospitals, newspapers, and many business enterprises. The result has been to make American Negroes to wide extent provincial, introvert, self-conscious and narrowly race-loyal.[41]

Even in 1950, despite no explicit reference to double consciousness, duality and marginality remained central themes in Du Bois's analysis of the Black experience. Yet Du Bois's analysis had taken another turn post-*Souls* that revealed his and our own evolving understanding of White supremacy. The racial caste system produces among Black people a kind of resolve that is evident in the building and maintenance of its own institutions—schools, religious life, media, and so much more. Yet at the same time, the focus of Black people in America to survive, to strive in the face of unrelenting White supremacy is necessarily so a singular one. The narrowness in which the racialized social structure focuses their attention makes it difficult for Black people in America to see the commonality they share with other people and struggles beyond their own and beyond this land. But Du Bois did not see this as inevitable. Though "decision in this matter has been lately determined by outer compulsion rather than inner plan," Du Bois did not rule out the possibility of an alternative.

That Du Bois would arrive at this point in 1950 is not surprising, given the global shift his scholarship and activism had taken over the previous three decades. The color line and its effects are not confined to America or to Black American life, though Black America remained even by 1950 central to Du Bois's analysis. By the 1930s, however, and most certainly after, Du Bois had come to understand how the color line affects even those upon which it confers its benefits. Most importantly, Du Bois began to see that any future for dismantling the color line would require the collective struggle of those groups at the bottom of the racial caste system, for while the color line provided them the superpower of second sight, it rendered those at the top of the system blind to its very existence. Transcendence is made possible through second sight. Thus, if White people can ever hope to get beyond the "vast hanging darkness" of the color line, they will require the assistance of those rendered unequal by its force and structure.

The contemporary relevance of Du Bois's post-*Souls* analysis of the Veil and second sight is quite clear. The propaganda machine of the Right has taken aim at nearly all forms of commentary that challenge the hegemony of the color line and America's privileged position in the geopolitical sphere. Right-wing media and politicians at all levels of local, state, and federal government are actively pursuing legislation to prohibit all criticism of the nation and its historic dependence upon exploitation and domination within public education, including higher education. Should these actors ultimately be successful, we would expect that the "vast hanging darkness" of the color line would only increase, further incapacitating the vast majority of White people from acting against it. Yet we would also anticipate that as the Veil further envelops our institutions, including education, the superpower of second sight would only grow in strength. In true dialectic fashion, White supremacy ultimately digs its own grave.

Whither the Jew Post-*Souls*?

And what of the Jewish figure post-*Souls*? As I argue in chapters 3 and 4, in the immediate years following Du Bois's return from Berlin, the figure of the Jew haunted his theorizing of Black duality and marginality. Yet in the decades after *Souls*, that haunting becomes less distinct, and Du Bois's direct references to Jews' plight are sparse across the early to mid-twentieth century. Historian Clive Webb characterizes Du Bois's lack of writing on the matter as "silence" and situates that silence within the larger context of early twentieth-century Black intellectuals. Many, Webb argues, shared Du Bois's affinity, even infatuation, with German cultural life. Consequently, as the realities of German life in the period leading up to and during Hitler's ascent to power became more apparent, these Black intellectuals became especially hesitant to speak on these and other matters concerning the plight of Germany's Jews. Webb reminds us that prior to Hitler's regime, German intellectuals spoke eloquently and forcefully on Black people's struggles under the American racial caste system. Arthur Feiler, for example, was the widely respected editor of Germany's most distinguished newspaper in the early twentieth century, the *Frankfurter Zeitung*. Feiler once wrote that in America, "one can study with horror how injustice, once perpetrated by a people, continues in later generations to consume it like a destructive poison."[42]

Likewise, Eve Darian-Smith argues that Du Bois, like his Black contemporaries, largely refrained from engaging in the swelling rumors of Jewish persecution under the Third Reich. It is not difficult to imagine that Du Bois—a Germanophile since his days at Fisk—was shocked by the swell of barbarous rumors emerging from the German nation-state in the post–World War I years. In his "Postscript" column for *The Crisis* magazine in May 1933, Du Bois gave voice to this sentiment while also alluding to the likely truth of the rumors:

> It seems impossible in the middle of the twentieth century [that] a country like Germany could turn to race hate as a political expedient. Surely, the experience of America is enough to warn the world. And yet so long as children are taught to believe in hierarchy of races, and in the innate superiority of certain racial groups, just so long it will be possible to appeal to the racial animosity for political effect. The absurdity of it in the case of Germany is too patent to recall. One has only to think of a hundred names like Mendelssohn, Heine, and Einstein, to remember but partially what the Jew has done for German civilization. It all reminds the American Negro that after all race prejudice has nothing to do with accomplishment or desert, with genius or ability. It is an ugly, dirty thing. It feeds on envy and hate.[43]

If by 1933 Du Bois was willing to acknowledge the likelihood of the German atrocities, his 1936 trip to Nazi Germany solidified his and others' worries. Du Bois could no longer minimize or ignore what he bore witness to with his own eyes. Writing for the Black American newspaper the *Pittsburgh Courier* upon his return, Du Bois demanded his Black readership to pay attention by paralleling the plight of Germany's Jews with that of Black people in the United States: "In the case of the Jews, one meets something different, which an American Negro does not readily understand. Prejudice against Jews in Germany comes nearer being instinctive than color prejudice." Continuing with an equal mix of clarity and pessimism in his prognosis, Du Bois stated, "There has been no tragedy in modern times equal in its awful effects to the fight on the Jew in Germany. It is an attack on civilization, comparable only to such horrors as the Spanish Inquisition and the African slave trade."[44]

This passionate plea notwithstanding, Du Bois's post-*Souls* reflections upon the Jewish question and the relationship it shared with his thinking and writing on the global color line remained complex. By 1944 the *Auschwitz Protocols*, written by two former prisoners, had shone a bright light upon the horrors of camp life. German authorities had begun liquidating some of their camps and transferring the remaining prisoners to others. As part of its efforts to increase international pressure upon the Nazi regime, the American Jewish Committee (AJC) authored the "Declaration of Human Rights," aimed at addressing the Holocaust and Jews' suffering. In October, the AJC's then president, Joseph Proskauer, wrote to Du Bois to share a draft of the declaration. "We feel sure that the sentiments expressed [in the declaration] are not only those of the Committee," wrote Proskauer, "but those held by thousands of distinguished and thoughtful Americans of all faiths. We, therefore, urge that you join with us in signing this declaration. . . . To this end, will you please sign and return one copy in the enclosed self-addressed envelope; the other copy we believe you will want to keep for your own records."[45]

Du Bois's reply, written in November, expressed misgivings about the bent of the letter and the request to sign it. "I have received your declaration of human rights," Du Bois began, "and want to say frankly that I am greatly disappointed."[46] Du Bois pulled no punches, picking apart the declaration paragraph by paragraph:

> You say under paragraph two of your creed: "No plea of sovereignty shall ever again be allowed to permit any nation to deprive those within its borders of these fundamental rights in the claim that these are matters of internal concern." How about depriving people outside the borders of a country of their rights? . . .
>
> Under paragraph five you appeal for sympathy for persons driven from the land of their birth; but how about American Negroes, Africans and Indians who have not been driven from the land of their birth, but nevertheless are deprived of their rights? Under paragraph six you want redress for those who wander the earth but how about those who do not wander and are not allowed to travel and nevertheless are deprived of their fundamental rights? . . .
>
> In other words, this is a very easily understood declaration of Jewish rights but it has apparently no thought of the rights of Negroes, Indians and South Sea Islanders. Why then call it the Declaration of Human Rights?[47]

Michael Rothberg suggests that we understand Du Bois's candid reply through the lens of his intellectual journey to that point. By 1944 Du Bois's perspective was one where the maintenance of the color line entailed specific social and historical projects. The universalist human rights paradigm, like that urged by the AJC, then, fell flat for Du Bois, who at this point was insisting upon the specificity of European colonialist and imperialist atrocities against a variety of peoples, not just Jews.[48]

Yet just five years later, a trip to Poland suggested that the figure of the Jew continued to shape his thinking on the color line. While in Poland, Du Bois toured the infamous site of the Warsaw ghetto uprising. He had previously visited the Polish countryside as a young academic in 1893 and then again during his 1936 trip to Germany. It was this last trip, however, that seemed to affect the older Du Bois the most. In April 1952, at the invitation of *Jewish Life* magazine as part of its "Tribute to the Warsaw Ghetto," Du Bois discussed his Polish experiences. He recalled the totality of his three visits. Yet it was clear from his words how deeply affected he had been by seeing the rubble that remained from Jewish resistance: "I have seen something of human upheaval in this world: the scream and shots of a race riot in Atlanta; the marching of the Ku Klux Klan; the threat of courts and police; the neglect and destruction of human habitation; but nothing in my wildest imagination was equal to what I saw in Warsaw in 1949. I would have said before seeing it that it was impossible for a civilized nation with deep religious convictions and outstanding religious institutions; with literature and art; to treat human beings as Warsaw had been treated."[49] The tour of the Warsaw site was as revealing for Du Bois's understanding of the plight of Black people as it was for his understanding of the Jewish question:

> The result of these three visits, and particularly of my view of the Warsaw ghetto, was not so much cleaner understanding of the Jewish problem in the world as it was a real and more complete understanding of the Negro problem. In this first place, the problem of slavery, emancipation, and caste in the United States was no longer in my mind a separate and unique thing as I had so long conceived it. It was not even solely a matter of color and physical and racial characteristics, which was particularly a hard thing for me to learn, since for a lifetime the color line had been a real and efficient cause of misery. . . . No, the race problem in which I was interested cut across lines of color and physique and belief and status and was a matter of cultural patterns, perverted teaching and human hate and prejudices which reached all sorts of people and caused endless evil to all men. So that the ghetto of Warsaw helped me to emerge from a certain social provincialism into a broader conception of what the fight against race segregation, religious discrimination and the oppression by wealth had to become if civilization was going to triumph and broaden in the world.[50]

Du Bois's visit to Warsaw, then, reveals again an evolving understanding of the Veil and the problem of the color line. The race problem for Du Bois, crystallized by way of Polish Jews' resistance to Nazism, is imbricated with a range of destructive global forces: capitalism, imperialism, religious intolerance, colonialism, and even environmental destruction. Just as his German education allowed him to overcome what he saw as a narrow provincialism in order to understand the race problem as a global phenomenon, Du Bois's trip to Warsaw—and his direct encounter with the aftermath of Jewish resistance—provided for him a greater understanding of the plight of Black people in the United States and the relationship between their suffering and the suffering of others the world over.

Post-*Souls*, then, the figure of the Jew remained an important one for Du Bois's intellectual journey, even while his own thinking on the matter became more complex than in prior decades. Still, the consistency with which Du Bois situated the struggles of both Jews and Black people within the context of external, global forces was far from the mainstream perspective of his day. How, then, did Du Bois's contemporaries in the social and behavioral sciences think about the Jewish question? How did they understand it in relation to the struggles of other groups within the racialized social structure?

The Jewish Question Post-*Souls*:
A Failure in Perspective

Early twentieth-century scholars echoed some of Du Bois's themes concerning duality and marginality. A few even offered parallels between the experiences of Black Americans and Jews in both western Europe and the United States. Yet where Du Bois differed most from his contemporaries was in his own understanding of second sight as a condition born from the Veil and as a kind of gift. His contemporaries often failed to see the positive benefits of this condition and did not properly locate its roots in the social system itself. Instead, they framed Black duality and marginality as a kind of pathological condition born from inferior racial stock or a stubborn unwillingness to break from a backward culture. Indeed, some early twentieth-century scholars went so far as to claim that chattel slavery provided Black people more integration and positive benefits than emancipation ever could. These scholars directly challenged Du Bois's own contention that enslavement itself was responsible for many of the deleterious conditions of postemancipation Black America.

None of the claims made by Du Bois's contemporaries are surprising to students of twentieth-century intellectual history. Scientific racism was, for most of the early and middle decades, still the dominant paradigm. What is sociologically fascinating, however, is how the so-called goal posts were shifted by scientific racism's adherents in lieu of new evidence that challenged their claims of biological and cultural inferiority.

In my own previous work, I have argued that science was and remains the principal driving force in the making and maintenance of what sociologists Michael Omi and Howard Winant term "racial projects." A racial project "is simultaneously an interpretation, representation, or explanation of racial dynamics, and an effort to reorganize and redistribute resources along particular racial lines. Racial projects connect what race means in a particular discursive practice and the ways in which both social structures and everyday experiences are racially organized, based upon that meaning."[51]

Omi and Winant's own theorizing of racial projects gives primacy to the state in shaping racial meanings. They write, for example, that racial meanings are "con-

structed and transformed sociohistorically through competing political projects."
In my own work, however, I build upon sociologist Karen Knorr Cetina's idea
of epistemic cultures to identify an epistemic culture of race and racism within
nineteenth- and twentieth-century science, including social science. By epistemic
culture, I mean to draw attention to how an expert system was shaped and maintained in service of scientific racism, permeating and facilitating Western society's
ongoing production of racial categories and their meanings.[52]

Scientific racism is far from obsolete, but it is also no longer a dominant paradigm in the social, behavioral, or even biological sciences. Most scientists reject
the idea that race is biological. While some social and behavioral scientists still
give credence to the idea that racial differences are cultural and then—explicitly
or implicitly—organize racial categories in a hierarchy based upon cultural differences, their perspective is a minority one. Yet in Du Bois's time, this was far from
the case. Across the early and mid-twentieth century, meaning was invested into
the supposed reality of racial categories—Black, White, Jew, and others. As a result, the analysis of human affairs in terms of racial differences both emerged from
and was supported within university laboratories, classrooms, seminars, conferences, and writings of those in the biological and social sciences.[53]

To illustrate this point, I combed through the early volumes of the *American Journal of Sociology* (*AJS*), the oldest continuing publication for sociological research and writing in the world and among the most prestigious. The early
volumes—those spanning the end of the nineteenth century through the first four
decades of the twentieth century—are filled with musings on the so-called Negro question, the challenges of racial and ethnic assimilation into White society,
the causes of continued racial inferiority, and its consequences for national unity.
Taken as a whole, the early volumes constitute a key component of the epistemic
culture of scientific racism within the social sciences and, by extension, wider society. During its early decades the *AJS* published a variety of contributions, not all
of which were by social scientists or experts. Nevertheless, the journal's pages were
dedicated to advancing their claims, no matter how unscientific, even for that era.
In this way, the *AJS* helped to produce and maintain hegemonic ideas concerning the veracity of racial categories and the meanings invested within them. Prestigious outlets such as the *AJS* legitimized these ideas, helping them to become common sense.

Political scientist Paul Reinsch, writing for the *AJS* in 1905, exemplifies the racial common sense of this period: "Without going into the question of origins, it is
clear that conditions of environment and historical forces have combined in producing certain great types of humanity which are essentially different in their characteristics. To treat these as if they were all alike, to subject them to the same meth-

ods of government, to force them into the same institutions, was a mistake of the nineteenth century which has not been carried over into our own." Reinsch, like many of his White contemporaries, was willing to shift away from biological explanations of racial inferiority that dominated the previous century. Instead, he understood racial differences as part historical, part environmental, and part cultural. Reinsch, for example, argued, on the one hand, that among Black children "after the age of puberty development soon ceases, the expectations raised by the earlier achievements are disappointed, and no further intellectual progress is to be looked for." Yet in explaining this so-called developmental stagnation, Reinsch wrote, "We can hardly avoid the conclusion that it is due rather to social, political, and climatic conditions than to the physiological, personal incapacity of the negro."[54]

Elsewhere, Mississippi politician and writer Alfred Holt Stone, among the most public and staunch proponents of scientific racism, wrote for the *AJS* that

> I know of no race in all history which possesses in equal degree the marvelous power of adaptability to conditions which the negro has exhibited through many centuries and in many places. His undeveloped mental state has made it possible for him to accept conditions, and to increase and be content under them, which a more highly organized and sensitive race would have thrown off, or destroyed itself in the effort to do so. This ability to accept the status of slavery and to win the affection and regard of the master race, and gradually but steadily to bring about an amelioration of the conditions of the slave status made possible the anomalous and really not yet understood race relations of the antebellum South.[55]

Stone's paper is worth discussing in part because of Du Bois's personal connection to it and because the trajectory of the paper helps illustrate how ideas gain and keep currency within an epistemic culture by way of professional organizations and professional outlets.

Though his paper was published in 1908, Stone first presented it to the American Sociological Society at its 1907 annual meeting in Madison, Wisconsin. In the months leading up to its presentation, however, Stone and Du Bois exchanged several letters related to the paper and to other matters. They had a cordial though contentious relationship, evidenced by public and private disagreements concerning the conditions of Black America. The society's secretary and treasurer at the time, C. W. Veditz, had extended Du Bois an invitation in October of that year to "participate in a discussion of A. H. Stone's paper on race friction in the South. . . . I would like to add my own personal request that you be with us. The new Society desires but one thing: the Truth, the whole Truth, and nothing but the Truth." Du Bois ultimately declined the invitation. However, he did review

Stone's paper, and in a letter to Stone shortly before the society's meeting, Du Bois informed his colleague, "I think it by all means [is] the fairest paper that you have [ever] written and strikes a note which I have not seen in your other papers. If this spirit of discussion could be held to in the race problem, I am sure we should accomplish great things."[56]

While Du Bois declined the invitation to join the society and participate in its meeting, he did send his comments on Stone's paper to be read at the meeting. However, the comments arrived too late to include in the discussion that followed Stone's presentation. Veditz, writing to Du Bois on stationery for the American Economic Association shortly after the conclusion of the American Sociological Society's meeting, informed Du Bois that with Stone's consent, Du Bois's comments would appear in print in the May 1908 issue of the *AJS* as part of a collection of responses to Stone's paper from his peers.[57]

The sheer number and range of commentaries regarding Stone's paper that were published in the May 1908 issue of the *AJS* reflect a broad and significant interest in Stone's claims. Many of those who offered remarks ultimately agreed with Stone's thesis, that "race friction" was increasing between Black and White people in the United States, though they took some small issue with the causes of that friction, in particular, Stone's position that race friction was not necessarily the result of Black people's enslavement less than a half-century prior. Professor U. G. Weatherly of the University of Indiana, for example, stated, "While agreeing heartily with Mr. Stone's contention that race friction between whites and blacks was not a necessary offspring of slavery, I think it can be shown that certain elements of the problem are inseparably connected with the later history of slavery." Importantly, though, Weatherly agreed with Stone's more general position in his paper that Black people are socially and culturally inferior to White people. "On the side of cultural and institutional development," Weatherly wrote, "the negro's history was almost a blank until he was brought to America as a slave. Whatever achievement he has since made has been upon models which he has taken from the whites."[58]

Du Bois's own remarks, which, although he was the most prolific sociological writer of his era, represent his only published writing for the *AJS*, reveal remarkable poise, given some of the more absurd claims made by Stone. Furthermore, Du Bois used the space of the *AJS* to actively advocate for ongoing work with the Atlanta Sociological Laboratory. Importantly, his comments also indicate that even by the early twentieth century the global shift within his own intellectual trajectory was well under way.

Du Bois began much like his other contemporaries, agreeing that Stone's general thesis that race friction between Black and White people in the United States was on the rise. Yet, Du Bois remarked, there remain three questions to wrestle with: "First, is the old status of acknowledged superiority and inferiority between the white and black races in America no longer possible? Secondly, are the race differences in this case irreconcilable? And thirdly, is racial separation practicable?"[59]

In answer to the first question, Du Bois shifted the focus away from the commonsense racialism of the time, that racial superiority is inherent, even if not strictly biological. Instead, Du Bois turned his attention to the system of slavery, which "denied growth or exception on the part of the enslaved and kept up that detail by physical force." Stone, in his own writing, had argued that slavery provided Black people with protected status on account of their inferiority. That is, slavery was benevolent. Du Bois, however, forcefully responded that not only was slavery not benevolent, but it was also responsible for Black people's unequal conditions postemancipation. "Emancipation," he wrote, "was simply the abolition of the grosser forms of that physical force."[60]

Du Bois took the second question as his opportunity to make a case for the strength of his own research program in Atlanta: "We find ourselves facing a field of science rather than opinion. As I have often said before, it is a matter of serious disgrace to American science that with the tremendous opportunity that it has had before it for the study of race differences and race development . . . almost nothing has been done." Du Bois continued: "When we at Atlanta University say that we are the only institution in the United States that is making any serious study of the race problems in the United States, we make no great boast because it is not that we are doing so much, but rather that the rest of the nation is doing nothing, and that we can get from the rest of the nation very little encouragement, co-operation, or help in this work." The question or rather accusation of Black inferiority was one Du Bois was willing to entertain as an empirical question. This was likely due to the fact that Du Bois knew that science—even racist science—was a language his contemporaries could not so easily dismiss. This is why he noted that when it came to accusations of Black inferiority, "the data upon which the mass of men, and even intelligent men, are basing their conclusions today, the basis which they are putting back of their treatment of the Negro, is a most ludicrous and harmful conglomeration of myth, falsehood, and desire." Du Bois, ever insightful, reminded Stone and his reading audience that "the very same arguments that are brought to prove the impossibility of white men and Negroes living together, except as inferior and superior, were also brought to prove that white men of differing rank and birth could not possibly exist in the same physical environment without similar subordination."[61]

To the third question—whether the separation of races is of practical concern—Du Bois revealed the global shift in his own thinking by pointing toward developments taking place outside of the American context. Everywhere, he in-formed Stone and his audience, contact between so-called racial groups was in-creasing. This was in no small part due to the colonial and imperial expansion of American and European empires. "Europe has insisted upon the opening of Af-rica," he wrote. "If the world can enter Asia, why cannot Asiatics enter the world?" The separation of so-called racial groups is not practical, then, because the expan-sion of the global economy requires labor, and empire demands that that labor come from elsewhere.[62]

Du Bois saved his most biting remarks for his conclusion. Stone, in his own paper, suggested a kind of inevitability toward conflict between White and non-White people. Quoting extensively from Du Bois's 1904 essay, "The Future of the Negro Race in America," Stone noted that Du Bois and others, in demanding full and fair equality between White and non-White people, were advocating for the abolition of the color line. To this, Stone quoted the American sociologist Edward A. Ross, from his highly influential *Foundations of Sociology*: "The superiority of a race cannot be preserved without pride of blood and an uncompromising attitude toward the lower races. . . . Whatever may be thought of the latter policy, the net result is that North America from the Bering Sea to the Rio Grande is dedicated to the highest type of civilization; while for centuries the rest of our hemisphere will drag the ball and chain of hybridism."[63] In what most likely was a direct response to Stone's racist appeals, Du Bois pulled no punches in noting the danger of such appeals in the early twentieth century, as violence toward Black people, including lynching, was reaching an apex. "Finally, rhetoric like that quoted by Mr. Stone is not in itself of particular importance," Du Bois wrote, "except when it encourages those Philistines who really believe that Anglo-Saxons owe their pre-eminence in some lines to lynching, lying, and slavery, and the studied insult of their helpless neighbors. God save us from such social philosophy!"[64]

Despite such a strong critique, by Du Bois's own account, Stone had pre-sented a fair discussion of racial conflict for that era, one that Du Bois himself thought—should others engage similarly—might engender a much-needed dis-cussion among social scientists. Whatever hopes Du Bois might have had for his other contemporaries is tempered when reviewing their commentary, which was far less "fair" than Stone's. For example, the same year Stone's paper was published, the *AJS* also published a paper entitled "A Southern View of Slavery." The author, H. E. Belin, was a South Carolinian with no social-scientific training of which to speak.

Belin's paper offered a full-force defense of slavery grounded in the mythology of the Lost Cause: "Belonging to the fast-thinning ranks of a generation which links together the South of past and present, being closely in touch with the old regime, and having a personal knowledge of conditions then existing, I desire, in the interests of historic truth, to present as concisely as possible an inside view of the institution of slavery." Slavery, according to Belin, was an ethical imperative based upon "the radical and essential difference between the races." Furthermore, Belin argued that any claims such as Du Bois's own that suggest that slavery produced retrogradation among Black people were "fallacy pure and simple." Rather, slavery, "so far from degrading the negro, has actually elevated him industrially, mentally, and even morally, the term of his involuntary tutelage to the white race raising him to a vastly higher level than that ever occupied by his kinsmen in Africa."[65]

Belin's defense was echoed by another paper published in the *AJS* that year, written by noted feminist author Charlotte Perkins Gilman. In her essay, entitled "A Suggestion on the Negro Problem," Gilman without any hint of irony portrayed White people as the victims of Black people's freedom: "We have to consider the unavoidable presence of a large body of aliens, of a race widely dissimilar and in many respects inferior, *whose present status is to us a social injury.* If we had left them alone in their own country this dissimilarity and inferiority would be, so to speak, none of our business."[66] To remedy this situation, Gilman suggested that what would be best for the nation and for Black people—a distinction commonplace among early and mid-twentieth-century American social scientists—was slavery by another name:

> Let each sovereign state carefully organize in every county and township an enlisted body of all negroes below a certain grade of citizenship. Those above it—the decent, self-supporting, progressive negroes—form no problem and call for nothing but congratulation. But the whole body of negroes who do not progress, who are not self-supporting, who are degenerating into an increasing percentage of social burdens or actual criminals, should be taken hold of by the state.... [T]hose old enough to work should be employed as follows: enough should be placed on farms to provide for the entire body. These farms should be model farms, under the best management, furnishing experiment stations, and bases for agricultural instruction, as well as the food for the whole army and all its officials; and where cotton and such products were raised, they would be a further source of income.... What this amounts to is simply state organization of the negro, under conditions wholly to his advantage, and therefore to ours. Some persons, hasty in speech, will now be asking "Who is to pay for all this?" To which the answer is "The same who paid for all the comforts and luxuries of the South in earlier years—the working negro."[67]

There can be no doubt that Belin and Gilman represent the remaining vestiges of scientific racism, which, in the case of Gilman, masquerades (poorly) as White

benevolence. Still other White contemporaries of Du Bois turned increasingly toward cultural and social explanations for what they perceived as Blacks' inevitable
inferiority and inability to assimilate and adapt to White society. Such a view was
summarized by Chicago School sociologist and past president of the American Sociological Association Ellsworth Faris. Faris's paper, entitled "The Mental Capacity
of Savages" and published in the *AJS* a decade after Belin's and Gilman's own writings, suggested that while Black children's mental capacity was on average the same
as that of their White peers, their culture was to blame for any differences in mental capacity when they reached adulthood:

> The hypothesis that has been forming, therefore, in recent years concerning the
> mind of so-called primitive man, meaning the uncivilized races of the present day,
> is that in native endowment the savage child is, on the average, about the same in
> capacity as the child of civilized races. Instead of the concept of different stages
> or degrees of mentality, we find it easier to think of the human mind as being, in
> its capacity, about the same everywhere, the difference in culture to be explained
> in terms of the physical geography, or the stimuli from other groups, or the unac-
> countable occurrence of great men.[68]

Previously, Faris's colleague at the University of Chicago, William I. Thomas,
had placed his own emphasis on "the social rather than the biological and economic aspects" of the so-called Negro problem. Black people, according to
Thomas, had been ill-prepared for freedom. Meanwhile, those abolitionists who
advocated for their emancipation had failed to predict "the loss of control involved
in the disturbance of old habits, nor make a proper allowance for the time element
involved in education into new habits." Interestingly, to buttress his claims Thomas
quoted extensively from Du Bois's *Philadelphia Negro*, in particular, a passage in
which Du Bois described the shortcomings of the Black middle class. Thomas
found himself in agreement with Du Bois that the Black middle class ought to take
up the mantle of leadership among all Black Americans. Yet, quoting Du Bois, the
Black middle class refused this responsibility on the grounds that it would mean
them drawing the very color line that their class status was meant to reject.[69]

Thomas's liberal quoting from Du Bois was part of an interesting phenomenon
within the pages of the *American Journal of Sociology* in its early decades. Along
with *The Philadelphia Negro*, there were several explicit references to *The Souls of
Black Folk* and Du Bois's Atlanta papers. In the early twentieth century, then, Du
Bois's themes of Black duality and marginality were considered by his peers, even if
uncritically.

Moreover, a small but significant number of Du Bois's contemporaries also
drew upon the figure of the Jew in order to frame their discussions of Black duality

and marginality. Yet, unlike Du Bois, their own framing reinforced the dominant perspective of that time that both Jews' and Blacks' duality was the result of their inherent inability or stubborn unwillingness to break from their backward cultural ways and embrace modern White society.[70]

This perspective is exemplified by Mississippi-born sociologist and Dartmouth professor John Moffat Mecklin in both his 1913 *AJS* paper, "The Philosophy of the Color Line," and his 1914 book, *Democracy and Race Friction*, which contains an only slightly revised version of the former. In "The Philosophy of the Color Line," Mecklin attempted to locate whether and how White people could coexist with non-White groups. For Mecklin, a healthy relationship between White people and other "backward race[s]" was only possible upon "the unconditional acknowledgment of the supremacy of the white group."[71] The maintenance of the color line, for Mecklin, required the active subordination of Black people's agency and suppression of their civil and political rights. Like Stone, Belin, and others, however, Mecklin viewed this subordination as a necessary and even good thing, as Black people were considered too new to democracy to be able to participate in it without knowing their second-class status within:

> The "color line" is the result of this effort of the ruling group to make the black constantly aware of his subordinate status and actually to restrict him to it in the absence of legal means for so doing. The real motive here was not so much to humiliate the black or to perpetuate the social habits of slavery; the determining factor was the practical necessity of finding and maintaining a modus vivendi between a race with long training in the exercise of democratic liberties and another utterly without training and forced by disabilities of its own to occupy indefinitely a subordinate place in the social order. The problem was exactly that faced by the English in South Africa, namely, "the construction of a government which, while democratic as regards one of the races, cannot safely be made democratic as regards the other."[72]

The biological essentialist claims of Mecklin's nineteenth-century predecessors echoed throughout his writing as Mecklin advanced the cultural essentialist claims that were commonplace among Du Bois's twentieth-century contemporaries. On the one hand, Mecklin wrote that White civilization had to be protected from the threat of intermarriage, as it "would eliminate entirely the dualism of the social mind in the most natural and complete fashion." On the other hand, Mecklin stated that "it seems hard that the Negro should be required to attain selfhood as best he can outside the higher cultural possibilities of the white group and subordinated to that group." Nevertheless, Mecklin was firm in his belief that purity— whether biological or cultural—was real and had to be fiercely guarded. White people, according to Mecklin, could not be asked to make "the supreme sacrifice of its ethnic purity which is the bearer of its social heritage and, therefore, the ultimate guarantee of the continuity of its peculiar type of civilization." In conclusion, Mecklin declared: "We are now prepared to understand why the full and complete social integration of the Negro is impossible. Such social integration as does exist must be based upon mutual concessions and compromises. The conditions of the greatest harmony will be, as already suggested, where the weaker group accepts unconditionally the will of the stronger group. Conditions of friction will inevitably occur where the weaker group refuses to accept these conditions."[73]

In *Democracy and Race Friction*, published just one year later, Mecklin continued where he left off in "The Philosophy of the Color Line": "The absence of a higher social consciousness observed in the African negro is responsible more than anything else for those weaknesses of the American negro which have subjected him to such severe criticism. . . . [A] number, perhaps the majority, of American negroes do not yet share in any intimate and vital sense in those higher ideals of the community which are the measure of values in the life of the individual and the springs of action for the social will."[74] Note here the comparison to Du Bois's theorizing of Black duality and marginality, as well as the significant differences. Like Du Bois, Mecklin argued that Black people were incompatible with America—both its ideology and its social organization. Yet whereas Du Bois located the root of this problem in the racialized social structure, for Mecklin the problem was an interior one. Black people, according to Mecklin, were incompatible with the very ideals of America because those ideals were rooted in White Western culture, to which Black people were socially and culturally inferior.

Interestingly, Mecklin drew upon Du Bois's early body of scholarship to make this very point, all while taking swipes at Du Bois in the process:

> The text books set before negro children are usually the same as those prepared for the white and are filled with pictures idealizing the Anglo-Saxon type and the social environment of the white child, whereas differences of race, if nothing more, make it impossible for the negro child to attain this ideal. This is his "social copy," and yet he is censured if as mature man or woman he despises his own race and surrenders his self-respect in abject imitation of the white. The shock of disillusionment which must come when he finds that it is all a false dream and that he lives "within the Veil" will be by no means as tragic for the average negro as it was for the sensitive nature of Du Bois, but it will be real nevertheless.[75]

Here, Mecklin implied that Black duality, or double consciousness, was the result of Black people's "slavish imitation of the white's civilization and the tendency to ignore differences in race and social status."[76]

Mecklin quoted at length from Du Bois's *Philadelphia Negro* in his own description of the role race prejudice played in the daily lives of Black people, even while dismissing Du Bois himself as "sensitive and egoistic." Moreover, Mecklin also paralleled American anti-Black racism with anti-Semitism in western Europe and Germany: "The strenuous process of age-long social repression undergone by the Jew the Negro could doubtless never survive."[77]

Finally, Mecklin's discussion of individuals from mixed-race backgrounds put on full display his and many of his White contemporaries' belief that Black duality was inheritable and irreconcilable: "The great contributors to human progress have always had back of them the temperamental characteristics of a pronounced racial type. . . . [C]ontinuity of culture, then, depends in a very profound sense upon the continuity of the racial type of which that culture is an expression. Race in its widest sense is, like the individual, a psychophysical unity. . . . It is no accident of history that mongrel peoples are almost always characterized by instability of political institutions and a general inchoateness of civilization." Mecklin continued: "The atmosphere in which the mulatto lives is not one that is psychologically healthful. It is an atmosphere of protest; the mulatto is himself an incarnated protest against the racial separation of the color line. Dr. Du Bois has given us a glimpse into the dualism of the soul from which this spirit of protest arises."[78] Mecklin then quoted at length from *The Souls of Black Folk* and Du Bois's famed passage on double consciousness before writing:

> It would of course be committing the psychologist's fallacy upon a gigantic scale to read the ideas of *The Souls of Black Folk* into the minds of the masses of the negroes of the South, and yet it doubtless voices the feelings of a cultured few largely of the mulatto class. The state of mind it reflects is not a happy one since it breathes of pessimism and half-concealed race hatred. Du Bois tells us how as a boy, when he realised that he lived "within the Veil," he was happiest when he excelled his pale-faced mates in his books, at a foot-race, or even when he would "beat their stringy heads." As the years brought widening knowledge and a fuller realization of the odds that were against him and his race in the fight, he describes how "the shades of the prison house closed round about us all: walls straight and stubborn to the whitest, but relentlessly narrow, tall and unscalable to sons of night who must plod darkly on in resignation, or beat unavailing palms against the stone, or steadily, half-hopelessly, watch the streak of blue above."[79]

Democracy and Race Friction, like many other early and mid-twentieth-century writings on race and racial conflict, portrays duality and marginality as a particular kind of pathos. Like nineteenth-century racialists, Mecklin and many other White social scientists viewed both Blacks and Jews as unable or unwilling to fully break from their own traditions and embrace White Western culture. On account of their inability or unwillingness to abandon their own cultural ways of life, Blacks and Jews were understood as destined to experience duality as a debilitating condition.

What makes this perspective even more fascinating is that whereas Mecklin posited Black duality as quasi inheritable and irreconcilable, he offered a completely different perspective on the roots of extreme hatred among White southerners. Nearly a decade after *Democracy and Race Friction*, Mecklin published *The Ku Klux Klan: A Study of the American Mind*. He had traveled extensively, conducting both interviews and surveys, in order to understand "the most spectacular of all the social movements in American society since the close of the World War" with what one reviewer of the book described as a "skillful, though rather flowery, pen."[80]

Whereas in his earlier writings Mecklin argued that racial conflict was inevitable as long as so-called inferior racial groups refused to accept the will of the so-called stronger group, he offered a significantly different explanation for the extreme racial hatred that proliferated among Klan membership. The "average man of native American stock who fills the ranks of the Klan" is not mentally inferior or culturally backward. Rather, their reasons for joining an organization Mecklin himself described as only flourishing on account of "false issues, by magnifying hates and prejudices, or by exploiting misguided loyalties" were rooted in external circumstances, not inherent pathos. The typical Klan member "is tossed about in the hurly-burly of our industrial and so-called democratic society. Under the stress and strain of social competition he is made to realize his essential mediocrity. Yet according to traditional democratic doctrine he is born free and the equal of his fellow who is outdistancing him in the race. Here is a large and powerful organization offering to solace his sense of defeat by dubbing him a knight of the Invisible Empire for the small sum of ten dollars. Surely knighthood was never offered at such a bargain!"[81] One cannot help but wonder, while reading *Democracy and Race Friction* alongside *The Ku Klux Klan*, whether and how Mecklin's perspective on Black duality might have differed had he considered what the stress and strain of social competition within a racialized social structure does for Black people. As Du Bois so forcefully showed across his scholarship, Black people were not even afforded the basic recognition of free and equal under America's so-called democratic doctrine.

If Mecklin's portrayal of Black duality and marginality as a particular kind of pathos represents a somewhat extreme and contentious position in relationship to Du Bois's own, Chicago School sociologist Robert Park's "marginal man" thesis presented the more mainstream and palatable version. Park's thesis is particularly relevant for comparison to Du Bois because Park's thesis centered on the experiences of Jewish immigrants in the United States. Even prior to the publication of his marginal man thesis, Park made clear that social structure matters when it comes to race prejudice. Park did not locate the roots of race prejudice in the so-called inferior mental composition of Jews, Black people, or other racialized groups. Rather, race prejudice was a matter of skin color and the values, norms, and ideas attached to its spectrum. Writing, for example, on the symmetry between anti-Black and anti-Asian prejudice for the *American Journal of Sociology* in 1914, Park stated:

> It is not because the Negro and the Japanese are so differently constituted that they do not assimilate. If they were given an opportunity the Japanese are quite as capable as the Italians, the Armenians, or the Slavs of acquiring our culture, and sharing our national ideals. The trouble is not with the Japanese mind but with the Japanese skin. The Jap is not the right color. The fact that the Japanese bears in his features a distinctive racial hallmark, that he wears, so to speak, a racial uniform, classifies him. He cannot become a mere individual, indistinguishable in the cosmopolitan mass of the population, as is true, for example, of the Irish and, to a lesser extent, of some of the other immigrant races. The Japanese, like the Negro, is condemned to remain among us an abstraction, a symbol, and a symbol not merely of his own race, but of the Orient and of that vague, ill-defined menace we sometimes refer to as the "yellow peril." This not only determines, to a very large extent, the attitude of the white world toward the yellow man, but it determines the attitude of the yellow man to the white. It puts between the races the invisible but very real gulf of self-consciousness.[82]

While Park's analysis certainly moved the field further away from the biological essentialism that defined much of it in the late nineteenth and early twentieth centuries, Park's marginal man thesis in particular significantly contributed to the cultural essentialism that emerged as replacement. With regard to Jews, for example, Park's marginal man thesis sought to position their hybridity as a matter of irreconcilable cultural ideals—one distinctly modern, the other distinctly inferior. Once emancipated, Park writes, among the Jews "there appeared a new type of personality, namely, a cultural hybrid, a man living and sharing intimately in the cultural life and traditions of two distinct peoples.... The emancipated Jew was, and is, historically and typically the marginal man." Similar to Du Bois's analysis of Black Americans, Park understood Jews as unable to reconcile the warring ideals of Jewish and American customs. Yet whereas Du Bois located the root of this conflict in the racialized social structure of American society, Park's suggestion here is that assimilation, should it happen, would resolve what is largely theorized as an internal tension.[83]

The dominance of Park's thesis and its more general cultural essentialist framework for mid-twentieth-century analyses of racial conflict cannot be understated. Park's marginal man thesis would be further extended across the mid-twentieth century by one of his own students, Everett V. Stonequist. Stonequist advanced the "duality-as-pathos" perspective by suggesting that the marginal man exists in psychological uncertainty. The marginal man is "poised in the psychological uncertainty between two (or more) social worlds; reflecting in his soul the discords and harmonies, repulsions and attractions of these worlds." Stonequist leaves no doubt of the degree to which such a personal problem reflects a pathos: "The intensity of the inner conflict varies with the situation itself, the individual experience with this situation, and perhaps certain inherited traits. With some individuals, it appears to be a minor problem; in such cases one cannot speak of a 'personality type.' It is only in those cases where the conflict is intense and of considerable duration that the personality as a whole is oriented around the conflict."[84] And, as Park did, Stonequist made it clear that the Jew was most likely to exhibit the pathological tendencies of this "personality type":

> The Jew is likely to be a typical marginal man.... He is the perennial immigrant. His children are apt to have the second-generation problems. Popularly regarded as a race, the Jews are felt to be unassimilable.... Centuries of social conflict, combined with their tenacious historical memories, have produced a group consciousness which in turn suspects and resists assimilation tendencies which go beyond a certain point. It is little wonder, then, that the Jew becomes the classic illustration of this problem, just as he has been the most articulate in expressing it.[85]

Like Germany in the late nineteenth century, the early to mid-twentieth century saw a gradual and significant increase in the number of Jews first entering into American colleges and universities and then into the professions. By the mid-twentieth century, Jews had obtained noticeable success in the social, behavioral, and medical sciences. How, then, did mid-twentieth-century Jewish social scientists think and write about Jewish duality and marginality? How did their thinking and writing differ, if they did indeed differ, from those of their non-Jewish counterparts?

Particularly leading up to and immediately following the World War II era, some Jewish social and behavioral scientists such as Kurt Lewin turned toward the controversial concept of self-hatred to explain how duality and marginality affect the collective Jewish psyche. Others, including psychologist Irving Sarnoff, proposed a model for theorizing American anti-Semitism that posited that the source of Jewish self-hatred was located in Jews' identification with their aggressors. For Sarnoff, the post–World War II environment was the perfect soil in which self-hatred could take root. "In so far as Jews are concerned," Sarnoff wrote in 1951, "the contemporary American scene appears to fulfill all three of the above prerequisite conditions."[86] He continued:

> Firstly, there is widespread antisemitism among majority group members. This negative attitude wanes in intensity from the crudely destructive outcries of the "lunatic fringe" category of bigots to the discreet practice of "gentleman's agreement" housing restrictions. Secondly, Jews are, in every sphere of life, ultimately dependent upon the good will of majority group members who control our social institutions. The granting or withholding of ratification of such needs as education, work, and living quarters is sometimes determined by the degree of prejudice motivating the particular educator, employer, or landlord whose approval the individual Jew is obliged to obtain. Finally, no Jewish person, unless he renounces membership in the minority group into which he is born and succeeds in "passing" as a non-Jew, can avoid personal experience with the social fact of antisemitism.[87]

Sarnoff, not unlike Du Bois, understood that the American social scene is where anti-Semitism (and, in the case of Du Bois, anti-Black racism) takes shape. However, for Sarnoff this social situation exposes Jews—unless they denounce their Jewishness—to the social fact of anti-Semitism. On the one hand, then, Jews could avoid anti-Semitism and self-hatred so long as they denounce their Jewishness. For Black people, the social fact of the color-caste system makes this near impossible, even to this very day. Yet what Sarnoff's argument also suggests is that Jews as Jews are incompatible with what it means to be American. Their duality and marginality are not matters of religious difference; instead, they illustrate just how tightly tethered whiteness is to the idea of nationhood and national citizenship.[88]

Lest readers think these were simply academic debates, even in the mid-twentieth-century popular imagination, the image of the Jew as distinctly not White and thus not American was routine. As Eric Goldstein shows in his *The Price of Whiteness: Jews, Race, and American Identity*, this theme was central to the material of Arthur Miller's 1945 novel *Focus* and Laura Z. Hobson's *Gentleman's Agreement* both in its best-selling novel form, first published in *Cosmopolitan* in 1946 in serial form, and in its widely praised movie version of 1947, with Gregory Peck as the undercover journalist who passed himself off as "Jewish." Hobson's novel exposed the overt racism directed at Jews in American society, prefiguring journalistic exploits such as the 1961 exposé by John Howard Griffin, *Black

Like Me. The idea of American Jews becoming White over the course of the twentieth century is thus an evolving image, one tied to economic mobility.

Elsewhere, while writing for the popular Jewish periodical *Commentary Magazine*, anthropologist Harold Orlansky suggested that Jews' marginal status begins in their childhood and paralleled it with the experiences of Black children who first begin to recognize the differences in appearance from their White peers: "It is enough to describe the Jewish group as an underprivileged minority in a marginal social position, and the individual Jew, like the light mulatto, as a typical marginal man. . . . The Jewish child cannot help taking as his own, society's evaluation of the Jewish stereotype. We have then the primary form of inferiority feeling and its consequence, self-hatred. 'I could bite my arm when I see how black it is,' a colored girl once said." Summarizing the early and mid-twentieth-century psychological, anthropological, and sociological literature on Jews' personality, Orlansky concluded that its principal features include feelings of inferiority, self-hatred, and neurosis, among others: "Apparently a great deal of ambivalence inheres in Jewish character—both within the Jewish group, where one individual may be as timid as another is aggressive, and within the individual, where submissive and aggressive tendencies may wage constant emotional war." Even as we move into the post–World War II period, then, commonly held beliefs in Jewish inferiority and internal strife ground popular and scientific perceptions of Jewish difference.[89]

Orlansky's observation is also interesting because, on the one hand, like Park and Stonequist, he clearly saw both the Jew and the mixed-race individual as the prototypical marginal men. On the other hand, the experience of Jews who cannot help but see and understand themselves through society's own evaluation of their Jewish status is indicative of the Du Boisian analysis of duality and marginality posited in *Souls* some fifty years prior. Even in Orlansky's quoting of the Black child who, supposedly after internalizing society's evaluation of her Black skin, wishes to bite her own arm, there are echoes of Du Bois's reflections on his own experience with a White schoolgirl, "a tall newcomer" who refused his offer for a card exchange. "Then it dawned upon me with a certain suddenness," Du Bois recalled, "that I was different from the others; or like, mayhap, in heart and life and longing, but shut out from their world by a vast veil."[90]

But whereas Park, Stonequist, Orlansky, and others suggested that the natural outcome of this observation is the internalizing of others' negative evaluations and potential self-hatred, Du Bois's reflections suggest a wider range of possible responses:

> I had thereafter no desire to tear down that veil, to creep through; I held all beyond it in common contempt, and lived above it in a region of blue sky and

great wandering shadows. That sky was bluest when I could beat my mates at examination-time, or beat them at a foot-race, or even beat their stringy heads. Alas, with the years all this fine contempt began to fade; for the words I longed for, and all their dazzling opportunities, were theirs, not mine. But they should not keep these prizes, I said; some, all, I would wrest from them. Just how I would do it I could never decide: by reading law, by healing the sick, by telling the wonderful tales that swam in my head,—some way.[91]

Du Bois does acknowledge, however, that for other Black children, "the strife was not so fiercely sunny." For some, "their youth shrunk into tasteless sycophancy, or into silent hatred of the pale world about them and mocking distrust of everything white; or wasted itself in a bitter cry, Why did God make me an outcast and a stranger in mine own house?"[92]

Anti-Black racism may lead to the internalization among Black people of White people's negative perceptions and evaluations. Yet it can and does also produce resistance, even if in the form of "silent hatred" and "mocking distrust." For, ultimately, Du Bois understood that while White people might define the ideals of their nation through the color line, America is, for Black people, the house they helped build.

CONCLUSION

Besides my regular work I have been following the political
movements of the country. The rise of anti-semitism, which
has much in common with our own race question, is of
considerable interest to me.

    —W. E. B. Du Bois to the John F. Slater Fund, March 1893

The result of these three visits [to Germany], and particularly
of my view of the Warsaw ghetto, was not so much clearer
understanding of the Jewish problem in the world as it
was a real and more complete understanding of the Negro
problem.... [T]he ghetto of Warsaw helped me to emerge
from a certain social provincialism into a broader conception
of what the fight against race segregation, religious
discrimination and the oppression by wealth had to become if
civilization was going to triumph and broaden in the world.

    —W. E. B. Du Bois, "The Negro and the Warsaw Ghetto"

       These two passages, separated by nearly sixty years of
significant global political, social, and economic shifts, not to mention intellectual
development in Du Bois himself, reflect the general thrust of this book: Du Bois's
early theorizing on race and racism was inspired by his experiences with and reflections upon western European anti-Semitism. Du Bois said as much in his letter to the benefactors of his German education in 1893. A decade later, in *The Souls
of Black Folk*, his German education and experiences shaped his view of the color
line as a global phenomenon. This much is evident even four decades later, when

in *Dusk of Dawn* Du Bois reflected upon his two years of study at the University of Berlin. Finally, having returned to both Germany and neighboring Poland after the war, an elderly Du Bois once again made it clear that the violent and deadly race prejudice Jews suffered at the hands of their German compatriots provided him with clarity beyond just western Europe's "Jewish question." Western European anti-Semitism provided Du Bois with the lens through which to better theorize race and racism as global phenomena. Contrary to much of the scholarship on Du Bois's intellectual project, Germany's "Jewish question" served as a key analytical construct from which Du Bois theorized the conditions of Black Americans at the turn of the twentieth century and beyond.

Du Bois's use of the German Jewish experience to make sense of the Black experience is an unfortunate omission in the large body of resurgent Du Boisian scholarship that this book has sought to remedy. Beyond the quest to remedy this intellectual history, however, a larger question looms: What can a reexamination of this relationship between anti-Semitism and anti-Black racism tell us about our present day? Is there more to this line of inquiry beyond reinterpreting the historical record or enriching Du Bois's intellectual history?

While I wrote this chapter, half of the United States was literally on fire, while the other half seems perpetually underwater from record-setting hurricanes and rising sea levels. The Dixie wildfire, which began in northern California in July 2021, had burned nearly 860,000 total acres by September and then was only half-contained. Smoke from the fires reportedly spread as far west as Colorado. Meanwhile, the Caldor fire, which began in August 2021, burned alongside the Dixie fire in northern California. According to Chief Thom Porter of the California Department of Forestry and Fire Protection, no fire was known before to have burned from one side of the Sierra to the other. The Caldor and Dixie fires both achieved that feat.[1]

Hurricane Ida, with its Category 4 winds and rain, wreaked havoc across the Louisiana Gulf Coast in early September 2021, displacing thousands of residents, most of whom are poor and Black. A sanitation worker strike in New Orleans, Louisiana, that began the year before over worker demands for sick leave and paid time off continued amid the hurricane recovery efforts. The result left nearly a third of New Orleans residents—mostly Black, many of whom are poor—without trash pickup for weeks after the storm, with the city estimating some fifty-four thousand tons of debris and trash still left to clear as of the writing of this sentence. One former city councilman, describing to the *Washington Post* the "unbelievable" stench of the city in the aftermath of the hurricane, stated, "I am covered in maggots. I've never seen maggots this big."[2]

The COVID-19 pandemic and its deadly Delta variant raged and spread across the globe. At the time that I finished this chapter, more than 650 million people around the world had contracted the virus. The global death toll surpassed 6.65 million. While more than 5.4 billion total vaccine doses have been administered around the world, vaccination rates by country vary tremendously and follow a historical pattern of vaccine distribution that favors the United States and European nation-states at the expense of African nations and its diaspora. According to the *New York Times'* Global Vaccine Tracker, as of June 22, 2022, nearly six hundred million vaccine doses had been administered in the United States, yet only 23 percent of the entire continent of Africa had received at least one dose; far fewer are fully vaccinated. In the island nation of Haiti, the total number of vaccine doses administered to its eleven million people is fewer than 290,000.

Well before COVID, Black and Brown people the world over were disproportionately victims of war, disease, and famine that are the direct consequences of European and American empires and their insatiable desire for expansion. As America finally withdraws its last military troops from its decades-long war in Afghanistan, thousands of Afghan refugees fleeing the impending rule of the Taliban await on whether they will find solace within the United States and European Union allied nations. Meanwhile, politicians and pundits, including what many might consider centrists, on both sides of the Atlantic warn of a "great replacement" that will occur should these nations provide asylum. Austria's chancellor Sebastian Kurz categorically ruled out allowing any more refugees into his nation, while Switzerland's government refuses to accept large groups directly from the war-torn nation. In the United States, the governors of both Wyoming and South Dakota have refused to accept any Afghan refugees, while governors from eleven other states, including most of the U.S. South, have yet to state their position one way or the other. Meanwhile, the enormously popular Fox News television pundit Tucker Carlson warns his viewers of a conspiracy to "flood swing districts with refugees that they know will become loyal Democratic voters. They're opening the southern border to over two hundred thousand illegal immigrants per month."[3] Meanwhile, President Joe Biden not only failed to stop the previous deportation regime but also has been a willing accomplice, as his administration solicits bids from private firms to provide Haitian and Spanish-speaking guards for a migrant detention facility at the infamous Guantánamo Bay.[4]

Apart from climate change, few questions are as important to our current moment as the continued significance of the color line: the ongoing production, maintenance, and refashioning of racial order through both law and custom. For well over a century now, scholars have debated and discussed Du Bois's astute prediction from *The Souls of Black Folk*. Now amid the third decade of the twenty-first century, the problem of the color line not only persists but appears as bright as ever.

In addition to the above examples, the twenty-first century has born witness to a massive global refugee crisis. Those fleeing war-torn countries for safe haven are forced to navigate the shifting sands of race and face enormous resistance from White Western nation-states that increasingly tether religious differences with racial meanings, producing the racialized threats the global War on Terror seeks to eliminate by any means necessary.[5] Elsewhere, populist movements across Europe and North America use the idea of race as a key vehicle through which to channel massive outrage and champion racist political actions that threaten both the philosophical and material foundations of liberal democracy.[6]

In the United States, it seems, punditry is evidently cursed with a short-term memory, or perhaps it is even allergic to the historical record. The campaign and subsequent presidential administration of Donald Trump and its overt White nationalist politics remain discussed among most Americans as little more than an aberration. Few national correspondents seem to give much if any thought to the fact that the detention camps for migrant children created by the Trump administration were the (il)logical extension of the rapid militarization of the U.S.-Mexico border following the September 11, 2001, terrorist attacks. Likewise, the majority of Americans struggle to connect the wave of Black protests and rebellions that swept the nation following the public murder of George Floyd in the summer of 2020 with America's decades-long War on Drugs and the growth of its carceral state under Presidents Reagan, Bush I, Clinton, Bush II, and Obama, its first Black president. Indeed, despite nearly all evidence to the contrary, American media insisted for the better part of eight years that the election of America's first Black president was clear evidence that American society had become postracial.[7]

As we take stock of our new century more than two decades into it, a Du Boisian analysis of our color line today remains as urgent as ever. We must account not only for the reemergence of populist White nationalisms in Europe and the United States but also for their reverberations from the past to the present. To restate my oft-made point throughout this text, we must attend to the "roots" and "routes" of our present moment. The roots of religious and racial resentment are well known. The routes already taken, especially across the twentieth century, are matters of historical and sociological inquiry. The routes to be carved are less determined. We are, in many ways, standing in the eye of a conjectural hurricane: a moment of indeterminacy in which the outcomes are still within the bounds of our intellectual and political practice should we fully commit to the struggle.[8]

To Du Bois's credit, he understood the critical need for a structural analysis of the global color line, one that took seriously not only how social forces produce debilitating affects among marginalized peoples but also the radical resistance to those forces. Moreover, he deftly demonstrated that no group ultimately triumphs underneath the constraints of the color line. The Veil is debilitating to all because it enables inhumane practices over time, rendering even Whites who profit from its maintenance—socially, economically, and even psychologically—as unrecognizable to themselves and others. Racism, incompatible with the human condition, will seed its own destruction. But when, and at what human cost? Double consciousness, both gift and curse, is a by-product of the color line. While arguably necessary for the color line's eradication, double consciousness remains insufficient on its own to overcome the structural constraints imposed by global racial domination.

Social theorist Benjamin Bowser asks, "If Du Bois's double consciousness exists, who has it; who does not; under what circumstances does it develop or wane; do other racial/ethnic groups have it?" For anyone who spends an entire life embedded within the American racial caste system, Bowser argues that double consciousness is a "predictable outcome of this structural arrangement." Moreover, if consciousness is indeed shaped by our social conditions, as Marx so famously opined, then as social conditions change, so too would our consciousness. In considering the codification of political and civil rights for Black people in the United States, Bowser maintains that a new articulation of our social structure would likely produce multiple, even distinct, racial consciousnesses among Black Americans.[9]

I find Bowser's reading of both double consciousness and its potential too hopeful. Bowser, in my estimation, mistakes changes to the structure of White supremacy as matters of degree when in fact they are matters of kind. Racial domination is not teleological. What the color line lacks in linearity it makes up for in its violent luminescence, a kind of structured spontaneity in which pain and death are visited and revisited upon those born on the wrong side of the Veil through various combinations of vigilantism, state-sponsored terrorism, and militarism across the centuries. While certain forms of violence today are arguably less overt than in decades and centuries past, the expansion of western European and American empire has made White supremacist violence global in both its scale and mundanity. Du Bois, for instance, lived through a period of American history in which the lynchings of Black people were so frequent as to become expected. Indeed, many texts—both fictitious and real—portray a kind of common knowledge about when, where, and how Black people can move and live (hell, even breathe) to avoid what otherwise would be the inevitability of their demise. Today, a similar commonplaceness accompanies the renderings of mass incarceration and disenfranchisement of Black and Latino people in America. How many of us, for example, have heard the oft-repeated statistic that between one-fourth and one-third of Black men will spend some portion of their adult lifetime in prison? Globally, there is an expectedness to the anxieties of White Western nations at the first hint of increased foreign presence within their borders.[10]

The European continent today, as it did during the nineteenth and twentieth centuries, remains marked by significant political unrest, social anxiety, and economic uncertainty. Political turmoil and civil war have resulted in an unprecedented number of asylum seekers from war zones in Afghanistan, Iraq, Somalia, and Syria to countries such as Sweden and Germany. The War on Terror has created a fertile ground in policy circles for Samuel P. Huntington's 1993 "clash of civilizations" thesis to take root, turning the rather limited threat of fundamentalist terrorism into an existential crisis for Western nations that mirrors late nineteenth-century existential concerns over Jews' incorporation into European nations' body politic and the consequences for national culture.[11]

The coinciding of intensified terrorism in parts of Europe with the sharp increase in asylum seekers fuels a growing belief that these two phenomena are linked, if not causal, stokes pessimism toward multiculturalism and primes emergent White nationalist movements in Europe and the United States. In May 2019 right-wing nationalist parties, running on fears over immigration and the dilution of national culture, won more than 20 percent of the votes in their parliamentary elections in five European countries. In France, a spokesperson for the French government's antiracism and anti-Semitism body stated, "We are witnessing the resurgence of a virulent, far-right identity politics that does not hesitate to put its beliefs into action." In Hungary, the far-right Fidesz Party, led by prime minister Viktor Orbán, ran rancorous public campaigns demonizing both migrants and Jews. As a result, 42 percent of Hungarians believed Jews held too much sway over the worlds of finance and international affairs. In Germany, there is a recrudescence of anti-Semitism, Islamophobia, and nativism largely in response to the more than one million refugees and migrants who have sought shelter from war, oppression, and famine since 2015. Members of Germany's Far Right decried this wave of immigrants and actively foment hate against refugees, Muslims, and Jews. Since 2015 anti-Semitic attacks have surged by more than 60 percent as more militant extremist groups call for outright violence against Muslims, refugees, and Jews, including "the desecration of Jewish institutions and attacks against Jewish people."[12]

Across the Atlantic, xenophobia, anti-Semitism, and Islamophobia are mainstream within U.S. politics. In 2015 Donald Trump openly campaigned for president on an anti-immigrant platform that included closing the U.S.-Mexico border to migrants and banning immigrants from majority Muslim nations. As a consequence, public polling now identifies a partisan "Trump effect" on Americans' attitudes toward Muslims. Elsewhere, researchers find that Americans who endorse anti-Muslim stereotypes, dehumanizing narratives, and attitudes that blame Muslims collectively for violence committed by individuals who identify as part of their faith are more approving of discriminatory policies targeting Muslims, more likely to support state and nonstate violence against civilians, and more likely to favor authoritarian measures in response to perceived security threats. The number of active hate groups in the United States is the highest in twenty years, with the most significant growth among White nationalist organizations, which saw a 48 percent increase from the year prior.[13]

And then there is the absolute terrorist violence: the 2015 murder of nine Black churchgoers by Dylann Roof in Charleston, South Carolina; the 2018 murder of eleven worshipers at Pittsburgh's Tree of Life or L'Simcha Congregation, the single deadliest attack on Jews in U.S. history; the 2019 murder of twenty-three people at a Walmart store in El Paso, Texas, the single deadliest attack on Latinos in contemporary American history; and in May 2022, the murder of ten shoppers at a Tops supermarket in a predominantly Black neighborhood in Buffalo, New York. Eighteen-year-old Payton S. Gendron drove several hours from his hometown in Conklin, New York, to the Tops supermarket, dressed in military-style clothing and body armor and armed with an AR-15 assault rifle. Prior to the shooting, Gendron published a 180-page manifesto online that laid out specific plans to attack Black people and repeatedly cited a Far Right conspiracy theory that White Americans are being replaced through immigration, interracial marriage, and even violence.[14]

Meanwhile, both 2020 and 2021 bore witness to the continued use of militarized police forces against U.S. citizens protesting state-sanctioned violence toward Black men and women, including in Washington, D.C., just steps from the White House and the Capitol. Yet when nearly twenty-five hundred mostly White supporters of former president Donald Trump stormed the U.S. Capitol on January 6, 2021, in an attempted coup, the Republican National Committee characterized their deadly riot as "legitimate political discourse." Citizenship—the rights and duties afforded to those who are full members of the polity—has historically been defined through whiteness. The violent suppression of Black protest in front of the very same U.S. Capitol where a mostly White mob threatening to hang the vice president of the United States was met with relatively little resistance reveals the continuities of that perverse construction and the limits of liberal democracy itself.[15]

While the racialized social structure may reinvent itself across place and time, it remains defined through and against what it rejects. The post-9/11 era, like the late nineteenth and early twentieth centuries, is defined in large part through concerns over perceived threats to the White Christian body politic. In the latter eras, Jews and Blacks were the targets of White racial anxieties. Today, Muslims and immigrants serve as the primary focus of those same anxieties. In the United States, a retrenchment toward racial segregation in American public schools and neighborhoods reveals that while many White parents fancy themselves as color-blind, their neighborhood and school choices betray their sympathies.[16]

At the national level, Black people remain unemployed at roughly double the rates of their White peers, a statistic that is remarkable in its consistency across decades of both economic stagnation and growth. In 2019 the typical White family has eight times the wealth of the typical Black family and five times the wealth of the typical Hispanic family. America's color line is perhaps made most visible, however, when an attempt to encroach it is made and subsequently met with significant White backlash. Even the most assimilated Black persons are reminded that they are Black first and American only when it's convenient, the moment they are stopped by the police while driving, walking, talking, or simply standing still in their predominantly White neighborhood. Moving up in America remains an unequal process burdened by the weight of the Veil. Double consciousness, from the original Du Boisian conceptualization to its many revisions over the years, remains an important construct through which to understand the duality, conflict, and contingency that accompany the presence and maintenance of the color line. Moreover, double consciousness remains an important analytic tool through which we can make some sense of the comparing and contrasting experiences of those groups who find themselves together on the wrong side of the Veil yet who because of the nature of the color line fail to recognize their shared unequal circumstances.

In September 2021 I returned to my hometown of Kansas City, Missouri, to attend the traveling exhibition about Auschwitz coproduced by Musealia and the Auschwitz-Birkenau State Museum. The exhibition was set up on the lower level of Kansas City's Union Station and contained well over seven hundred original objects. I attended this event with my uncle and my two cousins, one of whom works for the Jewish Community Relations Bureau of the American Jewish Committee.

Upon arriving at the entrance of the exhibit we were given a pair of headphones and our own audio guide device, which provided narration for over sixty different parts of the exhibition. As I made my way through the exhibit, listening to the audio narration while taking in the many displays from the 1400s through the end of World War II, I found myself reflecting once again upon Du Bois's words from 1952. Auschwitz is a story of Jewish pain and suffering. It is also a story of human cruelty, of the always present possibility that what so many thought impossible could indeed happen again. As I've shown across several chapters in this book, even in the late nineteenth century German Jews understood that their nation was always on the precipice of 1933. The Great War and Germany's devastating loss on the international stage provided the necessary ingredients for the emergence of Hitler and the resultant Nazi regime, with all its banal evil. Yet we would be mistaken to think the potential had not been there for generations prior.

About halfway through my trek through the exhibit, I came upon a reprint of a 1903 German cartoon, "Metamorphosis," the original of which is in the Musealia collection. The cartoon was from a German satirical weekly and across three frames depicts a Russian Jewish caricature transforming himself from a peasant into a member of the German middle class. In the first frame, the figure is hunched over, wearing all black, with a knapsack over one shoulder and a pile of clothing in tow. His beard and hat give away his traditional religious upbringing. In the second image his hat is gone, and his beard trimmed. He now wears spectacles and a patterned suit. Finally, the third image shows him once again in all black, but this time the clothing is refined. His posture is upright and tall. His thin mustache is generously waxed. He exudes confidence. In front of his body, he holds a painting upright with one hand; his other hand is raised. The thumb and index finger of that hand are brought together and remaining fingers are held up in a kind of haughty disdain.

On the one hand, the cartoon reveals how Jewish immigrants, many of whom were from poor rural villages, made a way for themselves in German society by forgoing their traditional upbringings. Yet at the same time, the cartoon reveals German anxieties around the Jews' seemingly uncanny ability to blend in, unnoticed, as a looming threat to German society and its ideals, which, as I've argued throughout, were antithetical to the figure of the Jew. Jews can only be German by abandoning their Jewishness. Jews can never be truly German because they are Jewish. This is why, for example, German nationalist Paul de Lagarde had advocated as early as 1886 for the forced deportation of Jews to the island of Madagascar, a plan revived by the Nazis in 1940 only to be replaced just two years later, and as a matter of convenience, with Hitler's Final Solution.[17]

Above the cartoon is a quote from the late nineteenth-century German Jewish writer Berthold Auerbach from 1880: "Antisemitism spreads like wildfire, to such an extent that one must be thankful for practically anyone who shows himself free of prejudice." Decades earlier, the protagonist of one of Auerbach's novels had astutely noted that in German society "the position of Jews has always been the barometer of humanity." As I reflected upon the quote above the cartoon and then later upon the observation of Auerbach's protagonist, I could not help but think of how Du Bois theorized the Veil and the physical and mental constraints it places upon both Black and White people the world over. In his 1947 "Appeal to the World" report, which Du Bois submitted to the United Nations on behalf of the NAACP, he wrote, "Therefore, Peoples of the World, we American Negroes appeal to you; our treatment in America is not merely an internal question of the United States. It is a basic problem of humanity; of democracy; of discrimination because of race and color; and as such it demands your attention and action. No nation is so great that the world can afford to let it continue to be deliberately un-just, cruel and unfair toward its own citizens."[18]

I argued earlier in this book that Du Bois's analysis of the "double problem" of German nationalism served as an important precursor for developing his theory of the "double problem" of American nationalism. Let me add now that when taken as a whole, Du Bois's analysis of Black double consciousness—by way of his anal-ysis of Germany's "Jewish question"—provides an evergreen framework through which to understand the kind of racism and xenophobia that typify emergent na-tionalist movements in the twenty-first century. Nations and their peoples do not exist naturally. They are "imagined communities," made possible through politi-cal, economic, and technological developments and through common myths and memories. Likewise, their imagining of themselves as one kind of unity also neces-sitates imagining that unity against other possible unities.[19]

Historically, the role of race within nationalism has been decisive. Though race does not manifest equally in all nationalist movements, there comes during the course of nationalist development a particular moment whereby race becomes a necessary tendency in its constitution. Elsewhere, I've described this process through the concept of racialized nationalism, whereby racial ideology—namely, the belief in racial purity—becomes rooted within nationalist movements and dis-course. This rooting creates an exclusionary brand of nationalism and national identity that is rooted in imagined purity. Members of these nationalist move-ments come to believe that as dutiful members of the nation-state, they must pro-tect the nation from any external or internal threats to that imagined purity.

Racialized nationalism situates membership in biological terms: cultural val-ues and practices are naturalized, inherently pure, and in need of vigorous defense through population control. Du Bois's theorizing of the color line and the double consciousness that results from residing on the other side of the Veil illustrates the sociopolitical conditions through which racialized nationalism emerges, as well as the effects it has on both those defined as "the people" of the nation-state and those defined against it.[20]

The structure of the Veil makes self-consciousness for Black people nearly impossible, structuring their understanding of themselves almost entirely "through the revelation of the other world." Today, racialized nationalism is enlivened through explicit appeals to xenophobia, anti-Blackness, Islamophobia, and anti-Semitism. These appeals discursively naturalize immigrants, Blacks, Muslims, and Jews as antithetical to the "soul" of the nation, corrosive to its national culture. As immigrants, Blacks, Muslims, and Jews are increasingly demonized, as they are constructed as threats to the imagined racial purity of the nation-state, the conflict between citizenship and belonging reaches a fever pitch.

To claim citizenship status under these conditions requires the subduction of one's group membership. Yet such subduction is futile for most whose skin bears the mark of Cain. Even for those who might physically pass, they must contend with the fact that cultural differences are also naturalized, and in turn, the collective spirit, or, in Du Bois's terms, the soul of these nations, becomes defined against those perceived as threats to its sanctity. Even for so-called model minorities, the assimilation demanded of them for their incorporation into the nation in which they already live, even when presented as national progress, is no more than a concession on behalf of the oppressed, a giving up of sorts of their collective strivings toward self-recognition. As it was across the entirety of the twentieth century, so it remains in the first several decades of this new century: the Veil continues to divide the world in two, one White, Western, and Christian world naturalized as universal and progressive and one non-White, non-Western, non-Christian world naturalized as irreconcilably particular and primitive.[21]

Philosopher Étienne Balibar argues that race and nation constitute a "reciprocity of determination" whereby each emerges from and is strengthened by the other. This strengthening occurs through both appeals to racial purity within the nation-state and appeals to racial dominion over the rest of the world. In the nineteenth and twentieth centuries, German nationalism used anti-Semitism to confer political and cultural unity. Germans—though an already heterogeneous ethnic plurality—were imagined as having a common cultural tradition that stretched back to antiquity. Meanwhile, Jews were organized under this wave of German nationalism as the common internal enemy. Yet this all took place within the context of Germany seeking the expansion of its reign across the non-European world. Likewise, in the United States the systematic institution of segregation coincided with America's entry into world imperialist competition.[22]

Yet there is an exterior set of conditions to racialized nationalism for which we must account and for which Du Bois's later writings offer important insights. As American imperialism emerged from the ashes of European colonialism following

Hitler's defeat, Du Bois shifted his consideration of racialized nationalism to the processes through which it constructs the sociopolitical subjectivity of those outside of the nation-state.

In his *The World and Africa*, Du Bois located the rise of European nation-states as dependent upon the discursive and then material transformation of Africa and Asia into geographic areas rich in material resources but lacking in intellectual, moral, and even spiritual substance. The justification for enslavement and capitalist exploitation and then colonialism was the ongoing reimagining of Africa as without a people: "All that was human in Africa was deemed European or Asiatic. Africa was no integral part of the world because the world which raped it had to pretend that it had not harmed a man but a thing." The plundering of Africa and its people was a matter of nation-building in Europe. World War I was for Du Bois "a war over spheres of influence in Asia and colonies in Africa." White supremacy, its imbrication with global capitalism, and the resulting maintenance of the Veil, or color line, "made civilized man commit suicide in a mad attempt to hold the vast majority of the earth's peoples in thrall to the white race—a goal to which they still cling today, hidden away behind nationalism and power politics."[23]

Racialized nationalism remains, as it was in the nineteenth and twentieth centuries, the hegemonic form of nationalism in the twenty-first century, which means that racialized nationalism imposes a tendency toward biological notions of racial purity on all other forms of nationalism. Racialized nationalism is both a supernationalist and supranationalist project. As a supernationalist project, racialized nationalism seeks purity above all else and must isolate and then eliminate those elements that are exogenous. Yet there are no criteria of appearance or behavior that allow for the recognition of what constitutes "pure" or "impure." That is, the Veil is not constituted by any characteristics intrinsic to those living behind it. Rather, the Veil is constituted through legal-juridical conventions and maneuvers. What and who constitute "pure" remain unmarked but can be determined by their contrast with the alleged visibility of the impure: the Jew, the Black, the immigrant, the Muslim. This has the unintended effect, however, of constantly casting doubt on what is pure. As Balibar instructs us, "The fact that the 'false' is too visible will never guarantee that the 'true' is visible enough." Thus in the quest for supernationalism, racialized nationalism inevitably shrinks the category of nationality and thereby destabilizes the national "soul."[24]

At the same time, racial signifiers such as "Jew," "Muslim," and "Black" allow racialized nationalism today to extend beyond the territorial boundaries of the nation-state and organize transnational bonds of solidarity based on "common threats," be they "globalists," "terrorists," or "cultural invaders." While many of these appeals against common "stateless" enemies appear as veiled appeals to cultural racism, underlying these appeals is a form of bioracism that stresses the importance of maintaining strict national borders so as to preserve and accumulate the aptitudes and abilities of those within them for the sake of "civilization." Hungary's prime minister, Viktor Orbán, for example, announced the building of a second barrier along the Hungarian-Serbian border because "too much mixing" of Hungary's ethnic character "would not enhance the value of the country but downgrade it instead, and toss it into chaos." The Veil, then, functions on a supranational scale to construct each threat as both a universal and particular threat to the collective soul of the "pure" nation.[25]

Finally, Du Bois's later analyses reveal how racialized nationalism's relationship to capitalist hegemony actively undermines democratic principles. Extending a state's democratic base as wide as possible poses a significant threat to its ruling class. Du Bois recognized this in his analysis of the German political condition following the collapse of the Weimar Republic and subsequent rise of the Nazis. To expand the democratic base and appeal to the larger German working class would have destroyed the financial standing of Hitler's industrial backers. But to offer the image of the Jew as the physical manifestation of German rot and decay was to substitute a nationalist struggle for a class struggle, stressing solidarity between workers and industry based upon Deutschtum, or "Germanness."

Today, parallels abound that vary only by intensity or degree rather than kind: from former U.S. president Donald Trump's pandering to rural White working classes by playing upon their twofold fears of Black working-class spillage from inner cities and migrant labor spillage from Latin America, to the manufactured moral panics concerning asylum seekers and refugees in Germany, Britain, France, and other EU nations. In each instance, the Veil sutures biological notions of racial purity to civic membership, giving rise to discursive representations of the nation's soul as under siege from Black and Brown labor and further shrinking the category of national membership.

It would be irresponsible to not also acknowledge how the tethering of White supremacy to global capitalism is rapidly accelerating the degradation of our planet. A recent report by the United Nations' Intergovernmental Panel on Climate Change warns that we are reaching a crucial tipping point in which the threat of worsening floods, droughts, wildfires, and ecosystem collapse will grow considerably. Those populations and communities most vulnerable to the threats of accelerated climate change are disproportionately poorer, Black, and indigenous. They will suffer most from the effect of flooded homes, neighborhoods, and villages; food shortages due to crop failures; and vanishing sources of drinking water. And their suffering, in a cruel twist of fate, will be cast as the very reasons they are unfit for citizenship in the nations in which they seek refuge. White supremacist global capitalism, then, actively makes the very racialized subjects it seeks to control.[26]

There is hope in the Du Boisian framework, however. Recall that the double consciousness generated through the irreconcilable strivings of non-Whites seeking to fulfill two souls—one of self-recognition and the other full membership within the White nation-state—is not just debilitating, it is also a second sight, a way of being in the world that is diasporic and full of potential for emancipatory possibilities. I am reminded, for example, of when protestors filled the streets of Saint Louis, Missouri, following the shooting death of Black teenager Michael Brown by White police officer Darren Wilson. As these protestors were met with the blunt and brutal force of the state—police and military personnel in full riot gear riding in armored vehicles and firing rubber bullets and tear gas—Palestinians residing in the West Bank and Gaza used social media to advise protestors on how to cope with tear gas and to express their support. Today, as the movement for Black Lives Matter once again confronts the American military-police assemblage in cities across the country, Black and Brown people in London, Toronto, Berlin, and elsewhere take to their own streets in solidarity. What these moments signify is a collective recognition of oppressed people's diasporic, multifocal experiences with racialized nationalism and its imperialists instruments, experiences rooted in and structured by the Veil.

Even more than a century removed from his well-known observations about the Veil and double consciousness, Du Bois's insights remain prescient. His framework continues to offer both scholars and activists the tools necessary to document, describe, and explain the radical possibilities that can emerge from Ferguson, Minneapolis, the West Bank, and elsewhere. Moreover, Du Bois's framework also allows us to theorize these possibilities where they do not exist quite yet. Yet to do so, we must attend to the shifting territorial and ideological demarcation of the color line and its imbrication with nationalist movements on both sides of the Atlantic. Like Du Bois, we must strive to "see the race problem in America, the problem of the peoples of Africa and Asia, and the political development of Europe as one." In doing so, we not only produce greater understanding of the causes and consequences of racialized nationalism but also better equip ourselves and others to contest them.[27]

Like the observation of nineteenth-century Jewry from Auerbach's novel, today the unjust and racist treatment of Black people anywhere is a measure of our collective humanity everywhere. The injustices of nineteenth- and twentieth-century Germany produced among its Jewry a profound sense of anxiety, of rootlessness, of irreconcilable strivings. Yet the modern history of Jews in Germany and elsewhere is still one of striving, even when it appears futile. Likewise, the injustices committed against Black people in the United States, from the "original sin" of chattel slavery, to the failures of Reconstruction and the subsequent reign of racial terrorism, to the present-day carceral state, produce among Black Americans a profound sense of disappointment, of trauma, of anger and rebellion. The history of Black people in the United States remains a history of striving toward a set of unrealized ideals that have been fashioned through the long legacy of collective Black pain and suffering. In each instance, Black Americans and German Jews have served as the barometer for who can be a full member of their respective societies. At the same time, both Black Americans and German Jews have served as the world's measure of its collective capacity to meet injustice with justice. To date, the world has yet to fully meet that challenge. Nevertheless, the souls of Black folk, like the souls of Jews, ever strive onward.

NOTES

INTRODUCTION. On Roots and Routes

1. Du Bois, *Autobiography*; Dietrich, "At the Dawning"; Du Bois, *Dusk of Dawn*, 80.

2. Du Bois, "Pan-African Association."

3. Draft of Du Bois's reply to A. C. McClurg, June 10, 1903, series 1A: General Correspondence, MS 312, W. E. B. Du Bois Papers, Special Collections and University Archives, University of Massachusetts Amherst Libraries. Hereafter cited as Du Bois Papers.

4. Francis G. Browne to W. E. B. Du Bois, March 19, 1903–5, Du Bois Papers.

5. June 10, 1903, is the date of the quote. The letters are from Browne, filed in the archives as coming from A. C. McClurg and Co. The letter noting the development of a fourth edition is dated May 1, 1904; the letter in regard to translated editions is dated April 14, 1905. All in Du Bois Papers.

6. Invitation from Ida B. Wells-Barnett to discuss *The Souls of Black Folk*, June 2, 1903, https://credo.library.umass.edu/view/full/mums312-b001-i255; Camillus Phillips to W. E. B. Du Bois, April 30, 1904, Du Bois Papers.

7. From Dietrich, "At the Dawning," 322.

8. Hallie E. Queen [Jackson] to W. E. B. Du Bois, February 11, 1907, Du Bois Papers.

9. Queen to Du Bois, February 11, 1907.

10. Winifred Myser to W. E. B. Du Bois, March 18, 1908, Du Bois Papers.

11. Gilroy, *Black Atlantic*.

12. Du Bois, "Lecture Notebook"; Du Bois, *Autobiography*, 127.

13. Morris, *Scholar Denied*; Wright, *First American School*; Zamir, *Dark Voices*, 109.

14. Mannheim, *Ideology and Utopia*; Shils, "Ideology and Utopia."

15. Appiah, *Lines of Descent*; Barkin, "Berlin Days"; Barkin, "W. E. B. Du Bois' Love Affair"; Lemke, "Berlin and Boundaries"; Weger, "Berlin Years."

16. Appiah, *Lines of Descent*; Hunter, *Black Citymakers*; Morris, *The Scholar Denied*; Wright,

First American School; Max Weber to W. E. B. Du Bois, April 17, 1905, Du Bois Papers; Du Bois, "Preface to the Jubilee Edition."

17. Charles A. Ellwood to W. E. B. Du Bois, May 14, 1903, Du Bois Papers; Mary Roberts Smith to W. E. B. Du Bois, February 24, 1903, Du Bois Papers.

18. F. W. Taussig to W. E. B. Du Bois, 1892, Du Bois Papers; F. W. Taussig to W. E. B. Du Bois, May 10, 1907, Du Bois Papers; American Economic Association to W. E. B. Du Bois, November 7, 1905, Du Bois Papers; Taussig, *Principles of Economics*, 236.

19. Morris, *Scholar Denied*; Wright, *First American School*; Appiah, *Lines of Descent*.

20. Morris, *Scholar Denied*, 50; Collins, *Sociology of Philosophies*.

21. Hunter, "Du Boisian Sociology."

22. McKee, *Sociology*; Feagin and Vera, *Liberation Sociology*.

23. Gilman and Thomas, *Are Racists Crazy?*; James M. Thomas, "Racial Formation"; James M. Thomas, "Race, Nation"; Mills, *Racial Contract*; Glenn, *Unequal Freedom*; Omi and Winant, *Racial Formation*; Winant, *New Politics of Race*; HoSang, LaBennett, and Pulido, *Racial Formation*; Dollinger, *Black Power*.

24. Sander L. Gilman, "Jews and Mental Illness"; Gilman and Thomas, *Are Racists Crazy?*; Hacking, "Double Consciousness."

25. Du Bois, "The Present Condition"; Prager and Telushkin, *Why the Jews?*; Pulzer, *Rise of Political Anti-Semitism*; Du Bois, *Philadelphia Negro*; Du Bois, *Black Reconstruction*.

26. Du Bois, *Suppression*; Du Bois, *Autobiography*; Du Bois, *Worlds of Color*.

27. Du Bois, *Dusk of Dawn*; Wright, *First American School*; Du Bois, *World and Africa*.

28. Kendhammer, "DuBois the Pan-Africanist"; Meer, "W. E. B. Du Bois, Double Consciousness"; Reed, *W. E. B. Du Bois and American Political Thought*; Burden-Stelly and Horne, *W. E. B. Du Bois*.

29. Du Bois, "Diary of My Steerage Trip," June 2, 1894.

30. Blackmon, *Slavery by Another Name*.

31. Du Bois, *Souls of Black Folk*, 2.

32. Du Bois, "Superior Race," 60.

33. Karabel, *The Chosen*, 99; Sarna, *American Judaism*, 219; Eric L. Goldstein, *Price of Whiteness*.

34. Gilman and Thomas, *Are Racists Crazy?*; James M. Thomas, "Du Bois, Double Consciousness"; James M. Thomas, "Race, Nation."

CHAPTER 1. Race, Science, and Madness

1. The letter is included in Mitchill, *Medical Repository*, 366–89.

2. Mitchill, *Medical Repository*, 185–86.

3. Du Bois, "Strivings"; Hacking, "Double Consciousness."

4. Dwight, "Facts Illustrative," 431.

5. Dwight, "Facts Illustrative," 431–32.

6. Dwight, "Facts Illustrative," 433; Du Bois, *Souls of Black Folk*, 3.

7. Dwight, "Facts Illustrative," 433; Bell, "Genealogical Shifts"; Itzigsohn and Brown, "Sociology and the Theory."

8. Skae, "Case of Intermittent Mental Disorder," 10–12; see also Hacking, "Double Consciousness."

9. Plumer, "Mary Reynolds," 812.

10. Elliotson, "Dual Consciousness," 96–97.

11. Bruce, "W. E. B. Du Bois and the Idea."

12. Tuke, "On the Mental Condition," 68, emphasis mine.

13. Hyslop, "On 'Double Consciousness,'" 785.

14. See Hyslop, "Discussion."

15. Baird, "Some Observations on Insanity," 530–31.

16. Beadles, "Insane Jew," 732–33.

17. Beadles, "Insane Jew," 736–37.

18. Sander L. Gilman, "Jews and Mental Illness"; Gilman and Thomas, *Are Racists Crazy?*; Richards, *Race, Racism and Psychology*; James M. Thomas, "Medicalizing Racism"; Winston, *Defining Difference*.

19. Winant, *Racial Conditions*, xiii; see also Jacobson, *Whiteness*; Baum, *Rise and Fall*.

20. Hahn Thomas, "Difference"; Heng, "Jews"; Meer, "Racialization"; James M. Thomas, "Racial Formation"; Sander Gilman, *Jew's Body*, 18.

21. Sander Gilman, *Jew's Body*, 39; James M. Thomas, "Racial Formation," 1751.

22. Fanon, *Black Skin, White Masks*; Gilman and Thomas, *Are Racists Crazy?*; Mamdani, *Citizen and Subject*; Mills, *Racial Contract*; Robinson, *Black Marxism*; Young, *Colonial Desire*.

23. Gilman and Thomas, *Are Racists Crazy?*; Young, *Colonial Desire*.

24. Blumenbach and Banks, *De Generis Humani Varietate Nativa*; Gilman and Thomas, *Are Racists Crazy?*; Mead, *Movements of Thought*, 176.

25. Sander L. Gilman, "Jews and Mental Illness," 151; Legge, *Jews, Turks, and Other Strangers*; Kieval, "Importance of Place"; Prager and Telushkin, *Why the Jews?*; Pulzer, *Rise of Political Anti-Semitism*.

26. Erb, *Über die wachsende Nervosität*, 22; Kraepelin, "Zur Entartungsfrage," 748; see also Gilman and Thomas, *Are Racists Crazy?*

27. Jan Goldstein, "Wandering Jew"; Efron, *Defenders of the Race*; Charcot, *Clinical Lectures*, 11–12.

28. Brill and Karpas, "Insanity," 379.

29. Brill and Karpas, "Insanity."

30. Brill and Karpas, "Insanity," 579; Fishberg, *Materials*, 5.

31. Jaspers, *General Psychopathology*.

32. Binet, *On Double Consciousness*; Hyslop, "Discussion"; Pinsker, *Auto-Emancipation!*; Burgl, *Die Hysterie*, 19.

33. Sander L. Gilman, *Jewish Self-Hatred*; Sander L. Gilman, "Jews and Mental Illness"; Gilman and Thomas, *Are Racists Crazy?*

34. See Boudin in *Bulletins*; see also "Medical News."

35. Gilman and Thomas, *Are Racists Crazy?*

36. Jarvis, "Insanity."

37. Jarvis, "Insanity," 10.

38. Jarvis, "Insanity"; Jarvis, "On the Supposed Increase"; Gilman and Thomas, *Are Racists Crazy?*

39. "À propos du procès-verbal," quoted in Sander L. Gilman, "Jews and Mental Illness," 152; see also Gilman and Thomas, *Are Racists Crazy?*

40. Beard, "Neurasthenia," 217.

41. Charcot, *Clinical Lectures*; Binet, *On Double Consciousness*, 18.

42. Mosse, "Max Nordau, Liberalism"; Presner, "Clear Heads, Solid Stomachs"; Moshe Zimmerman, "Muscle Jews."

43. Sander L. Gilman, "Jews and Mental Illness"; Deutsch, "First U.S. Census"; see also, for example, Mays, "Human Slavery."

44. Harrowitz, *Tainted Greatness*; Byrnes, "Bloom's Sexual Tropes"; Englander, *Evident Most Frequent Appearances*, 123; see also Sander L. Gilman, "Jews and Mental Illness."

45. Byrnes, "Bloom's Sexual Tropes," 310; for claims of different forms of anti-Semitism, including political anti-Semitism, see Brustein, *Roots of Hate*; Schorsch, *Jewish Reactions*.

46. Pinsker, *Auto-Emancipation!*, 3.

47. Pinsker, *Auto-Emancipation!*, 3.

48. Pinsker, *Auto-Emancipation!*, 6.

49. Pinsker, *Auto-Emancipation!*, 13; Mosse, "Max Nordau, Liberalism"; Presner, "Clear Heads, Solid Stomachs."

50. Shumsky, "Leon Pinsker," 44; see also Volovici, "Leon Pinsker's *Autoemancipation!*"

51. Shumsky, "Leon Pinsker," 44.

52. Pinsker, *Auto-Emancipation!*, 81–82.

53. See also James M. Thomas, "Du Bois, Double Consciousness."

CHAPTER 2. The Du Boisian Reformulation

1. In 2017 I was awarded a summer residential fellowship with the W. E. B. Du Bois Center at the University of Massachusetts at Amherst. The Du Bois Center is located in the W. E. B. Du Bois Library, as are Du Bois's complete papers. I remain incredibly grateful for the two months I spent in this archive and for the wonderful staff of both the library and the Du Bois Center.

2. Mannheim, *Ideology and Utopia*; Shils, "Ideology and Utopia"; see also Berger and Luckmann, *Social Construction*.

3. Dennis, "Double Consciousness," 26; see also Dennis, "Du Bois's Concept"; and Dennis, "Continuities and Discontinuities."

4. William James, *Principles of Psychology*, vol. 1; Mead, *Mind, Self, and Society*; Cooley, *Human Nature*; see also Harter, "Construction and Conservation."

5. William James, *Principles of Psychology*, 1:293.

6. Du Bois, *Dusk of Dawn*, 133.

7. William James, *Principles of Psychology*, 1:294.

8. For the claim on Du Bois and psychology, see Dennis, "Double Consciousness." In further consideration of James and Du Bois, Shamoon Zamir argues for serious consideration of James's influence on Du Bois's intellectual project by way of James's lectures on ethics and morality (*Dark Voices*).

9. William James, *Principles of Psychology*, 1:375.

10. William James, *Principles of Psychology*, 1:377, 380.

11. William James, *Principles of Psychology*, 1:391.

12. William James, *Principles of Psychology*, 1:391.

13. William James, *Principles of Psychology*, 1:391.

14. William James, *Principles of Psychology*, 1:392; see also Susan Wells, "Discursive Mobility."

15. Du Bois, *Autobiography*, 133, 143. Elsewhere, James Campbell argues that Du Bois's fondness for James may have been greater than James's for Du Bois. Yet Campbell also insists that the parallels between James's writings on fractured social selves and Du Bois's own formulation of double consciousness are too close to ignore or dismiss ("Du Bois and James").

16. Du Bois, "Preface to the Jubilee Edition," x; Du Bois, *Autobiography*; Lutz, *American Nervousness*, 262.

17. William James, *Varieties of Religious Experience*, 167–68; Du Bois, *Souls of Black Folk*, 3.

18. Lemke, "Berlin and Boundaries," 46; Du Bois, *Autobiography*, 50.

19. Appiah, *Lines of Descent*; Barkin, "Berlin Days"; Barkin, "W. E. B. Du Bois' Love Affair"; Lemke, "Berlin and Boundaries"; Weger, "Berlin Years"; James M. Thomas, "Race, Nation."

20. Brustein, *Roots of Hate*, 78, 80, 87; Mosse, *Germans and Jews*, 39; Weiss, *Ideology of Death*, 43.

21. Brustein, *Roots of Hate*, 97, 99; Steiman, *Paths to Genocide*, 122.

22. Brustein, *Roots of Hate*, 99; see also Mosse, *Toward the Final Solution*.

23. Brustein, *Roots of Hate*, 132; for an overview of Lagarde's anti-Semitism, see Stern, *Politics of Cultural Despair*.

24. Mendel, *Textbook of Psychiatry*, 114, 63.

25. Hajdu, "Note from History"; Du Bois, *Autobiography*, 182; Barkin, "W. E. B. Du Bois' Love Affair."

26. Hajdu, "Note from History"; Frank, "Jews"; Stocking, *Race*, 167.

27. Andrew Zimmerman, "Anti-Semitism"; Andrew Zimmerman, *Anthropology and Antihumanism*. Kümmel's German text is described and analyzed in Andrew Zimmerman, "Anti-Semitism." As an aside, Leonard Glick provides a critical reading of Boas's writings that reveals that the anthropologist maintained a deep ambivalence toward his German Jewish identity. Indeed, Boas's own position on the necessity of a kind of Jewish assimilation that leaves little, if any, traces of Jewishness shares many common features with Virchow and other progressive Germans of that era. See Glick, "Types Distinct."

28. Finkelstein, *Emil du Bois-Reymond*, 219.

29. Finkelstein, *Emil du Bois-Reymond*, 220nn38–39.

30. Abraham, *Max Weber*, 49; Abraham, "German-Jewish History"; Tal, *Christians and Jews*.

31. Du Bois, *Autobiography*; Barkin, "Berlin Days."

32. Barkin, "Berlin Days," 83, 85.

33. Orizu, "German Influence," 42. For this claim, compare Du Bois, "Present Condition," 172, with Treitschke, *Politics*, 312.

34. Dorpalen, *Heinrich von Treitschke*, 227.

35. Appiah, *Lines of Descent*; Morris, *Scholar Denied*; Clark, "Adolf Wagner," 379.

36. Du Bois, "Autobiography," 125–26.

37. W. E. B. Du Bois to the John F. Slater Fund (fragment), ca. March 1893, Du Bois Papers.

38. From Woodard, *W. E. B. Du Bois: The Native Impulse,* 26.

39. Barkin, "Berlin Days," 96; Lemke, "Berlin and Boundaries," 64; Appiah, *Lines of Descent.*

40. Du Bois, *Autobiography,* 109, 20–21.

41. Du Bois, *Autobiography,* 156.

42. W. E. B. Du Bois to the Congregational Sunday-School, September 29, 1892, Du Bois Papers.

43. W. E. B. Du Bois to the John F. Slater Fund, March 1893, Du Bois Papers; Woodard, *W. E. B. Du Bois,* 26.

44. Du Bois, *Autobiography,* 179; Du Bois, *Dusk of Dawn,* 47.

45. For the roots of contemporary racism in the laboratories of nineteenth-century science, see Young, *Colonial Desire.*

CHAPTER 3. Germany, Anti-Semitism, and the Problem of the Color Line

1. James M. Thomas, "Racial Formation"; Cetina, *Epistemic Cultures*; Young, *Colonial Desire.*

2. Ajala, "Nature of African Boundaries"; Kendhammer, "DuBois the Pan-Africanist"; Mamdani, *Citizen and Subject*; Shepperson, "Centennial."

3. Mannheim, *Ideology and Utopia*; Shils, "Ideology and Utopia"; Berger and Luckmann, *Social Construction.*

4. Barkin, "Berlin Days"; Appiah, *Lines of Descent*; Zamir, *Dark Voices.*

5. Pulzer, *Rise of Political Anti-Semitism,* 7.

6. Baron, "Impact of the Revolution"; Sondhaus, "Schwarzenberg, Austria"; Pulzer, *Rise of Political Anti-Semitism*; Niewyk, *Jews in Weimar Germany,* 5.

7. Pulzer, *Rise of Political Anti-Semitism,* 18; Barkin, "Berlin Days," 95–96.

8. Pulzer, *Rise of Political Anti-Semitism,* 22–23; Barkin, "Berlin Days," 81.

9. Pulzer, *Rise of Political Anti-Semitism,* 27; Niewyk, *Jews in Weimar Germany*; Mosse, *Germans and Jews.*

10. Pulzer, *Rise of Political Anti-Semitism,* 32; see Mills, *Racial Contract.*

11. Mills, *Racial Contract*; James M. Thomas, "Re-upping the Contract."

12. Pulzer, *Rise of Political Anti-Semitism,* 38nn7–8. I am indebted to and reliant upon Pulzer and others for their translations of German texts; for the original, see Frantz, *Der National-liberalismus,* 34–35; and for similar assessments of Frantz and his writings, see McDaniel, "Constantin Frantz," and Philippson, "Constantin Frantz."

13. Du Bois, *Autobiography,* 127.

14. Du Bois, *Autobiography,* 127; Woodard, *W. E. B. Du Bois,* 26; Du Bois, *Dusk of Dawn,* 47.

15. Brustein, *Roots of Hate,* 43; Pulzer, *Jews and the German State,* 14; Richarz, *Jewish Life in Germany*; Niewyk, *Jews in Weimar Germany.*

16. For a detailed analysis of the phenomenon whereby racism became a marker of insanity across the twentieth century, see Gilman and Thomas, *Are Racists Crazy?*

17. Lampert, "Race, Periodicity"; Loomba, "Periodization, Race, and Global Contact"; Sander Gilman, *Jew's Body,* 18; James M. Thomas, "Racial Formation."

18. Mendes-Flohr and Reinharz, *Jew in the Modern World*; Voigtländer and Voth, "Persecution Perpetuated."

19. Frankel, *Damascus Affair*; Jacobs and Forsyth, "Damascus Affair"; *Times* quote from "Damascus Blood Libel."

20. Brustein, *Roots of Hate*, 5–6, 46.

21. Brustein, *Roots of Hate*, 107; Wertheimer, *Unwelcome Strangers*.

22. Pulzer, *Rise of Political Anti-Semitism*.

23. Lindemann, *Esau's Tears*; see also Lindemann, *Anti-Semitism before the Holocaust*; and Niewyk, *Jews in Weimar Germany*.

24. Niewyk, "Solving the 'Jewish Problem,'" 339; Brustein, *Roots of Hate*, 87; Pulzer, *Rise of Political Anti-Semitism*.

25. The original source of Stöcker's speech is Adolf Stöcker, "Unsere Forderungen an das moderne Judentum" [Our demands of modern Jewry], in *Das moderne Judenthum in Deutschland, besonders in Berlin: Zwei Reden in der Christlich-socialen Arbeiterpartei* [Modern Jewry in Germany, particularly in Berlin: Two speeches to the Christian Social Workers' Party], 2nd ed. (Berlin: Wiegandt und Grieben, 1880), 4–20. The English translation for this speech is provided by Richard S. Levy in his *Antisemitism in the Modern World: An Anthology of Texts* (Lexington, Mass.: D. C. Heath, 1991), 58–66.

26. Pulzer, *Rise of Political Anti-Semitism*, 94n11; Marr, *Victory of Judaism*, 19, 30–35; Brustein, *Roots of Hate*, 130–31.

27. Quoted in Pulzer, *Rise of Political Anti-Semitism*, 51.

28. Pulzer, *Rise of Political Anti-Semitism*, 95n14.

29. Pulzer, *Rise of Political Anti-Semitism*, 96n19.

30. Pulzer, *Rise of Political Anti-Semitism*, 53, 96, 227; Lagarde, *Mitteilungen*, 346, emphasis added.

31. Dühring, *Jewish Question*, 61; Pulzer, *Rise of Political Anti-Semitism*, 53.

32. Sander L. Gilman, "Wandering Imaginations," 51; Du Bois, *Autobiography*, 122, 177, 184; Brustein, *Roots of Hate*, 6; Fields, "Individuality and the Intellectuals," 439.

33. The original source of the Tivoli program is Wilhelm Mommsen and Günther Franz, *Deutsche Parteiprogramme I: Die konservativen Parteien von den Anfängen bis 1918* [German party programs I: The conservative parties from their beginnings to 1918] (Leipzig: Teubner, 1932), 25–27, translated by Pulzer in *Rise of Political Anti-Semitism*, 119.

34. Pulzer, *Rise of Political Anti-Semitism*, 119, 122n8. It is also important to note that the Conservatives had long been regarded as de facto anti-Semitic; as early as 1883 one of their members had claimed, "We have taken on ourselves the entire odium of the antisemitic movement in order to revitalize the Christian conscience of the people and lay the ethical foundation for the solution of the social question" (120n5). The *Preussische Jahrbücher* correctly observed that "basically the Conservatives have always been antisemitic" (120n6).

35. Hyman, "History of European Jewry"; Niewyk, "Solving the 'Jewish Problem'"; Rürup, "Jewish Emancipation and Bourgeois Society."

36. Du Bois, *Autobiography*, 127.

37. Du Bois, *Autobiography*, 127, emphasis mine.

38. Du Bois, "Present Condition," 171–72.

39. Du Bois, "Present Condition," 175.

40. Itzigsohn and Brown, "Sociology and the Theory"; Itzigsohn and Brown, *Sociology of W. E. B. Du Bois*; James M. Thomas, "Du Bois, Double Consciousness."

41. Du Bois, "Present Condition," 175. Du Bois's use of the phrase "cake of custom" is likely attributed to the British intellectual Walter Bagehot, who coined the term in the mid-nineteenth century. The phrase refers to the set of customs or cultural practices that take root in a society. We might think of them being baked into a society's general organization like a cake.

42. Du Bois, "Present Condition," 175; James M. Thomas, "Du Bois, Double Consciousness."

43. James M. Thomas, "Race, Nation"; Appiah, *Lines of Descent*.

44. Du Bois, "Diary of My Steerage Trip," June 2, 1894; Barkin, "W. E. B. Du Bois' Love Affair."

45. Compare Du Bois, "Present Condition," 172, with Treitschke, *Politics*, 312; Du Bois, "The Present Condition," 182.

46. Baldwin, "Letter from a Region."

47. Du Bois, *Autobiography*, 127; Du Bois, "Winds of Time"; Du Bois, "Realities in Africa," 722.

CHAPTER 4. Post-*Souls*, Veiled Mysteries

1. The influence for this chapter title is derived from Du Bois's characterization of Jewish travelers he encountered on his return voyage to the United States from Germany in 1894. He wrote in his diary, "In spite of all I have seen the Jew remains a half veiled mystery to me. I should be the last to join in any prejudice against him both from principle & from the acquaintance I've had with noble individuals in his race.... I have great hopes and great admiration for the Jew people only I see that their national development is over widely different obstacles than those of my nation" (Du Bois, "Diary of My Steerage Trip," June 2, 1894). No other scholar has so thoroughly documented the contributions of the Atlanta Sociological Laboratory as Professor Earl Wright II. See Wright, *First American School*; Wright, *Jim Crow Sociology*; Wright, "Using the Master's Tools"; Wright and Calhoun, "Jim Crow Sociology." Du Bois published his trilogy between 1957 and 1961. I've consulted the Oxford University editions, edited by Professor Henry Louis Gates Jr. See Du Bois, *Ordeal of Mansart*; Du Bois, *Mansart Builds a School*; Du Bois, *Worlds of Color*.

2. Du Bois, *Black Reconstruction*. The late Cedric Robinson, in *Black Marxism*, properly historicizes Du Bois's contribution to historical materialism, as well as the broader Black radical tradition. See also Bertholf, "Listening to Du Bois's 'Black Reconstruction'"; Itzigsohn, "Class, Race, and Emancipation"; Saman, "Du Bois and Marx."

3. Quoted from Bertholf, "Listening to Du Bois's 'Black Reconstruction,'" 78.

4. See the full reprint in C. L. R. James, "Black Jacobins and Black Reconstruction"; also see Itzigsohn, "Class, Race, and Emancipation."

5. Du Bois, *Dusk of Dawn*, 47; Du Bois, *World and Africa*.

6. Brewer, review of *The World and Africa*, 386; Woodson, review of *Color and Democracy*, 343.

7. Dennis, "Du Bois's Concept"; Dennis, "Continuities and Discontinuities"; Dennis, "Double Consciousness"; Dennis, "W. E. B. Du Bois"; Rampersad, *Art and Imagination*.

8. Itzigsohn and Brown, *Sociology of W. E. B. Du Bois*; Itzigsohn and Brown, "Sociology and the Theory"; Du Bois, "Forum of Fact and Opinion"; see also James M. Thomas, "Du Bois, Double Consciousness."

9. See Itzigsohn and Brown, "Sociology and the Theory"; and Itzigsohn and Brown, *Sociology of W. E. B. Du Bois*.

10. Du Bois, "Diary of My Steerage Trip," June 2, 1894.

11. Du Bois, "Present Condition"; Pulzer, *Rise of Political Anti-Semitism*, 53; Dühring, *Jewish Question*, 61.

12. Du Bois, *Souls of Black Folk*, 1.

13. Cohen, "'Wandering Jew'"; Hasan-Rokem and Dundes, *Wandering Jew*; Du Bois, *Souls of Black Folk*, 1.

14. Du Bois, "Russia, 1926."

15. Saman, "Du Bois and Marx," 35–36.

16. Du Bois, "Present Condition," 175; Gruening, *These United States*.

17. Quotes are from the reprinted version of Du Bois, "From Georgia," 463.

18. Du Bois, "From Georgia," 463.

19. Du Bois, *Darkwater*, 23; Farebrother, "*The Crisis* (1910–1934)."

20. Du Bois, "Souls of White Folk"; Du Bois, "United War Work Campaign."

21. Lewis, *W. E. B. Du Bois*, 14; Du Bois, *Darkwater*, 39; see Goudsouzian and McKinney, *Unseen Light*.

22. Rudwick, *Race Riot*; McLaughlin, "Reconsidering."

23. Du Bois, *Darkwater*, 18.

24. Du Bois, *Darkwater*, 18–19.

25. Balfour, "*Darkwater*'s Democratic Vision," 543.

26. Du Bois, *Souls of Black Folk*; Itzigsohn and Brown, "Sociology and the Theory."

27. Du Bois, *Darkwater*, 17, quoted in Balfour, "*Darkwater*'s Democratic Vision," 544.

28. The literature on these matters is vast and constantly updated. For interested readers, here are a few studies that examine systemic racism and persistent racial inequality within the American context across a variety of institutional arrangements: Flippen, "Unequal Returns"; Goetz, "Gentrification"; Kent and Ricketts, "Wealth Gaps"; Reflective Democracy Campaign, "System Failure"; Sewell, "Racism-Race Reification Process"; Sewell and Jefferson, "Collateral Damage"; Shapiro, Meschede, and Osoro, "Roots."

29. Gilroy, *Black Atlantic*; Forney, "Souls of Black Folk"; Perkinson, "Gift/Curse."

30. Du Bois, "Revelations," 3.

31. Du Bois, "Revelations," 5; Du Bois, "From Georgia"; Robinson, *Black Marxism*.

32. Du Bois, "Revelations," 11–12.

33. Du Bois, "Revelations," 13.

34. Du Bois, "Revelations," 14.

35. Du Bois, "Revelations," 14.

36. The original essay is Du Bois, "Strivings of the Negro People," which, as noted in the introductory chapter, was only slightly revised for *The Souls of Black Folk*. See "The Souls of White Folk," from *Darkwater*.

37. Du Bois, "Revelations," 15, emphasis added.

38. Du Bois, "Revelations," 12.

39. See Du Bois, "Souls of White Folk"; Du Bois, *Darkwater*; and Du Bois, *Black Reconstruction* for Du Bois's discussion of the psychological and social wages of whiteness.

40. Du Bois, *Autobiography*, 411–12.

41. Du Bois, "Black United States," 12.

42. Webb, "Nazi Persecution"; see also Beck, "German Views"; Böker, "Arthur Feiler."

43. Du Bois, "Postscript," 116.

44. Darian-Smith, "Re-reading W. E. B. Du Bois," 487; Du Bois, "Forum of Fact and Opinion."

45. Rothberg, "W. E. B. Du Bois in Warsaw"; Joseph M. Proskauer, American Jewish Committee, to W. E. B. Du Bois, October 24, 1944, Du Bois Papers.

46. W. E. B. Du Bois to American Jewish Committee, November 14, 1944, Du Bois Papers.

47. Du Bois to American Jewish Committee, November 14, 1944.

48. Rothberg, "W. E. B. Du Bois in Warsaw," 175.

49. Du Bois, "Negro and the Warsaw Ghetto," 14.

50. Du Bois, "Negro and the Warsaw Ghetto," 14–15.

51. Gilman and Thomas, *Are Racists Crazy?*; Omi and Winant, *Racial Formation*, 56.

52. Omi and Winant, *Racial Formation*, 71; Cetina, *Epistemic Cultures*; Giddens, *Consequences of Modernity*; Gilman and Thomas, *Are Racists Crazy?*

53. Young, *Colonial Desire*; Gilman and Thomas, *Are Racists Crazy?*

54. Reinsch, "Negro Race and European Civilization," 148, 154.

55. Stone, "Is Race Friction," 692.

56. American Sociological Society to W. E. B. Du Bois, October 4, 1907, Du Bois Papers; W. E. B. Du Bois to Alfred Holt Stone, December 26, 1907, Du Bois Papers.

57. American Economic Association, January 14, 1908, Du Bois Papers.

58. Weatherly, "Discussion," 823–24.

59. Du Bois, "Discussion," 834.

60. Du Bois, "Discussion," 834–35.

61. Du Bois, "Discussion," 835–36.

62. Du Bois, "Discussion," 837.

63. Du Bois, "Future of the Negro Race"; Stone, "Is Race Friction"; Ross, *Foundations of Sociology*, 379.

64. Du Bois, "Discussion," 838.

65. Belin, "Southern View," 517.

66. Charlotte Perkins Gilman, "Suggestion," 78, emphasis added.

67. Charlotte Perkins Gilman, "Suggestion," 80.

68. Faris, "Mental Capacity," 618.

69. W. I. Thomas, "Race Psychology," 726, 736, 751; see Du Bois, *Philadelphia Negro*, 177.

70. For a notable exception to the commonsense perspective, see Howard, "Social Cost"; W. I. Thomas, "Race Psychology."

71. Mecklin, "Philosophy," 346.

72. Mecklin, "Philosophy," 347–48; Mecklin, *Democracy and Race Friction*.

73. Mecklin, "Philosophy," 356.

74. Mecklin, *Democracy and Race Friction*, 85–86.

75. Mecklin, *Democracy and Race Friction*, 99–100.

76. Mecklin, *Democracy and Race Friction*, 100.

77. Mecklin, *Democracy and Race Friction*, 124–25; Mecklin quotes from Du Bois, *Philadelphia Negro*, 325.

78. Mecklin, *Democracy and Race Friction*, 143–44.

79. Mecklin, *Democracy and Race Friction*, 143–44; Mecklin quotes here from Du Bois, *Souls of Black Folk*, 2–3. Throughout *Democracy and Race Friction*, Mecklin made it a point to take shots at Du Bois, mentioning him by name several times. While Mecklin's argument is indeed a weak one, especially with the benefit of hindsight, his mentioning of Du Bois by name is also a recognition of Du Bois's own significant stature in the field, even if Du Bois's perspective is one that Mecklin and others find disagreeable. Mecklin writes, for example, that there are those like Du Bois, "whose thought is so strongly tinged with pessimism and antagonism to the white race," who have become the spiritual leaders of Black people, to their collective detriment. "It is imperative . . . that his intellectual leaders supply him with ideals that shall inspire him with honest race pride and encourage more sympathetic relations with the whites. The militant race philosophy preached by a certain group of negro writers and thinkers is not one that the sincere friend of the negro would like to see him adopt" (156). Mecklin then suggests that Black people find their hope in the works of Booker T. Washington, "another great mulatto" (156).

80. Mecklin, *Ku Klux Klan*, 3; see Stephenson, "Ku Klux Klan," 301–2.

81. Mecklin, *Ku Klux Klan*, 240, 108.

82. Park, "Racial Assimilation," 610–11; see also Park, "Bases of Race Prejudice."

83. Park, "Human Migration," 892.

84. Stonequist, *Marginal Man*, 8.

85. Stonequist, "Problem of the Marginal Man," 9–10.

86. Sarnoff, "Identification," 203.

87. Sarnoff, "Identification," 203.

88. Sarnoff, "Identification"; Lewin, "Self-Hatred among Jews"; Lewin, *Resolving Social Conflicts*; see also Sander L. Gilman, *Jewish Self-Hatred*. For an analysis of the relationship between whiteness and nationhood, see James M. Thomas, "Race, Nation."

89. Orlansky, "Study of Man: Jewish Personality Traits"; see also Orlansky, "Study of Man: The Jews of Yankee City."

90. Du Bois, *Souls of Black Folk*, 2.

91. Du Bois, *Souls of Black Folk*, 2.

92. Du Bois, *Souls of Black Folk*, 3.

CONCLUSION

1. Wigglesworth and Smith, "'Unprecedented' Caldor, Dixie Fires."

2. Reckdahl and Bella, "New Orleans Hasn't Picked Up."

3. Lincoln, "Tucker Carlson Wonders."

4. Carter, "Democratic and Republican Administrations."

5. Garner and Selod, "Racialization of Muslims"; Selod, "Citizenship Denied."

6. Hockenos, "Central Europe's Right-Wing Populism"; Polakow-Suransky, "Opinion: White Nationalism."

7. Bonilla-Silva, "Structure of Racism"; Doherty, Motel, and Weisel, "Sharp Racial Divisions"; Kaplan, *Myth of Post-racial America*.

8. My use of conjectural analysis borrows heavily from Stuart Hall's definition. See Hall, "Signification, Representation, Ideology"; Hall et al., *Policing the Crisis*.

9. Bowser, "Expanding W. E. B. Du Bois's Concept," 6–7.

10. Winant, *New Politics of Race*; Seamster and Ray, "Against Teleology"; Sentencing Project, "Report."

11. Huntington, "Clash of Civilizations?"; Lucassen, "Peeling an Onion"; Kumar, *Islamophobia*.

12. Lucassen, "Peeling an Onion"; *BBC News*, "Europe and Right-Wing Nationalism"; Arab American Institute, "American Attitudes."

13. Arab American Institute, "American Attitudes."

14. Bhutta et al., "Disparities"; Carol Anderson, *White Rage*; Franklin, "Parts"; Torchinsky, "Details Emerge."

15. Weisman and Epstein, "G.O.P. Declares."

16. Lichter, Parisi, and Taquino, "Toward a New Macro-segregation?"; Siegel-Hawley and Frankenberg, "Southern Slippage"; Underhill, "Managing Difference."

17. Schleunes, "Madagaskar für die Juden."

18. Baron, "Impact of the Revolution," 197n4; Du Bois, "Appeal to the World."

19. Benedict Anderson, *Imagined Communities*; Smith, *Nation in History*.

20. Hobsbawm and Ranger, *Invention of Tradition*; Balibar and Wallerstein, *Race, Nation, Class*; Smith, *Nation in History*.

21. Du Bois, *Souls of Black Folk*, 3; Balibar and Wallerstein, *Race, Nation, Class*, 25.

22. Balibar and Wallerstein, *Race, Nation, Class*, 52.

23. Du Bois, *World and Africa*, 4, 46, 50.

24. Balibar and Wallerstein, *Race, Nation, Class*, 60.

25. Husain, "Terror and Abolition."

26. Plumer and Zhong, "Stopping Climate Change."

27. Du Bois, *Dusk of Dawn*, 47.

BIBLIOGRAPHY

ARCHIVES

W. E. B. Du Bois Papers. MS 312. Special Collections and University Archives, University of Massachusetts Amherst Libraries.

PUBLISHED SOURCES

Abraham, Gary A. "German-Jewish History as a Paradigm for Understanding Nationalism." *Contemporary Jewry* 15, no. 1 (1994): 97–120.

——. *Max Weber and the Jewish Question: A Study of the Social Outlook of His Sociology.* Urbana: University of Illinois Press, 1992.

Ajala, Adekunle. "The Nature of African Boundaries." *Africa Spectrum* 18, no. 2 (1983): 177–89.

Anderson, Benedict. *Imagined Communities: Reflections on the Origin and Spread of Nationalism.* Rev. ed. London: Verso, 2016.

Anderson, Carol. *White Rage: The Unspoken Truth of Our Racial Divide.* New York: Bloomsbury USA, 2016.

Appiah, Kwame Anthony. *Lines of Descent: W. E. B. Du Bois and the Emergence of Identity.* Cambridge, Mass.: Harvard University Press, 2014.

"À propos du procès-verbal." *Bulletins de la Société d'Anthropologie de Paris* 1, no. 7 (1884): 698–701.

Aptheker, Herbert. *The Literary Legacy of W. E. B. Du Bois.* Millwood, N.Y.: Kraus International Publications, 1989.

Arab American Institute. "American Attitudes towards Arabs and Muslims." Arab American Institute, Washington, D.C., December 5, 2017. https://www.aaiusa.org/library/american-attitudes-towards-arabs-and-muslims-2017.

Baird, Harvey. "Some Observations on Insanity in Jews." *Journal of Mental Science* 54, no. 226 (1908): 528–32.

Baldwin, James. "Letter from a Region in My Mind." *New Yorker*, November 17, 1962, 59–144.

Balfour, Lawrie. "*Darkwater*'s Democratic Vision." *Political Theory* 38, no. 4 (2010): 537–63.

Balibar, Étienne, and Immanuel Wallerstein. *Race, Nation, Class: Ambiguous Identities*. London: Verso Books, 2011.

Barkin, Kenneth D. "'Berlin Days,' 1892–1894: W. E. B. Du Bois and German Political Economy." *Boundary 2* 27, no. 3 (October 2000): 79–101.

———. "W. E. B. Du Bois' Love Affair with Imperial Germany." *German Studies Review* 28, no. 2 (2005): 285–302.

Baron, Salo W. "The Impact of the Revolution of 1848 on Jewish Emancipation." *Jewish Social Studies* 11, no. 3 (1949): 195–248.

Baum, Bruce. *The Rise and Fall of the Caucasian Race: A Political History of Racial Identity*. New York: NYU Press, 2008.

BBC News. "Europe and Right-Wing Nationalism: A Country-by-Country Guide." November 13, 2019, sec. Europe. https://www.bbc.com/news/world-europe-36130006.

Beadles, Cecil F. "The Insane Jew." *Journal of Mental Science* 46, no. 195 (1900): 731–37.

Beard, George. "Neurasthenia, or Nervous Exhaustion." *Boston Medical and Surgical Journal*, April 29, 1869, 217–21.

Beck, Earl R. "German Views of Negro Life in the United States, 1919–1933." *Journal of Negro History* 48, no. 1 (January 1963): 22–32.

Belin, H. E. "A Southern View of Slavery." *American Journal of Sociology* 13, no. 4 (1908): 513–22.

Bell, Bernard W. "Genealogical Shifts in Du Bois's Discourse on Double Consciousness as the Sign of African American Difference." In *W. E. B. Du Bois on Race and Culture*, edited by Bernard W. Bell, Emily R. Grosholz, and James B. Stewart, 87–108. New York: Routledge, 2014.

Berger, Peter L., and Thomas Luckmann. *The Social Construction of Reality: A Treatise in the Sociology of Knowledge*. New York: Anchor, 1967.

Bertholf, Garry. "Listening to Du Bois's 'Black Reconstruction': After James." *South: A Scholarly Journal* 48, no. 1 (2015): 78–91.

Bhutta, Neal, Andrew C. Chang, Lisa J. Dettling, and Joanne W. Hsu. "Disparities in Wealth by Race and Ethnicity in the 2019 Survey of Consumer Finances." *FEDS Notes* (blog), September 28, 2020.

Binet, Alfred. *On Double Consciousness: Experimental Psychological Studies*. Whitefish, Mont.: Kessinger Publishing, 2010.

Blackmon, Douglas A. *Slavery by Another Name: The Re-enslavement of Black Americans from the Civil War to World War II*. New York: Anchor, 2009.

Blumenbach, Johann Friedrich, and Joseph Banks. *De Generis Humani Varietate Nativa*. 3rd ed. Göttingen, Germany: Vandenhoek und Ruprecht, 1795. https://doi.org/10.5962/bhl.title.35972.

Böker, Alexander. "Arthur Feiler and German Liberalism." *Social Research* 10, no. 4 (1943): 455–79.

Bonilla-Silva, Eduardo. "The Structure of Racism in Color-Blind, 'Post-Racial' America." *American Behavioral Scientist* 59, no. 11 (October 2015): 1358–76.

Boudin, M. "Sur l'idiatie et l'aliénation mentale chez les Juifs d'Allemagne." *Bulletin de la Société d'Anthropologie de Paris* 1, no. 4 (1863): 386–88.

Bowser, Benjamin. "Expanding W. E. B. Du Bois's Concept of Double Consciousness." *Perspectives* 29, no. 1 (December 2006): 6–8.

Brewer, W. M. Review of *The World and Africa*, by W. E. B. Du Bois. *Journal of Negro History* 32, no. 3 (1947): 384–87.

Brill, A. A., and Morris J. Karpas. "Insanity among the Jews." *Medical Record* 86 (April 1914): 577–79.

Bruce, Dickson D. "W. E. B. Du Bois and the Idea of Double Consciousness." *American Literature* 64, no. 2 (1992): 299–309.

Brustein, William I. *Roots of Hate: Anti-Semitism in Europe before the Holocaust.* Cambridge: Cambridge University Press, 2003.

Burden-Stelly, Charisse, and Gerald Horne. *W. E. B. Du Bois: A Life in American History.* Santa Barbara, Calif.: ABC-CLIO, 2019.

Burgl, Georg. *Die Hysterie und die strafrechtliche Verantwortlichkeit der Hysterischen: Ein praktisches Handbuch für Ärzte und Juristen.* Stuttgart: Ferdinand Enke, 1912.

Byrnes, Robert. "Bloom's Sexual Tropes: Stigmata of the 'Degenerate' Jew." *James Joyce Quarterly* 27, no. 2 (1990): 303–23.

Campbell, James. "Du Bois and James." *Transactions of the Charles S. Peirce Society* 28, no. 3 (1992): 569–81.

Carter, Niambi M. "Democratic and Republican Administrations Have Long Agreed on One Thing—Discriminating against Haitian Refugees." *Washington Post*, September 23, 2021.

Cetina, Karin Knorr. *Epistemic Cultures: How the Sciences Make Knowledge.* Cambridge, Mass.: Harvard University Press, 1999.

Charcot, J. M. *Clinical Lectures on Certain Diseases of the Nervous System.* Translated by E. P. Hurd. Detroit, Mich.: George S. Davis, 1888.

Clark, Evalyn A. "Adolf Wagner: From National Economist to National Socialist." *Political Science Quarterly* 55, no. 3 (1940): 378–411.

Cohen, Richard I. "The 'Wandering Jew' from Medieval Legend to Modern Metaphor." In *The Art of Being Jewish in Modern Times*, by Richard I. Cohen, 147–75. Philadelphia: University of Pennsylvania Press, 2013.

Collins, Randall. *The Sociology of Philosophies: A Global Theory of Intellectual Change.* Cambridge, Mass.: Belknap Press of Harvard University Press, 1998.

Cooley, Charles Horton. *Human Nature and the Social Order.* New York: C. Scribner's Sons, 1902.

"The Damascus Blood Libel (1840)." In *Encyclopedia Judaica.* Jewish Virtual Library, 2008. https://www.jewishvirtuallibrary.org/the-damascus-blood-libel.

Darian-Smith, Eve. "Re-reading W. E. B. Du Bois: The Global Dimensions of the U.S. Civil Rights Struggle." *Journal of Global History* 7, no. 3 (November 2012): 483–505. https://doi.org/10.1017/S1740022812000290.

Dennis, Rutledge M. "Continuities and Discontinuities in the Social and Political Thought of W. E. B. Du Bois." *Race and Ethnic Relations* 9 (July 1996): 3–23.

———. "Double Consciousness." In *The Wiley Blackwell Encyclopedia of Race, Ethnicity, and*

Nationalism. John Wiley & Sons, Ltd., 2015. https://doi.org/10.1002/9781118663202.
wberen187.

——— . "Du Bois's Concept of Double Consciousness: Myth and Reality." *Race and Ethnic Relations* 9 (July 1996): 69–90.

——— . "W. E. B. Du Bois: The Autobiographer as Sociological Theorist." *Perspectives* 29, no. 1 (December 2006): 3–5.

Deutsch, Albert. "The First U.S. Census of the Insane (1840) and Its Use as Pro-slavery Propaganda." *Bulletin of the History of Medicine* 15, no. 5 (May 1944): 469–82.

Dietrich, Lucas. "'At the Dawning of the Twentieth Century': W. E. B. Du Bois, A. C. McClurg & Co., and the Early Circulation of *The Souls of Black Folk.*" *Book History* 20, no. 1 (2017): 307–29.

Doherty, Carroll, Seth Motel, and Rachel Weisel. "Sharp Racial Divisions in Reactions to Brown, Garner Decisions." December 8, 2014, Pew Research Center. https://www.pewresearch.org/politics/2014/12/08/sharp-racial-divisions-in-reactions-to-brown-garner-decisions/.

Dollinger, Marc. *Black Power, Jewish Politics: Reinventing the Alliance in the 1960s.* Boston: Brandeis University Press, 2018.

Dorpalen, Andreas. *Heinrich von Treitschke.* New Haven, Conn.: Yale University Press, 1957.

Du Bois, W. E. B. "An Appeal to the World: A Statement of Denial of Human Rights to Minorities in the Case of Citizens of Negro Descent in the United States of America and an Appeal to the United Nations for Redress." Submitted by W. E. B. Du Bois and the NAACP to the UN on October 23. New York: National Association for the Advancement of Colored People, 1947. https://www.aclu.org/appeal-world.

——— . "Autobiography." June 1953. MS 312. W. E. B. Du Bois Papers, Special Collections and University Archives, University of Massachusetts Amherst Libraries.

——— . *The Autobiography of W. E. B. Du Bois: A Soliloquy on Viewing My Life from the Last Decade of Its First Century.* New York: International Publishers, 1968.

——— . *Black Reconstruction in America: An Essay toward a History of the Part Which Black Folk Played in the Attempt to Reconstruct Democracy in America, 1860–1880.* Edited by Henry Louis Gates Jr. The Oxford W. E. B. Du Bois. New York: Oxford University Press, 2014.

——— . "Black United States: Study of the Descendants of Africans in the United States." Draft, 1950. MS 312. W. E. B. Du Bois Papers, Special Collections and University Archives, University of Massachusetts Amherst Libraries.

——— . *The Correspondence of W. E. B. Du Bois.* Vol. 1, *Selections, 1877–1934*, edited by Herbert Aptheker. Amherst: University of Massachusetts Press, 1997.

——— . *Darkwater: Voices from within the Veil.* Mineola, N.Y.: Dover Publications, 1999.

——— . "Diary of My Steerage Trip across the Atlantic." June 2, 1894. MS 312. Series 10. Essays & Student Papers 1889–1896. W. E. B. Du Bois Papers, Special Collections and University Archives, University of Massachusetts Amherst Libraries.

——— . "Discussion of the Paper by Alfred H. Stone, 'Is Race Friction between Blacks and Whites in the United States Growing and Inevitable?'" *American Journal of Sociology* 13, no. 6 (May 1908): 834–38. https://doi.org/10.1086/211634.

———. *Dusk of Dawn: An Essay toward an Autobiography of a Race Concept.* New Brunswick, N.J.: Transaction Publishers, 1983.

———. "A Forum of Fact and Opinion: Race Prejudice in Nazi Germany." *Pittsburgh Courier,* December 19, 1936.

———. "From Georgia: Invisible Empire State." *Georgia Review* 66, no. 3 (2012): 462–64.

———. "The Future of the Negro Race in America." *East and the West* 2 (January 1904): 4–19.

———. "Lecture Notebook." 1896. MS 312. W. E. B. Du Bois Papers, Special Collections and University Archives, University of Massachusetts Amherst Libraries.

———. *Mansart Builds a School.* Edited by Henry Louis Gates Jr. and Brent Hayes Edwards. New York: Oxford University Press, 2014.

———. "The Negro and the Warsaw Ghetto." *Jewish Life: A Progressive Monthly* 6, no. 7 (1952): 14–15.

———. *The Ordeal of Mansart.* Edited by Henry Louis Gates Jr. and Brent Hayes Edwards. New York: Oxford University Press, 2014.

———. "Pan-African Association. To the Nations of the World, ca. 1900." July 23, 1900. MS 312. W. E. B. Du Bois Papers, Special Collections and University Archives, University of Massachusetts Amherst Libraries.

———. *The Philadelphia Negro: A Social Study.* New York: Schocken Books, 1899.

———. "Postscript." *The Crisis,* May 1933. National Association for the Advancement of Colored People, New York.

———. "Preface to the Jubilee Edition of *The Souls of Black Folk* (1953)." *Monthly Review* 55, no. 6 (November 2003). https://monthlyreview.org/2003/11/01/preface-to-the-jubilee-edition-of-the-souls-of-black-folk-1953/.

———. "The Present Condition of German Politics (1893)." *Central European History* 31, no. 3 (1998): 171–87.

———. "The Realities in Africa: European Profit or Negro Development?" *Foreign Affairs* 21, no. 4 (1943): 721–32.

———. "The Revelations of Saint Orgne the Damned." Commencement address, Fisk University, Nashville, Tenn., June 8, 1938. MS 312. W. E. B. Du Bois Papers, Special Collections and University Archives, University of Massachusetts Amherst Libraries.

———. "Russia, 1926." *The Crisis,* November 1926, 8.

———. *The Souls of Black Folk.* 1903; New York: Dover Publications, 1994.

———. "The Souls of White Folk." *The Independent,* August 18, 1910.

———. "Strivings of the Negro People." *Atlantic Monthly,* August 1897.

———. "The Superior Race (an Essay)." *The Smart Set: A Magazine of Cleverness* 70, no. 4 (1923): 55–60.

———. *The Suppression of the African Slave-Trade to the United States of America, 1638–1870.* Harvard's Historical Monograph Series. New York: Cosimo Classics, 2007.

———. "United War Work Campaign, ca. 1918." MS 312. W. E. B. Du Bois Papers, Special Collections and University Archives, University of Massachusetts Amherst Libraries.

———. "Winds of Time." *Chicago Defender,* December 18, 1945. MS 312. W. E. B. Du Bois Papers, Special Collections and University Archives, University of Massachusetts Amherst Libraries.

———. *"The World and Africa" and "Color and Democracy."* Edited by Henry Louis Gates Jr. New York: Oxford University Press, 2014.

———. *Worlds of Color.* Edited by Henry Louis Gates Jr. New York: Oxford University Press, 2007.

Dühring, Eugen. *The Jewish Question as a Racial, Moral and Cultural Question.* Translated by Alexander Jacob. Ostara Publications, 2019.

Dwight, Benjamin W. "Facts Illustrative of the Powers and Operations of the Human Mind in a Diseased State." *American Journal of Science* 1, no. 4 (1818): 431–33.

Efron, John M. *Defenders of the Race: Jewish Doctors and Race Science in Fin-de-Siècle Europe.* New Haven, Conn.: Yale University Press, 1994.

Elliotson, J. "Dual Consciousness." *Cornhill Magazine* 35 (January–June 1877): 86–105.

Englander, Martin. *The Evident Most Frequent Appearances of Illness in the Jewish Race.* Vienna: J. L. Pollak, 1902.

Erb, Wilhelm. *Über die wachsende Nervosität unserer Zeit: Akademische Rede zum Geburtsfeste . . . Karl Friedrich am 22.* Heidelberg: Universitäts-Buchdruckerei J. Höring, 1893.

Fanon, Frantz. *Black Skin, White Masks.* Rev. ed. New York: Grove Press, 2008.

Farebrother, Rachel. "*The Crisis* (1910–34)." In *The Oxford Critical and Cultural History of Modernist Magazines, Volume 2: North America 1894–1960*, edited by Peter Brooker and Andrew Thacker, online edition. Oxford: Oxford University Press, 2012.

Faris, Ellsworth. "The Mental Capacity of Savages." *American Journal of Sociology* 23, no. 5 (1918): 603–19.

Feagin, Joe R., and Hernan Vera. *Liberation Sociology.* 2nd ed. Boulder, Colo.: Paradigm Publishers, 2008.

Fields, Karen E. "Individuality and the Intellectuals: An Imaginary Conversation between W. E. B. Du Bois and Émile Durkheim." *Theory and Society* 31, no. 4 (2002): 435–62.

Finkelstein, Gabriel. *Emil du Bois-Reymond: Neuroscience, Self, and Society in Nineteenth-Century Germany.* Illustrated edition. Cambridge, Mass.: MIT Press, 2013.

Fishberg, Maurice. *Materials for the Physical Anthropology of the Eastern European Jews.* Lancaster, Pa.: New Era, 1905.

Flippen, Chenoa Anne. "Unequal Returns to Housing Investments? A Study of Real Housing Appreciation among Black, White, and Hispanic Households." *Social Forces* 82, no. 4 (2004): 1523–51.

Forney, Craig. "The Souls of Black Folk and the Soul of W. E. B. Du Bois." In *The Souls of W. E. B. Du Bois: New Essays and Reflections*, edited by Edward J. Blum and Jason R. Young, 85–109. Macon, Ga.: Mercer University Press, 2009.

Frank, Gelya. "Jews, Multiculturalism, and Boasian Anthropology." *American Anthropologist* 99, no. 4 (1997): 731–45.

Frankel, Jonathan. *The Damascus Affair: "Ritual Murder," Politics, and the Jews in 1840.* Cambridge: Cambridge University Press, 1997.

Franklin, Jonathan. "Parts of the Buffalo Shooter's Alleged Screed Were Copied from Other Sources." NPR, May 18, 2022, sec. Race.

Frantz, Constantin. *Der Nationalliberalismus und die Judenherrschaft*. Munich: M. Huttler, 1874.

Garner, Steve, and Saher Selod. "The Racialization of Muslims: Empirical Studies of Islamophobia." *Critical Sociology* 41, no. 1 (January 2015): 9–19.

Giddens, Anthony. *The Consequences of Modernity*. Palo Alto, Calif.: Stanford University Press, 1991.

Gilman, Charlotte Perkins. "A Suggestion on the Negro Problem." *American Journal of Sociology* 14, no. 1 (1908): 78–85.

Gilman, Sander L. *Jewish Self-Hatred: Anti-Semitism and the Hidden Language of the Jews*. Baltimore, Md.: Johns Hopkins University Press, 1990.

———. "Jews and Mental Illness: Medical Metaphors, Anti-Semitism, and the Jewish Response." *Journal of the History of the Behavioral Sciences* 20, no. 2 (April 1984): 150–59.

———. *The Jew's Body*. New York: Routledge, 1991.

———. "Wandering Imaginations of Race and Hysteria: The Origins of the Hysterical Body in Psychoanalysis." In *Performing Hysteria*, edited by Johanna Braun, 41–60. Leuven, Belgium: Leuven University Press, 2020.

Gilman, Sander L., and James M. Thomas. *Are Racists Crazy? How Prejudice, Racism, and Antisemitism Became Markers of Insanity*. New York: NYU Press, 2016.

Gilroy, Paul. *The Black Atlantic: Modernity and Double-Consciousness*. Cambridge, Mass.: Harvard University Press, 1993.

Glenn, Evelyn Nakano. *Unequal Freedom: How Race and Gender Shaped American Citizenship and Labor*. Cambridge, Mass.: Harvard University Press, 2004.

Glick, Leonard B. "Types Distinct from Our Own: Franz Boas on Jewish Identity and Assimilation." *American Anthropologist* 84, no. 3 (1982): 545–65.

Goetz, Edward. "Gentrification in Black and White: The Racial Impact of Public Housing Demolition in American Cities." *Urban Studies* 48, no. 8 (June 2011): 1581–1604.

Goldstein, Eric L. *The Price of Whiteness: Jews, Race, and American Identity*. Princeton, N.J.: Princeton University Press, 2008.

Goldstein, Jan. "The Wandering Jew and the Problem of Psychiatric Anti-Semitism in Fin-de-Siècle France." *Journal of Contemporary History* 20, no. 4 (1985): 521–52.

Goudsouzian, Aram, and Charles W. McKinney Jr., eds. *An Unseen Light: Black Struggles for Freedom in Memphis, Tennessee*. Lexington: University Press of Kentucky, 2018.

Gruening, Ernest Henry, ed. *These United States: A Symposium*. New York: Boni and Liveright Publishers, 1923.

Hacking, Ian. "Double Consciousness in Britain 1815–1875." *Dissociation* 4, no. 3 (1991): 134–46.

Hajdu, Steven I. "A Note from History: Rudolph Virchow, Pathologist, Armed Revolutionist, Politician, and Anthropologist." *Annals of Clinical and Laboratory Science* 35, no. 2 (2005): 203–5.

Hall, Stuart. "Signification, Representation, Ideology: Althusser and the Post-structuralist Debates." *Critical Studies in Mass Communication* 2, no. 2 (June 1985): 91–114.

Hall, Stuart, Chas Critcher, Tony Jefferson, John Clarke, and Brian Roberts. *Policing the Crisis:*

Mugging, the State and Law and Order. 35th anniversary ed. Hampshire: Red Globe Press, 2013.

Harrowitz, Nancy A. *Tainted Greatness: Antisemitism and Cultural Heroes.* Philadelphia, Pa.: Temple University Press, 1994.

Harter, Susan. "The Construction and Conservation of the Self: James and Cooley Revisited." In *Self, Ego, and Identity: Integrative Approaches,* edited by Daniel K. Lapsley and F. Clark Power, 43–70. New York: Springer, 1988.

Hasan-Rokem, Galit, and Alan Dundes, eds. *The Wandering Jew: Essays in the Interpretation of a Christian Legend.* Bloomington: Indiana University Press, 1986.

Heng, Geraldine. "Jews, Saracens, 'Black Men,' Tartars: England in a World of Racial Difference." In *A Companion to Medieval English Literature and Culture c.1350–c.1500,* edited by Peter Brown, 247–69. London: John Wiley & Sons, 2007.

Hobsbawm, Eric, and Terence Ranger, eds. *The Invention of Tradition.* Cambridge: Cambridge University Press, 1992.

Hockenos, Paul. "Central Europe's Right-Wing Populism." *The Nation,* May 5, 2010.

HoSang, Daniel Martinez, Oneka LaBennett, and Laura Pulido, eds. *Racial Formation in the Twenty-First Century.* Berkeley: University of California Press, 2012.

Howard, George Elliott. "The Social Cost of Southern Race Prejudice." *American Journal of Sociology* 22, no. 5 (March 1917): 577–93.

Hunter, Marcus Anthony. *Black Citymakers: How the Philadelphia Negro Changed Urban America.* New York: Oxford University Press, 2015.

———. "Du Boisian Sociology and Intellectual Reparations: For Coloured Scholars Who Consider Suicide When Our Rainbows Are Not Enuf." *Ethnic and Racial Studies* 39, no. 8 (June 2016): 1379–84.

Huntington, Samuel P. "The Clash of Civilizations?" *Foreign Affairs* 72, no. 3 (Summer 1993): 22–49.

Husain, Atiya. "Terror and Abolition." *Boston Review,* June 11, 2020. https://bostonreview.net/race/atiya-husain-terror-and-abolition.

Hyman, Paula E. "The History of European Jewry: Recent Trends in the Literature." *Journal of Modern History* 54, no. 2 (1982): 303–19.

Hyslop, Theo. B. "A Discussion on Occupation and Environment as Causative Factors of Insanity." *British Medical Journal* 2, no. 2337 (1905): 941–45.

———. "On 'Double Consciousness.'" *British Medical Journal* 2, no. 2021 (1899): 782–86.

Itzigsohn, José. "Class, Race, and Emancipation: The Contributions of the Black Jacobins and Black Reconstruction in America to Historical Sociology and Social Theory." *CLR James Journal* 19, no. 1/2 (2013): 177–98.

Itzigsohn, José, and Karida Brown. "Sociology and the Theory of Double Consciousness: W. E. B. Du Bois's Phenomenology of Racialized Subjectivity." *Du Bois Review: Social Science Research on Race* 12, no. 2 (October 2015): 231–48.

———. *The Sociology of W. E. B. Du Bois: Racialized Modernity and the Global Color Line.* New York: NYU Press, 2020.

Jacobs, Joseph, and John Forsyth. "The Damascus Affair of 1840 and the Jews of America." *Publications of the American Jewish Historical Society,* no. 10 (1902): 119–28.

Jacobson, Matthew Frye. *Whiteness of a Different Color: European Immigrants and the Alchemy of Race.* Cambridge, Mass.: Harvard University Press, 1999.

James, C. L. R. "The Black Jacobins and Black Reconstruction: A Comparative Analysis." *Small Axe* 8 (September 2000).

James, William. *The Principles of Psychology.* Vol. 1. New York: Henry Holt and Company, 1890.

———. *The Varieties of Religious Experience: A Study in Human Nature.* New York: Modern Library, 1902.

Jarvis, Edward. "Insanity among the Coloured Population of the Free States." *American Journal of the Medical Sciences* 7 (January 1844): 3–15.

———. "On the Supposed Increase of Insanity." *American Journal of Psychiatry* 8, no. 4 (April 1852): 333–64.

Jaspers, Karl. *General Psychopathology.* Translated by J. Joenig and Marian Hamilton. 2 vols. Baltimore, Md.: Johns Hopkins University Press, 1997.

Kaplan, H. Roy. *The Myth of Post-racial America: Searching for Equality in the Age of Materialism.* Lanham, Md.: Rowman & Littlefield Education, 2011.

Karabel, Jerome. *The Chosen: The Hidden History of Admission and Exclusion at Harvard, Yale, and Princeton.* Boston: Houghton Mifflin Harcourt, 2005.

Kendhammer, Brandon. "DuBois the Pan-Africanist and the Development of African Nationalism." *Ethnic and Racial Studies* 30, no. 1 (January 2007): 51–71.

Kent, Ana Hernandez, and Lowell R. Ricketts. "Wealth Gaps between White, Black and Hispanic Families in 2019: St. Louis Fed." *St. Louis Fed on the Economy* (blog), January 5, 2021. https://www.stlouisfed.org/on-the-economy/2021/january/wealth-gaps-white-black -hispanic-families-2019.

Kieval, Hillel. "The Importance of Place: Comparative Aspects of the Ritual Murder Trial in Modern Central Europe." In *Comparing Jewish Societies,* edited by Todd M. Endelman, 135–65. Ann Arbor: University of Michigan Press, 1997.

Kraepelin, Emil. "Zur Entartungsfrage." *Zentralblatt für Nervenheilkunde und Psychiatrie* 31 (1908): 745–51. Reprinted in *Emil Kraepelin: Kraepelin in Heidelberg, 1891–1903,* edited by W. Burgmair, E. J. Engstrom, and M. M. Weber, 61–70. Munich: Belleville, 2005.

Kumar, Deepa. *Islamophobia and the Politics of Empire.* Chicago: Haymarket Books, 2012.

Lagarde, Paul de. *Mitteilungen.* Mainz, Germany: Dieterich, 1884.

Lampert, Lisa. "Race, Periodicity, and the (Neo–) Middle Ages." *MLQ: Modern Language Quarterly* 65, no. 3 (2004): 391–421.

Legge, Jerome S., Jr. *Jews, Turks, and Other Strangers: Roots of Prejudice in Modern Germany.* Madison: University of Wisconsin Press, 2003.

Lemke, Sieglinde. "Berlin and Boundaries: Sollen versus Geschehen." *Boundary 2* 27, no. 3 (October 2000): 45–78.

Lewin, Kurt. *Resolving Social Conflicts: Selected Papers on Group Dynamics.* 1st ed. New York: Harper & Brothers, 1948.

———. "Self-Hatred among Jews." *Contemporary Jewish Record* 4, no. 3 (June 1941): 219.

Lewis, David Levering. *W. E. B. Du Bois, 1868–1919: Biography of a Race.* 1st ed. New York: Holt Paperbacks, 1994.

Lichter, Daniel T., Domenico Parisi, and Michael C. Taquino. "Toward a New Macro-segregation? Decomposing Segregation within and between Metropolitan Cities and Sub-urbs." *American Sociological Review* 80, no. 4 (August 2015): 843–73.

Lincoln, Ross A. "Tucker Carlson Wonders If Afghan Refugees Are Part of a Democratic Plot to Steal Elections" (video), September 1, 2021. https://www.thewrap.com/tucker-carlson -wonders-if-afghan-refugees-are-part-of-a-democratic-plot-to-steal-elections-video/.

Lindemann, Albert S. *Anti-Semitism before the Holocaust*. 1st ed. New York: Routledge, 2000.

———. *Esau's Tears: Modern Anti-Semitism and the Rise of the Jews*. Cambridge: Cambridge University Press, 1997.

Loomba, Ania. "Periodization, Race, and Global Contact." *Journal of Medieval and Early Modern Studies* 37, no. 3 (September 2007): 595–620.

Lucassen, Leo. "Peeling an Onion: The 'Refugee Crisis' from a Historical Perspective." *Ethnic and Racial Studies* 41, no. 3 (February 2018): 383–410.

Lutz, Tom. *American Nervousness, 1903: An Anecdotal History*. Ithaca, N.Y.: Cornell University Press, 1991.

Mamdani, Mahmood. *Citizen and Subject: Contemporary Africa and the Legacy of Late Colonialism*. Princeton, N.J.: Princeton University Press, 1996.

Mannheim, Karl. *Ideology and Utopia: An Introduction to the Sociology of Knowledge*. Translated by Louis Wirth and Edward Shils. Mansfield Centre, Conn.: Martino Fine Books, 2015.

Marr, Wilhelm. *The Victory of Judaism over Germanism*. Translated by P. Mendes-Flohr and J. Reinharz. Bern: Rudolph Costenoble, 1879.

Mays, Thomas J. "Human Slavery as a Prevention of Pulmonary Consumption." *Transactions of the American Climatological Association* 20 (June 1904): 192–97.

McDaniel, Iain. "Constantin Frantz and the Intellectual History of Bonapartism and Caesarism: A Reassessment." *Intellectual History Review* 28, no. 2 (April 2018): 317–38.

McKee, James B. *Sociology and the Race Problem: The Failure of a Perspective*. Urbana: University of Illinois Press, 1993.

McLaughlin, Malcolm. "Reconsidering the East St. Louis Race Riot of 1917." *International Review of Social History* 47, no. 2 (August 2002): 187–212.

Mead, George Herbert. *Mind, Self, and Society: From the Standpoint of a Social Behaviorist*. Chicago: University of Chicago Press, 1967.

———. *Movements of Thought in the Nineteenth Century*. Chicago: University of Chicago Press, 1972.

Mecklin, John Moffatt. *Democracy and Race Friction: A Study in Social Ethics*. New York: Macmillan Company, 1914.

———. *The Ku Klux Klan: A Study of the American Mind*. New York: Harcourt, Brace, 1924.

———. "The Philosophy of the Color Line." *American Journal of Sociology* 19, no. 3 (1913): 343–57.

"Medical News." *British Medical Journal* 1, no. 1590 (1891): 1366–68.

Meer, Nasar. "Racialization and Religion: Race, Culture and Difference in the Study of Antisemitism and Islamophobia." *Ethnic and Racial Studies* 36, no. 3 (March 2013): 385–98.

———. "W. E. B. Du Bois, Double Consciousness and the 'Spirit' of Recognition." *Sociological Review* 67, no. 1 (January 2019): 47–62.

Mendel, Emanuel. *Text-Book of Psychiatry: A Psychological Study of Insanity for Practitioners and Students.* Philadelphia, Pa.: F. A. Davis Company, 1907.

Mendes-Flohr, Paul, and Jehuda Reinharz, eds. *The Jew in the Modern World: A Documentary History.* 2nd ed. New York: Oxford University Press, 1995.

Mills, Charles W. *The Racial Contract.* Ithaca, N.Y.: Cornell University Press, 1999.

Mitchill, Samuel Latham. *The Medical Repository (and Review of American Publications on Medicine, Surgery and the Auxiliary of Science).* New York: T. and J. Swords, 1817.

Morris, Aldon. *The Scholar Denied: W. E. B. Du Bois and the Birth of Modern Sociology.* Oakland: University of California Press, 2017.

Mosse, George L. *Germans and Jews: The Right, the Left, and the Search for a "Third Force" in Pre-Nazi Germany.* Detroit, Mich.: Wayne State University Press, 1987.

———. "Max Nordau, Liberalism and the New Jew." *Journal of Contemporary History* 27, no. 4 (1992): 565–81.

———. *Toward the Final Solution: A History of European Racism.* 1st ed. New York: Howard Fertig, 1997.

Niewyk, Donald L. *Jews in Weimar Germany.* 1st ed. New Brunswick, N.J.: Routledge, 2000.

———. "Solving the 'Jewish Problem': Continuity and Change in German Antisemitism, 1871–1945." *Leo Baeck Institute Year Book* 35, no. 1 (January 1990): 335–70.

Omi, Michael, and Howard Winant. *Racial Formation in the United States.* 3rd ed. New York: Routledge, 2014.

Orizu, Michaela C. "The German Influence on the Life and Thought of W. E. B. Du Bois." Master's thesis, University of Massachusetts Amherst, 2001.

Orlansky, Harold. "The Study of Man: Jewish Personality Traits." *Commentary Magazine,* 1946. https://www.commentary.org/articles/harold-orlansky/the-study-of-man-jewish-personality-traits/.

———. "The Study of Man: The Jews of Yankee City." *Commentary Magazine,* 1946. https://www.commentary.org/articles/harold-orlansky/the-study-of-man-the-jews-of-yankee-city/.

Park, Robert E. "The Bases of Race Prejudice." *Annals of the American Academy of Political and Social Science* 140 (November 1928): 11–20.

———. "Human Migration and the Marginal Man." *American Journal of Sociology* 33, no. 6 (May 1928): 881–93.

———. "Racial Assimilation in Secondary Groups with Particular Reference to the Negro." *American Journal of Sociology* 19, no. 5 (March 1914): 606–23.

Perkinson, James W. "The Gift/Curse of 'Second Sight.'" In *Shamanism, Racism, and Hip Hop Culture: Essays on White Supremacy and Black Subversion,* edited by James W. Perkinson, 45–83. Black Religion / Womanist Thought / Social Justice. New York: Palgrave Macmillan U.S., 2005.

Philippson, Johanna. "Constantin Frantz." *Leo Baeck Institute Year Book* 13, no. 1 (January 1968): 102–19.

Pinsker, Leon. *Auto-Emancipation!* Translated by D. S. Blondheim. New York: Maccabaean Publishing Company, 1906.

Plumer, Brad, and Raymond Zhong. "Stopping Climate Change Is Doable, but Time Is Short, U.N. Panel Warns." *New York Times,* April 4, 2022, sec. Climate.

Plumer, William S. "Mary Reynolds: A Case of Double Consciousness." *Harper's Magazine*, May 1860, 807–12.

Polakow-Suransky, Sasha. "Opinion: White Nationalism Is Destroying the West." *New York Times*, October 12, 2017, sec. Opinion.

Prager, Dennis, and Joseph Telushkin. *Why the Jews? The Reason for Antisemitism*. New York: Touchstone, 2003.

Presner, Todd Samuel. "'Clear Heads, Solid Stomachs, and Hard Muscles': Max Nordau and the Aesthetics of Jewish Regeneration." *Modernism/Modernity* 10, no. 2 (2003): 269–96.

Pulzer, Peter. *Jews and the German State: The Political History of a Minority, 1848–1933*. Detroit, Mich.: Wayne State University Press, 2003.

———. *The Rise of Political Anti-Semitism in Germany & Austria*. Cambridge, Mass.: Harvard University Press, 1988.

Rampersad, Arnold. *The Art and Imagination of W. E. B. Du Bois*. New York: Schocken, 1990.

Reckdahl, Kate, and Timothy Bella. "New Orleans Hasn't Picked Up Some People's Trash for Weeks Since Ida. They're Begging to Get Rid of the Stench." *Washington Post*, September 22, 2021.

Reed, Adolph L., Jr. *W. E. B. Du Bois and American Political Thought: Fabianism and the Color Line*. New York: Oxford University Press, 1999.

Reflective Democracy Campaign. "System Failure: What the 2020 Primary Elections Reveal about Our Democracy." May 2021. https://wholeads.us/research/system-failure-2020-primary-elections/.

Reinsch, Paul S. "The Negro Race and European Civilization." *American Journal of Sociology* 11, no. 2 (1905): 145–67.

Richards, Graham. *Race, Racism and Psychology: Towards a Reflexive History*. 2nd ed. New York: Routledge, 2012.

Richarz, Monika, ed. *Jewish Life in Germany: Memoirs from Three Centuries*. Bloomington: Indiana University Press, 1991.

Robinson, Cedric J. *Black Marxism: The Making of the Black Radical Tradition*. 2nd ed. Chapel Hill: University of North Carolina Press, 2000.

Ross, Edward Alsworth. *Foundations of Sociology*. London: Macmillan, 1905.

Rothberg, Michael. "W. E. B. Du Bois in Warsaw: Holocaust Memory and the Color Line, 1949–1952." *Yale Journal of Criticism* 14, no. 1 (2001): 169–89.

Rudwick, Elliott M. *Race Riot at East St. Louis, July 2, 1917*. Urbana: University of Illinois Press, 1964.

Rürup, Reinhard. "Jewish Emancipation and Bourgeois Society." *Leo Baeck Institute Year Book* 14, no. 1 (January 1969): 67–91.

Saman, Michael J. "Du Bois and Marx, Du Bois and Marxism." *Du Bois Review: Social Science Research on Race* 17, no. 1 (2020): 33–54. https://doi.org/10.1017/S1742058X20000089.

Sarna, Jonathan D. *American Judaism*. New Haven, Conn.: Yale University Press, 2004.

Sarnoff, Irving. "Identification with the Aggressor: Some Personality Correlates of Anti-Semitism among Jews." *Journal of Personality* 20, no. 2 (December 1951): 199–218.

Schleunes, Karl A. "'Madagaskar für die Juden': Antisemitische Idee und politische Praxis, 1885–1945." Review. *Shofar: An Interdisciplinary Journal of Jewish Studies* 17, no. 4 (1999): 134–35.

Schorsch, Ismar. *Jewish Reactions to German Anti-Semitism, 1870–1914.* New York: Columbia University Press, 1972.

Seamster, Louise, and Victor Ray. "Against Teleology in the Study of Race: Toward the Abolition of the Progress Paradigm." *Sociological Theory* 36, no. 4 (December 2018): 315–42.

Selod, Saher. "Citizenship Denied: The Racialization of Muslim American Men and Women Post-9/11." *Critical Sociology* 41, no. 1 (January 2015): 77–95.

Sentencing Project. "Report to the United Nations on Racial Disparities in the U.S. Criminal Justice System." March 2018. https://www.sentencingproject.org/reports/report-to-the -united-nations-on-racial-disparities-in-the-u-s-criminal-justice-system/.

Sewell, Abigail A. "The Racism-Race Reification Process: A Mesolevel Political Economic Framework for Understanding Racial Health Disparities." *Sociology of Race and Ethnicity* 2, no. 4 (October 2016): 402–32.

Sewell, Abigail A., and Kevin A. Jefferson. "Collateral Damage: The Health Effects of Invasive Police Encounters in New York City." *Journal of Urban Health* 93, no. S1 (April 2016): 42–67.

Shapiro, Thomas, Tatjana Meschede, and Sam Osoro. "The Roots of the Widening Racial Wealth Gap: Explaining the Black-White Economic Divide." Research and Policy Brief. Institute on Assets and Social Policy, Brandeis University, February 2013.

Shepperson, George. "The Centennial of the West African Conference of Berlin, 1884–1885." *Phylon* 46, no. 1 (1985): 37–48.

Shils, Edward. "'Ideology and Utopia' by Karl Mannheim." *Daedalus* 103, no. 1 (1974): 83–89.

Shumsky, Dimitry. "Leon Pinsker and *'Autoemancipation!'*: A Reevaluation." *Jewish Social Studies* 18, no. 1 (2011): 33–62.

Siegel-Hawley, Genevieve, and Erica Frankenberg. "Southern Slippage: Growing School Segregation in the Most Desegregated Region of the Country." Civil Rights Project. UCLA, September 2012.

Skae, David. "Case of Intermittent Mental Disorder of the Tertian Type, with Double Consciousness." *Northern Journal of Medicine* 3, no. 14 (June 1845): 10–13.

Smith, Anthony D. *The Nation in History: Historiographical Debates about Ethnicity and Nationalism.* Hanover, N.H.: Historical Society of Israel, 2000.

Sondhaus, Lawrence. "Schwarzenberg, Austria, and the German Question, 1848–1851." *International History Review* 13, no. 1 (1991): 1–20.

Steiman, L. *Paths to Genocide: Antisemitism in Western History.* Hampshire: Palgrave Macmillan, 1997.

Stephenson, George M. "*The Ku Klux Klan: A Study of the American Mind.* By John Moffatt Mecklin. (New York: Harcourt, Brace and Company, 1924. 244 p.)." *Journal of American History* 11, no. 2 (September 1924): 301–2.

Stern, Fritz R. *The Politics of Cultural Despair: A Study in the Rise of the Germanic Ideology.* Berkeley: University of California Press, 1974.

Stocking, George W., Jr. *Race, Culture, and Evolution: Essays in the History of Anthropology.* Chicago: University of Chicago Press, 1982.

Stone, Alfred Holt. "Is Race Friction between Blacks and Whites in the United States Growing and Inevitable?" *American Journal of Sociology* 13, no. 5 (March 1908): 676–97.

Stonequist, Everett V. *The Marginal Man: A Study in Personality and Culture Conflict*. New
    York: Scribner, 1937.

———. "The Problem of the Marginal Man." *American Journal of Sociology* 41, no. 1 (1935):
    1–12.

Tal, Uriel. *Christians and Jews in Germany: Religion, Politics and Ideology in the Second Reich,
    1870–1914*. Ithaca, N.Y.: Cornell University Press, 1975.

Taussig, F. W. *Principles of Economics*. New York: Macmillan Company, 1915.

Thomas, Hahn. "The Difference the Middle Ages Makes: Color and Race before the Modern
    World." *Journal of Medieval and Early Modern Studies* 31, no. 1 (January 2001): 1–38.

Thomas, James M. "Du Bois, Double Consciousness, and the 'Jewish Question.'" *Ethnic and
    Racial Studies* 43, no. 8 (June 2020): 1333–56.

———. "Medicalizing Racism." *Contexts* 13, no. 4 (Fall 2014): 24–29.

———. "Race, Nation, and the Color-Line in the Twenty-First Century: A Du Boisian Analy-
    sis." *Social Problems* 68, no. 2 (May 2021): 267–83.

———. "The Racial Formation of Medieval Jews: A Challenge to the Field." *Ethnic and Racial
    Studies* 33 (November 2010): 1737–55.

———. "Re-upping the Contract with Sociology: Charles Mills's Racial Contract Revisited a
    Decade Later." *Sociology Compass* 1, no. 1 (September 2007): 255–64.

Thomas, W. I. "Race Psychology: Standpoint and Questionnaire, with Particular Reference to
    the Immigrant and the Negro." *American Journal of Sociology* 17, no. 6 (1912): 725–75.

Torchinsky, Rina. "Details Emerge about the Suspect in the Buffalo Mass Shooting." NPR, May
    16, 2022, sec. National.

Treitschke, Heinrich von. *Politics*. 2 vols. Edited by Arthur Balfour. Translated by Blanche Dug-
    dale and Torben De Bille. New York: AMS Press, 1978.

Tuke, D. Hack. "On the Mental Condition in Hypnotism." *Journal of Mental Science* 29, no.
    125 (1883): 55–80.

Underhill, Megan R. "Managing Difference: White Parenting Practices in Socioeconomically
    Diverse Neighborhoods." *City & Community* 20, no. 2 (June 2021): 79–98.

Voigtländer, Nico, and Hans-Joachim Voth. "Persecution Perpetuated: The Medieval Ori-
    gins of Anti-Semitic Violence in Nazi Germany." *Quarterly Journal of Economics* 127, no. 3
    (2012): 1339–92.

Volovici, Marc. "Leon Pinsker's *Autoemancipation!* and the Emergence of German as a Lan-
    guage of Jewish Nationalism." *Central European History* 50, no. 1 (2017): 34–58.

Weatherly, U. G. "Discussion of the Paper by Alfred H. Stone, 'Is Race Friction between Blacks
    and Whites in the United States Growing and Inevitable?'" *American Journal of Sociology*
    13, no. 6 (May 1908): 823–25.

Webb, Clive. "The Nazi Persecution of Jews and the African American Freedom Struggle." *Pat-
    terns of Prejudice* 53, no. 4 (August 2019): 337–62.

Weger, Stacey. "The Berlin Years: The Influence of German Thought and Experience on the
    Development of Du Bois's Sociology." *Sociation Today* 7, no. 1 (2009): n.p.

Weisman, Jonathan, and Reid J. Epstein. "G.O.P. Declares Jan. 6 Attack 'Legitimate Political
    Discourse.'" *New York Times*, February 4, 2022, sec. U.S.

Weiss, John. *Ideology of Death: Why the Holocaust Happened in Germany*. Chicago: Ivan R.
    Dee, 1997.

Wells, Susan. "Discursive Mobility and Double Consciousness in S. Weir Mitchell and W. E. B. Du Bois." *Philosophy and Rhetoric* 35, no. 2 (2002): 120–37.

Wertheimer, Jack. *Unwelcome Strangers: East European Jews in Imperial Germany.* New York: Oxford University Press, 1991.

Wigglesworth, Alex, and Hayley Smith. "'Unprecedented' Caldor, Dixie Fires Are the First to Burn from One Side of the Sierra to the Other." *Los Angeles Times,* August 31, 2021, sec. California.

Winant, Howard. *New Politics of Race: Globalism, Difference, Justice.* Minneapolis: University of Minnesota Press, 2004.

———. *Racial Conditions: Politics, Theory, Comparisons.* Minneapolis: University of Minnesota Press, 1994.

Winston, Andrew S. *Defining Difference: Race and Racism in the History of Psychology.* Washington, D.C.: American Psychological Association, 2003.

Woodard, Fredrick. *W. E. B. Du Bois: The Native Impulse; Notes toward an Ideological Biography, 1868–1897.* Iowa City: University of Iowa Press, 1976.

Woodson, C. G. Review of *Color and Democracy: Colonies and Peace,* by W. E. B. Du Bois. *Journal of Negro History* 30, no. 3 (1945): 342–43.

Wright, Earl, II. *The First American School of Sociology: W. E. B. Du Bois and the Atlanta Sociological Laboratory.* Burlington, Vt.: Routledge, 2016.

———. *Jim Crow Sociology: The Black and Southern Roots of American Sociology.* Cincinnati, Ohio: University of Cincinnati Press, 2020.

———. "Using the Master's Tools: The Atlanta Sociological Laboratory and American Sociology, 1896–1924." *Sociological Spectrum* 22 (January 2002): 15–39.

Wright, Earl, II, and Thomas C. Calhoun. "Jim Crow Sociology: toward an Understanding of the Origin and Principles of Black Sociology via the Atlanta Sociological Laboratory." *Sociological Focus* 39, no. 1 (February 2006): 1–18.

Young, Robert J. C. *Colonial Desire: Hybridity in Theory, Culture and Race.* London: Routledge, 1995.

Zamir, Shamoon. *Dark Voices: W. E. B. Du Bois and American Thought, 1888–1903.* Chicago: University of Chicago Press, 1995.

Zimmerman, Andrew. *Anthropology and Antihumanism in Imperial Germany.* Chicago: University of Chicago Press, 2001.

———. "Anti-Semitism as Skill: Rudolf Virchow's 'Schulstatistik' and the Racial Composition of Germany." *Central European History* 32, no. 4 (1999): 409–29.

Zimmerman, Moshe. "Muscle Jews versus Nervous Jews." In *Emancipation through Muscles: Jews and Sports in Europe,* edited by Michael Brenner and Gideon Reuveni, 13–26. Lincoln: University of Nebraska Press, 2006.

INDEX

Afghanistan, 117, 120

Africa: colonization of, 58, 60, 74–75; decolonization of, 77–78, 85, 125–26

African Americans. *See* Blacks

American Jewish Committee (AJC), 94–95

American Journal of Sociology (*AJS*), 98–105, 109

American Socialist Party, 82

anti-Semitism: Auerbach on, 123–24; "blood libel" and, 27, 63; Brustein on, 47; of Christian Social Party, 48, 65–67; Christianity and, 25–26, 57; Du Bois on, 12, 51–52, 55, 115, 116; Du Bois-Reymond on, 49–50; Frantz on, 61; German exceptionalism and, 62–64; in Hungary, 120; Ku Klux Klan and, 13; Marr on, 67–68; Pinsker on, 35; self-hatred and, 110–11; Treitschke on, 50–51; Young Hegelians and, 46

Appiah, Kwame Anthony, 4, 7, 51, 58

Asian Americans, 109

Atlanta Sociological Laboratory, 4, 6, 76, 100–101, 138n1

Auerbach, Berthold, 123–24

Auschwitz exhibition (2021), 122–23

Bagehot, Walter, 138n41

Baird, Harvey, 23

Baldwin, James, 74

Balfour, Lawrie, 85–86

Balibar, Étienne, 125

Barkin, Kenneth, 5, 53, 58

Beadles, Cecil F., 23

Belin, H. E., 102–3

Bellamy, Edward, 71–72

Berlin Conference (1884–85), 58, 74–75

Biden, Joe, 117

Binet, Alfred, 33

Bismarck, Otto von, 65

Black Flame trilogy (Du Bois), 11, 76

Black Lives Matter, xi, 118, 128

Black Reconstruction in America (Du Bois), 10, 76–78, 82, 89, 91, 138n2

Blacks: emancipation of, 26, 101, 104; psychiatric disorders among, 31–37, 80; suffrage of, 72; voting rights of, 11, 73

Blanc, Louis, 71–72

"blood libel," 27, 63

Blumenbach, Friedrich, 27

Boas, Franz, 48–49, 135n27

Bourne, Ansel (aka A. J. Brown), 42

Bourne Trilogy films, 42

Bowser, Benjamin, 119

Brill, A. A., 29

Brown, Karrida, 79

Brown, Michael, 128

Browne, Francis G., 2

Brustein, William, 47

Burgl, Georg, 30

Bush, George H. W., 118

Bush, George W., 118

Byrnes, Robert, 34

Printed in the USA
CPSIA information can be obtained
at www.ICGtesting.com
CBHW030211130124
3429CB00006B/68